Ski Faster, Easier

Lee Borowski, MA

LEISURE PRESS

CHAMPAIGN, ILLINOIS

Library of Congress Cataloging-in-Publication Data

Borowski, Lee, 1941-
    Ski faster, easier.

    Includes index.
    1. Skis and skiing.   2.   Cross-country skiing.
I. Title.
GV854.B63   1986   796.93   85-23211
ISBN 0-88011-272-7

Developmental Editor: Susan Wilmoth, PhD
Production Director: Ernie Noa
Copy Editor: Olga Murphy
Typesetter: Brad Colson
Proofreader: Ann Bruehler
Text Layout: Janet Davenport
Interior Design: Julie Szamocki
Cover Design and Layout: Jack Davis
Printed by: United Graphics

Artwork: Bill Mathie
Cover photo courtesy of Lori Adamski-Peek. Special thanks to Sue
Long and Dan Simoneau.

ISBN: 0-88011-272-7

Printed in the United States of America

10   9   8   7   6   5   4   3   2   1

Leisure Press
A division of Human Kinetics Publishers, Inc.
Box 5076
Champaign, IL 61820

Acknowledgments

A special thanks to the following people: Peter Davis, our first coach, who gave us a good start. Marty Hall was a constant help, starting with his encouragement in the early years right up to the present with his communication as to what is happening on the international circuit. Errol and Beth Schluter helped immensely with our junior program. This not only included coaching but also day-in and day-out excellence in trail grooming by Errol and his associates in the Waukesha County park system.

Many of the coaching checkpoints and technique breakthroughs that are presented in this book were actually discovered by my son, Bret. My daughter, Lisa, was a tremendous help in proofreading and was an excellent sounding board, and my wife, Betsy, assisted with the proofreading, and was especially helpful in presenting the weekend tourer's point of view.

Steve Gaskill, Jim Page, Gary Larson, Peter Graves, Peter Ashley, and all of the U.S. Ski Team members and coaches contributed by coming to area clinics and offering their encouragement. Other contributors deserving recognition are Ed Trecker, who supplied many of the photos upon which the artwork was based, and Scott Oberbreckling and the coaching staff at the University of Alaska—Fairbanks for access to their World Cup video tapes.

A very special thank you is extended to the Milwaukee Nordic Ski Club, Bob Sandless, Dave Harrison, Ken Schoville, the USSA (both Central Division and National), and the United States Ski Team for providing a dream and an avenue for young skiers to pursue, and to all of the skiers, young and old, who helped in the evolution of a teaching technique.

Contents

Preface

Several years ago I was very fortunate to gain access to tapes of the cross-country competitors at the 1980 Olympic Games. Being active in coaching Milwaukee area skiers of all ages, I was very excited, for despite reading every available book and article, seeing many movies and attending various camps and clinics, I realized I had seen almost no footage of the top racers in the world. What I saw came as a shock. Not only did the existing films and literature not prepare me, but many of the books and articles were in direct contradiction to what the best skiers in the world were actually doing.

In addition, each of the individual competitors themselves appeared to ski differently—from the locomotive style of Thomas Wassburg to the fluid grace of Nikolai Zimyatov to the raw, lumbering power of Juha Mieto. Each obviously had a highly personalized style. However, as I pored over the tapes, early dismay rapidly disappeared as I discovered that in certain basic movements and positions these skiers were almost identical. Body types, pole lengths, and general physical mannerisms gave these athletes unique styles; but to my delight, the fundamentals remained constant.

Having identified these fundamentals, a series of coaching checkpoints was established. I felt I needed something solid against which I could compare an individual skier in order to upgrade his or her technique. Very often a novice can realize something is wrong; correcting it is another matter. When our family first began to ski, my wife would often laugh at me saying I "looked like a wounded turkey." She didn't know how to correct me, but she sure let me know something was wrong. These checkpoints then gave me a solid reference point: a way to positively correct deficient technique. In addition, they overcame one of the serious drawbacks of even the best ski literature—the lack of checks and balances needed to prevent "overlearning." Most conscientious students have a tendency to overlearn a skill until it becomes a flaw. In fact, many times a person will try to learn something he or she already does correctly, with disastrous results. These checkpoints then allow quick diagnosis and prevent overcorrection.

I was anxious to try them out on our young racers. However, while teaching these youngsters from ages 8 on up, one thing was soon apparent: They did not arrive alone. They needed transportation and usually were with dad, mom, or the entire family. Many times the dads or moms showed more interest than the kids themselves, so the youth racing group became a family affair. Add to this, various local skiers I coach from ages 21 to 73 whose common bond is a love for skiing and a desire to improve. Instead of teaching a group of "elite racers" only, a heterogeneous mixture of all ages and talents was the result. This hodgepodge of skiing humanity turned out to be a blessing in disguise. It forced a continuous rethinking and simplification of the basic skiing principles, the result being the development of a simple sequential buildup to sound biomechanical technique. The results were amazing: Our skiers of all abilities were learning in a simple graduated manner, never realizing that what they were accomplishing was supposedly difficult to do. This step-by-step approach to "world class" technique was the backbone of this book.

And then WHAM! Just when everything was in place, the world of cross-country skiing exploded—THE SKATE hit the scene. So back to the drawing board. But learning is a continuous process and to stop learning is to fall behind. The introduction of the skate just made it all the more important.

Fortunately, our source of world class tapes had increased dramatically. After much viewing of the likes of Bill Koch, Gunde Svan, Annette Boee, Marja-Liisa Himalaenen, Ove Aunli, plus many others, a new series of coaching checkpoints was developed. Several seasons of using these checkpoints passed. To our delight, the skate proved much easier to learn and the checkpoints proved extremely effective. This book contains these checkpoints and will provide the skater all he or she needs to know to develop a world class skate. In addition, the effect of the widespread use of the V-skate and marathon skate on equipment selection are discussed, as are waxing and training.

This book, however, is not only a technique manual. I have always been a little disappointed with books I have read in the past. They seemed to be aimed for other skiers. Marginal snow, no mountains, and proximity to large population centers pose special problems. Advice such as "roller ski up a mountain pass for 2 hours" or "get 60 hours on snow in November" left me rather cold. Our problems were never dealt with specifically. Learning to ski when there is little snow is difficult. Learning on roller skis is even harder, yet both can be accomplished with the proper knowledge. How do you train when the snow has melted and the roads are too icy to roller ski or run? What are the special learning differences between adults and youngsters? This book will deal with those problems encountered in a less than ideal environment.

Above all, I believe cross-country skiing is a sport for the entire family. Although this book had its origins in biomechanical research on the best skiers in the world and is designed to help a skier reach his or her potential, it is also meant to be a handbook for family skiing—one from which skiers can refer in order to help each other so that each may improve, regardless of the starting point. One may be thinking of the Olympics, while another may only be interested in an enjoyable tour through the local moraines. The only difficulty in writing a book like this could be that parts of the book may seem overly simple for advanced skiers and other parts too complex for beginners. That is a small sacrifice in producing a graduated book that can take a beginner to world class technique.

The common goal of every skier is to ski more efficiently. Skiing becomes more fun and less tiring, allowing the racer to ski faster or the tourer to enjoy a more pleasant outing. In either case, both experience the essential thrill of skiing—the glide. Their basic motion is the same; the racer is just more dynamic, conditioning being the main difference. So whether you enjoy pushing your body to its limits or simply absorbing the crunching sounds and sparkling sights of winter, good technique is the key to a more enjoyable experience. You will ski faster, easier.

Rhythmic Motion

1

Not for Beginners Only

"The first step in becoming a good skier or any athlete, for that matter, is to perform in a relaxed manner." I distinctly recall one adverse reaction when I made this statement at one of our local clinics. A friend of mine did not see relaxation in the techniques of the world class racers shown on the videotapes, especially in their finishing sprint. He felt relaxation was an integral part of the technique that was used by the average skier but not by the "elite" racer. He questioned, "How could that rapid thrusting to the finish be called relaxation?" Our only difference was in terminology—in the meaning of the word *relaxation*, not the physical motion itself.

By athletic relaxation I did not mean total relaxation, whereas he did. It is not skiing around like a wet noodle, arms and legs flapping in the breeze. Instead it is a fluid motion devoid of excess tension. The only muscles working are the ones that are needed, and these may be contracting quite explosively. The opposing or antagonistic muscles are completely relaxed, allowing the active muscles to perform efficiently. This principle applies to any sport and is a large part of what is called coordination, holding form, or effortless grace.

When the wrong muscles interfere, a stiff, tentative, or jerky motion results. The amount of energy wasted is enormous. Not only do the antagonistic muscles use energy themselves, they also oppose the correct muscles. That is why the novice skier or, even more so, the beginning roller skier becomes very tired in such a short time, even if in excellent condition.

Using the correct muscles while relaxing the unneeded ones is an important part of learning any new skill. This applies in golf, tennis, skiing, or crocheting.

In learning the coordination of cross-country skiing, going too fast, too soon is a mistake that is hard to resist. Disaster can strike. Vigorous skiing magnifies any awkwardness. Skiers can find themselves practicing contracting the wrong muscles in a forceful manner, actually using these muscles to stop themselves. Bad habits are easy to form and hard to break. Therefore the skier's goal should be to ski in a relaxed and coordinated manner. Speed can wait. During this phase, fear and tension are the enemies: confidence and relaxation, the friends. Being too tentative slows progress; instead, the skier should try to glide from ski to ski with self-assurance. Soon after feeling that those slippery skis will never be mastered, the beginning skier will be cruising down the trail wondering why it ever seemed difficult.

Many skiers never learn to ski in a relaxed manner; therefore, "Not for Beginners Only" is included as part of the title for this chapter. Fortunately, relaxed skiing is easy to spot. If you are one of the majority of skiers who do not have access to videotape or Polarvision, do not despair. Just have a friend or family member watch you ski. If you are stiff or tense, it will be obvious. If your friends and family are like mine, be ready for some good jibes. My family gives me that kind of "help" whenever they can.

Again, it doesn't pay to try to ski fast until you have stopped the muscles of your body from fighting each other. If you are a tense skier, make learning a relaxed stride your immediate goal, or it will be much harder to correct later. This does not mean you have to look like a plate of well-cooked spaghetti ready to flop all over the place; but even if you did, that would not be so bad. Once you have conquered relaxation, the brakes on muscle fighting muscle have been released. Then it is easy to turn on the afterburners. An excellent way to learn to ski relaxed without detracting from snow time is roller skiing in the summer (more about that in a later chapter).

It is impressive to see for the first time the smooth rhythm of the expert skier, floating over the snow, arms and legs working in perfect unison. This smoothness is even more apparent if the pace is a little slower as in a moderate workout or a 50-k race. Arms and legs exactly synchronized, this flowing rhythm, the *diagonal stride*, is the hallmark of the cross-country skier. The diagonal stride is the most difficult of the major cross-country movements to master, and will be discussed in the first several chapters of this book.

In the diagonal, the opposite arms and legs work together, much the same as running and walking. For example, as the left leg moves forward so does the right arm. At the same time, the right leg and left arm move to the rear in perfect unison. It should be a natural movement and usually is until fear or artificial mental control interferes (see Figure 1.1).

Figure 1.1 Basic coordination of the diagonal. The opposite arm and leg work together.

How well a person learns this rhythmic stride depends greatly on his or her mental image of what he or she is trying to do. I was amazed the first time my nephew Cory, at age 13, was on skis. He was fluid, dynamic, graceful, and powerful—easily one of the best skiers on the trail that day. When I asked him where he learned to ski so well, he replied that he was only imitating those skiers he had watched on the world championships televised on *Wide World of Sports.* In contrast, another youngster of the same age learned to ski by reading a book on cross-country skiing that his father checked out from the library. It was an excellent book, and it emphasized the concept of weight transfer through use of the phrase *hop and glide.* By the end of the season the whole family, including the youngster, was hopping around like jackrabbits. It was a pretty humorous sight. Fortunately, they went to Telemark Lodge for a weekend and received a little "shock therapy" when they skied behind some "elite" skiers who flowed down rather than hopped around the trails. Once this realization struck home, it still took some time and effort to get them straightened out. (Incidentally, the second youngster was my son.)

Nothing replaces seeing good skiers when first learning—not even this book. Being able to watch and absorb the motion of good technique on film or in person is critical. But don't throw this book away yet, for it will prove to be an excellent tool to help you ski as well as the best skiers, perhaps someday even better than them.

The Diagonal Stride

Before mastering the basics of a fluid diagonal, a few terms must be defined. What is the *kick?* Some authors define the kick as in soccer or football with the kicking leg being the one "kicked" forward. Most coaches, myself included, however, refer to the leg that is pushing the skier forward as the kicking leg. In the discussions here, the kicking leg is the one transmitting the force, the one moving to the rear, the one powering the skier because of its contact with the snow (see Figure 1.2 a and b).

The kicking leg pushes the gliding leg along with the body of the skier. Most skiers are continually trying to increase their joy of skiing by emphasizing the length of their glide. The tourer may do so in a leisurely manner, the racer in a more powerful one. Both, however, are trying to ski more efficiently. There is really no difference in what the racer and tourer are trying to accomplish, only in the amount of force or energy they use to do so.

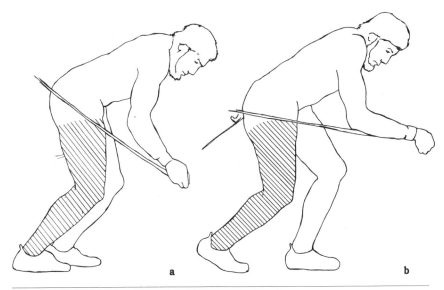

Figure 1.2   The kicking leg is the one that powers the skier.

Diagonal Stride Drills

The following sequence of snow drills are standard instructional fare, tried and proven successful by many instructors over the past. However, pay attention to the sequence in which they are presented, for they serve as a springboard for more advanced work. Any failure to master the relaxed coordination of the diagonal will only lengthen the learning period. Young children most often will not need these drills because they are usually so uninhibited that their muscles move naturally in an efficient motion (see Figure 1.3). Also remember that observing good skiers at this stage is very valuable.

Skiing Without Poles.   This standard drill is especially helpful to the skier who has trouble coordinating arm and leg movement. Many beginning skiers, out of fear, use the poles for balance, and thereby plant them at the wrong time. In the diagonal stride the left arm and right leg work together, as does the right arm and left leg. This is a natural walking movement, but on slippery skis, with poles in hands, strange things can happen. For now, however, drop the poles on the side of the trail, as you are only

Figure 1.3 Youngsters in their abandonment, pick up the natural movement easily.

attempting to achieve proper coordination; you will learn to use the poles for propulsion later.

As the left arm moves forward so does the right leg (see Figure 1.4). This should be checked periodically by glancing down at the hands and legs. Normally you should have your head up, looking down the track, but an occasional glance during this time will not hurt. If

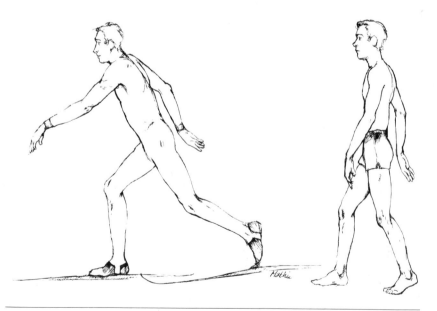

Figure 1.4 The coordination of the diagonal is much like walking and can be learned most easily by skiing without poles.

you can't get it right, kick off your skis. Then walk naturally down the trail (not in the tracks, please) until your natural walking motion shows you the proper arm and leg movements.

Then put your skis back on and start to ski slowly. You may even start by walking with your skis on. Once you have mastered the rhythm, start to glide a little, and you will soon be moving down the trail with childlike abandon. At this stage, your family, friends, or even a beginner will be able to detect whether or not opposite arms and legs are working in unison. You do not have to be a ski professional to analyze this motion. (By the way, many experienced skiers still do not have the proper timing.)

Continue practicing this drill until the diagonal motion becomes natural. Then pick up your poles and ski a few strides normally, checking to see if the arms and legs are still working properly. At this stage be sure to plant your pole tips near the heel of your foot but *not* in front of the toe. It is always a mistake for a beginner to plant the poles too far forward because they are then too easily available as crutches for balance. This will slow or most likely halt your progress in developing balance on the ski itself and will certainly destroy the natural rhythm of the body.

Again, when the left hand comes forward, so should the right knee and vice versa. Have a friend check you out. Practicing alternating back and forth between the poles and no poles will help your muscle memory and will enhance learning. It is a little easier to ski up a steeper incline where the glide and resulting insecurity will be less. The most difficult places to diagonal are the very fast conditions on the flats where good balance is needed because of the longer glide. This drill can also be done by gripping the poles in the middle while holding them parallel to the ground. Some people find this easier to do than skiing without poles altogether.

Skiing on a Steep Hill with Short Steps.　When we first started skiing, I noticed that our family looked much better going up a hill as opposed to skiing on the flats. Now, after teaching many beginners, I know that it is just easier to ski properly up a steeper hill.

Because the glide is shorter, the ski stride becomes more like a normal running stride.

If you have trouble coordinating the arms and legs in the diagonal, find a steeper hill, but not so steep as to cause a herringbone. As long as you take short steps up the hill, the arms and legs will usually work well together. The critical point is when the hill is crested. The short steps should be continued onto the flat, gradually allowing glide to occur. For now, do not increase the length of the steps, just let the ski glide after each short step. Again, make sure your pole is planted no farther forward than the toe. Have someone watch you to see if your natural diagonal deteriorates on the flat. If it does, it's usually because you are trying to plant the pole too far forward, so it's back to the bottom of the hill. Continue this process until you are able to make the transition from hill to flat in good style.

At this time it is appropriate to introduce one of those seemingly small items that are all important when learning a skill: the grip. In golf it is almost impossible to be good without the proper grip. In cross-country skiing, the grip of the hands on the pole plays the same important role, except it is the nongrip, or release, that is important here.

For relaxed and natural skiing, the arms must be able to move in a manner free of tension. Grasping the poles during the entire movement creates tension. The poles should be lightly cradled as the tip is planted in the snow but released in the follow-through—almost. The "almost" refers to the slight pressure of the thumb and forefinger on the shaft. However, the other fingers do not grip the pole in the follow-through. The light regripping occurs just before the pole is planted. At first it will feel as if those poles are swinging wildly all over the place, but after a while this feeling will disappear, and the pay-off will be relaxed skiing.

To achieve pole release, adjust pole straps properly. If the straps are too tight, the end of the pole will dig into the back of the hand between the thumb and forefinger (see Figure 1.5—strap so tight that pole is not allowed to hang vertically). If the strap is too loose, the thumb and forefinger will not be able to control the pole as the pole handle will swing away from the hand.

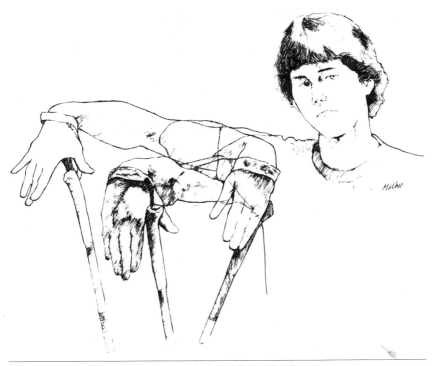

Figure 1.5   Three pole strap adjustments from left to right. Too loose, just right, too tight.

Figure 1.5 shows a good method to check for proper strap adjustment. Then, how far back should the arms travel? For now, try to let the hands move past the hips for at least a foot. At this stage, the actual amount of movement is unimportant. What we are trying to prevent is the typical beginner's flaw of gripping the poles tightly and stopping the pole push before the hands reach the hips. This type of motion causes tightness and will stop the development of a fluid stride.

Short-Step Skiing . . . The Next Phase.   Jogging on skis is the next step. If you are still having trouble coordinating arms and legs on the flats, spend time "trotting" on skis. It is easier for the arms and legs to work properly when running than while skiing, so jog on your skis for a while. As you get more proficient, allow the skis to glide after the short steps. Again, be sure to plant the pole with a bent arm and the tip near the heel of the boot. Eventually, the stride will lengthen and become the normal cross-country diagonal. How it evolves is important. At this stage keep the steps short while increasing the glide. It is important to realize that the trotting phase is only temporary, however. (I have seen skiers who never get out of this stage.) The purpose of the trotting phase is to coordinate the arms and legs. It is not an end in itself. For running on skis is just that—*running.* For that matter, you may as well put on the jogging shoes and pound the icy winter pavement, for you have given up the unique and exhilarating part of cross-country skiing—the glide.

Your first goal, especially in your initial season on snow, is relaxed rhythmic motion with the arms and legs in fluid unison. Spend some time on this. Once it is ingrained, the advanced work is much easier to learn. If you do not master this natural rhythm as a beginner, it will undoubtedly haunt you for some time, if not for the rest of your skiing days. Too much emphasis on speed before you master fluidity will result in more tension and in what skiers call thrashing. Sometimes even the best racers are guilty of thrashing.

Off-Season Drills

If the season ends before you master arm and leg synchronization, or if you are reading this in the off-season, do not despair. You can learn the proper arm and leg motions more easily in the warmer months. This is usually called dryland training. However, because one of our drills is done in water, we will call it off-season training. The following two off-season drills are very similar in execution and purpose, although one occurs on land and the other in water.

Hill Running with Poles. Beginners and intermediates have had great success using this technique. At a slow to moderate speed, you stride up a hill keeping your feet low to the ground. The main emphasis is on technique, although conditioning will be an added bonus. Again, you should watch your arms and legs to be sure that they are working together. As the left arm comes forward so does the right leg, and vice versa. It is much easier to master arm and leg coordination without skis. The movement is more natural because balancing is not a problem. Once you master the coordination, continue the drill with the prime goal becoming conditioning rather than technique.

Two things will help your hill running look and feel more like skiing: First, make sure you run with your feet low to the ground, almost brushing the grass; second, when the pole is planted, keep the arms in a flexed position—about 90° to 120°. Learning this natural arm position at the beginning will make some of the advanced material easier to learn. One of the most common flaws is to ski with the arms too straight in the front (see Figure 1.6). Unfortunately, this straight arm technique was an accepted method of teaching only a few years ago and still crops up occasionally. The reasons why a straight arm technique is inefficient will be explained in later chapters. I do not know of one top international competitor who skis with arms straight in front, but a number of good national skiers do.

Figure 1.6(a) Good pole running technique.   **Figure 1.6(b)** Some beginners keep their arms too straight when running.

Skiing in water.   The second off-season drill is to practice skiing in water about up to your thigh. Obviously, no skis or boots are needed for this drill. Stride through the water, timing it so that your arms and legs are working diagonally. Again, check to see that the opposite hand and knee come forward together. Imagine you are skiing and make sure your coordination is right.

Two years ago, I witnessed a graphic example of the results from practicing this drill. Of all the people with whom I have worked in skiing, my own father was most difficult. Whether it is my fault or his, it sure takes us a long time to communicate, even about the simplest things. However, at age 71, he really surprised me last ski season, which was only his third. He was doing quite well the season before, but his arms were not working in unison with his legs. While we were swimming one day last summer, I showed him how to practice the correct coordination in water. Expecting him to reject my suggestion, I forgot about it. Imagine my surprise the next winter when I saw my dad skiing in much better form than he did the previous season, and this accomplished during his first week on snow. He then admitted that he had spent some time during his daily swims and learned how to use his arms and legs properly. Besides, it was also good exercise for him. If a 71-year-old beginner can master this in the water of summer, it must be a good drill.

If you spend some time on these drills in the summer, your skiing in the winter can be more enjoyable, too. Then when the snow comes and you're on the trail skiing, just imagine you are in the water or on the hill. Start with short strides and try to obtain the same feeling as in the off-season drills. Using your imagination is a big help. Your work will pay off because this ski technique on snow amazingly resembles that of running with poles and in water.

Common Errors of the Diagonal

People's fears and inhibitions developed over a lifetime are difficult to change quickly. This is especially true for men who usually find it easier to use their muscles at the wrong time, thus creating the tension of muscle fighting muscle. The previous drills are excellent in helping to develop the basis of a relaxed and coordinated technique, but some feedback is still important. Therefore, included are some of the common errors of beginning adult skiers, which also may occasionally be seen in some youngsters.

The most common flaw of "grown-ups" is the *foot glued to the track syndrome.* Rigidly moving down the

track, these skiers' feet never lose contact with the
security of the ground; thus, they do not really enjoy
the abandon of good skiing. The ski should lift free of
the track because of the natural follow-through of the
kick. This lifting should take no real effort on the part
of the skier, but tight muscles cause some strange
things. Once aware of this problem, the cure usually
comes in two stages. First, the skier should allow his
or her foot to lift in the back. This often starts as an
artificial movement, imposed by will rather than a
reaction to the natural momentum of the kick. Most
likely, insecurity will strike again as the skier loses
balance, and the trail foot will return to the ground
(usually with a resounding slap) too early, well behind
the other kicking foot. (Stage 1.) The final improvement in this area occurs when the skier develops the
confidence and balance to stay on the glide ski long
enough to allow his or her trail foot to hit the ground
next to the kicking one. This breakthrough occurs not
when the skier mentally forces him- or herself to bring
the trail foot next to the kicking one, but rather when
balance and relaxation allow him or her to do so.
Taking shorter steps and keeping the weight on top of
the glide ski is an excellent way to learn this balance.

The second most common error of adult skiers is
placing the foot in cold water and usually accom-
panies the foot glued to the track syndrome (see
Figures 1.7 and 1.8). Placing the foot in front and
holding the body back, these skiers sort of shove themselves forward with the kicking leg, never really
getting much weight over the gliding ski. They also
usually use the poles much too early—for balance
rather than propulsion. To correct this, skiers should
attempt to hurl their entire body forward. This can be
quite disconcerting to beginners, for it usually takes
quite awhile to gain that degree of abandonment. However, as skiers grow in confidence, this becomes easier
to do. These skiers should feel that their body weight
is on top of the glide ski. Soon they will be throwing
their body forward and will wonder why it seemed so
hard to do in the first place. This also is much easier
learned if the skiers do two things. First and very
importantly, they should bend the arms at the elbow.
This bend should be exaggerated for a while if the
skiers are guilty of the foot in cold water flaw. Second,

Figure 1.7 ''Foot glued to the track'' is a common beginners' flaw. Allow the foot to naturally follow through to the dotted line.

Figure 1.8 The skier on the left is afraid to commit his weight to the glide ski. It is the ''foot in cold water'' syndrome. The cure exhibited on the right is to take short steps and to keep your weight on the glide ski.

they should stick to short steps while learning to balance on skis.

Wrapping it up

Many beginners and casual tourers can be found in the densely populated Milwaukee-Chicago area. The majority of skiers in this area fail to ski with proper arm and leg coordination. How do you correct this type of skiing? If you want to citizen race or even just ski more efficiently, the drills mentioned earlier in the chapter are the answer. Do some skiing without poles each time you go out until your arms and legs work in correct harmony. Try to balance comfortably on the glide ski. This should be done on a slight hill. Then find a moderate hill where the glide is not so long and it is easier to relax. Commit your weight to the glide ski and allow your arms and legs to work properly. Remember, as the right arm comes forward so does the left leg—diagonally; they move back in unison also. The same goes for the left arm and right leg.

The first goal of the aspiring skier, then, is to ski with relaxed rhythm, arms and legs working in perfect unison. Any attempt to go too fast before this is accomplished will only accentuate the tension and errors already being committed will make mastering good technique even harder. I was a wounded turkey for many years before I learned to relax or was even able to stomach seeing myself on videotape. Actually, it is still painful watching myself because I never seem to look as good as I would like. It is really tough to break ingrained habits.

I am always impressed when I see a group of skiers skiing together smoothly. Once on the trails of Winter Park in Minoqua, Wisconsin, I glanced up to see three skiers angling up a hill, visible through a break in the trees. It was a beautiful sight. They looked like three graceful birds sweeping up to the horizon. When I caught up with this group, I was surprised to see that they were really intermediate ski-ers, not experts as they seemed from a distance. But they were fluid, skiing naturally in a rhythmic motion, and were bound to improve—even if they had no desire to do so. They were partaking in what is the best part of the sport—gliding along in harmony with the trail, enjoying the snow covered woods of northern Wisconsin. These types of experiences, almost Zen-like in nature, are heightened by the ability to relax on the skis and to subconsciously enjoy the thrill of gliding across the countryside. Best of all, this experience is well within reach of the average skier.

For the younger skier, a relaxed style comes easily. However, for the older skier, especially the men, it is not always so. We have young skiers who, in their first year of skiing display world class technique. Whether or not they develop the endurance to become a world champion is another matter. The point is that young skiers, if they are not overcoached, often ski exceptionally well in a short time. If the older skiers could somehow stop their minds from interfering with the natural efficiency of their bodies, they, too, would learn more quickly. When coaching adults, that is why we ask them not to try too hard to improve. Trying too hard creates tension and tight muscles and that delays the learning process. If only the muscles needed are used, no tightness should be felt because tension results from the contraction of muscles that are superfluous to the motion. Excess tension means the activity is not being executed properly. Keeping a goal or two in the back of the mind is better than too much intense concentration, especially if a good skier is around to imitate once in a while.

One of the greatest factors in Bill Koch's success is his ability to relax on his skis. His skating ability, downhill perfection, and muscular strength are well known, but the most noticeable thing about Koch's skiing when viewed with a number of other world class competitors is his total relaxation as he glides up a hill. He seems to ski more effortlessly than his competitors. He rests the trail leg and arm completely as he glides along the trail. It almost seems as if he has an unfair advantage. The goal of any skier should be to attain this level of relaxation of the parts of the body that are not actually contracting at the time. Skiing would then be easier and more enjoyable.

In the following chapters advanced techniques will be discussed. But a word or two of warning: Do not try the concepts of those advanced chapters unless you have mastered the relaxed rhythm of the basic diagonal. Then realize, again, that to successfully perform the techniques that will hurl and power your body down the track, you must be in good condition; otherwise, your efforts will be restricted to very short bursts of world class diagonaling with long stretches of recuperation or just plain heavy breathing. But on the positive side, those techniques, used in moderation and dictated by the skier's physical condition, can allow anyone to ski faster, easier.

Main Concepts

1. Relaxed fluid motion is the goal of any athlete, especially, the beginning skier.
2. The opposite arm and leg flow in perfect unison in the diagonal stride. When the left hand is forward, so is the right knee (foot). They continue moving in unison as does the right arm and left leg.
3. Short-step skiing, especially up an incline, alternated with skiing without poles is the best way to learn the coordination of the diagonal stride.
4. Training during the off-season using on-land or in-water ski drills can improve your skiing technique.
5. It is important to master the timing of the diagonal before moving on to more advanced skills.

Riding The Glide Ski

2

You Can't Defy Gravity

Proper balance on the gliding ski is the "missing link" as far as many skiers and even teaching manuals are concerned. Why is proper balance so important? First of all, it is the glide phase that separates cross-country skiing from running. The glide is the most attractive part of our sport. Its flow makes the skier feel as one with the surroundings, and it is where the skier is paid back for his or her effort during the kick. If the skier is not in balance, almost all is lost: The glide is cut short, and much of the exhilaration of skiing is gone.

Beginners or intermediates will often fall off their skis early because they lack proper balance. A telltale sound is the slap of the trailing ski behind the glide foot. Some experienced skiers actually ride the ski rather successfully but may still be in an unbalanced position. Although they do not fall off their glide ski early, they still cut their glide short by their corrections and extra movements to stay on their ski. In addition, the extra forces they generate are passed through the ski to the snow and cause pressure on the gliding surface, thereby slowing the glide. Learning proper balance would save them much time in their races and would allow them to use energy for propulsion rather than for balance. In both cases, however, the beginner and the expert run into trouble because their mass is not centered over the glide ski. You can't defy the law of gravity.

One note of warning: *Master the proper rhythm of arms and legs working together before attempting extensive work on riding the glide ski.* Younger skiers will usually be ready for this phase right away;

however, for older skiers, too much emphasis on getting on top of the glide ski can destroy the progress made in chapter 1. In no case should it be attempted before mastering the short-step diagonal. Another reason for starting with short-step skiing, or jogging on skis, is to keep the body on top of the skis. This develops the proper coordination and, at the same time, begins to teach a natural balance on the glide ski.

Before describing the glide position, its place in the total picture should be explained. Cross-country skiing is a power-explosion sport. During the kick, the leg is used to propel the body forward. Then the legs rest as the arms perform their muscular duty, pushing the skier along the track on a balanced glide ski. The lower body is almost motionless while the arms maintain the momentum generated by the kick.

The Glide Position

The glide phase itself is divided into two parts (see Figure 2.1). As the kicking leg leaves the ground, the skier enters the first, or *free glide*, position of this phase. During this short period before the pole is planted, the skier glides from the power of the kick alone. Because of friction with the snow, the skier is constantly slowing down during this phase. Therefore, it is imperative that the pole is planted as soon as possible to stop this process of deceleration.

Once the pole is planted, the skier enters the second gliding phase—the *pole-assisted glide.* It is this phase that separates the greats from the also-rans.

Figure 2.1 **(a)** End of the kick, start of the free glide; **(b)** free glide; **(c)** pole plant, end of free glide and start of pole glide; and **(d)** pole glide.

Elite skiers competing at the world class level have a very short free glide and a very powerful pole glide. Contrast this to the average skier who has almost no pole glide, relying on free glide alone. This results in an inefficient stop-and-start motion. The skier free glides, slows down almost to a stop, and kicks again to free glide, the arms being almost useless except for balance. The expert keeps momentum by planting the pole as soon as the hand is forward, and has very little stop-and-start motion. The next kick starts while the skier is still moving at a good rate. *It is important for the self-coached skier to remember to keep the rhythm of arms and legs working together, planting the pole as soon as the hand is forward.*

The most common error at this time is to try to extend the glide while delaying the pole plant. Most skiers consciously, unless told otherwise, attempt to get a long free glide. Once a late pole plant has become a habit, look out. It could take a full season of skiing to undo what would have been easy to correct at the beginning. It is by far the most common error for intermediate skiers who have already developed some balance on their glide skis. Whatever else you do, be sure that when the knee and opposite hand come forward, the pole is planted immediately. It is ironic that the beginner usually plants his pole way too early—for balance, whereas the intermediate plants his pole too late—for glide.

At this time, do not extend the glide drastically. Rather, work to obtain a balanced glide position, letting the increased glide come naturally. How to develop a powerful kick and longer glide will be explained in later chapters. For now, learning a balanced position while preserving the arm and leg motions is the goal. Wait a while for the power applications. Above all, get the pole planted without delay when the hand and knee come forward. Although you are probably tired of hearing this, it will be mentioned again, because it is that important.

Analyzing the Glide

When analyzing the glide position, start from a side view. One of the first noticeable things about a group of world class skiers is that their postures vary greatly. Some such as Bill Koch, Lars Erik Erikson, and Odvar Braa are more upright in the supposed "Norwegian Style." Yet even within their own teams, great variations arise. Pall Gunner Mickelsplass skis with the more bent-over style that is sometimes credited to the Russians. Then again, on the Russian team Yuri Burlakov and Evgeni Beliaev ski as upright as any of the Norwegians. Finally there is the ever-changing Juha Mieto. Conclusion? Quite a bit of lee-way exists as to how upright a person can ski. The fine tuning of an expert's forward lean depends on value judgment. Is the skier really projecting all of his or her energy down the track? This sometimes takes the eye of an expert coach and individual experimentation to find the position that allows not only relaxation on the ski, but also a powerful thrust down the track.

Skiing Postures for the Stride

Before you panic looking for that expert coach, there is much you can do on your own with the help of your friends. Go with your own natural posture as you start skiing. As you get faster, you will probably fall into a more bent-over posture naturally. Necessary at this time is a balanced posture that will allow you to experience an exceptional glide (see Figure 2.2).

There are many possible balanced positions such as the skier in Figure 2.2. The skier may be able to be balanced over a straight leg, but for most people, any fast progress would be difficult. In addition, the skier would have to rebend his or her legs constantly in order to kick powerfully. An overly straight glide leg is not a good position, not even for a tourer, because even though it is a seemingly more restful position, the skier must raise and lower his or her body weight as he or she bends his leg for each kick. This is the equivalent of going up and down a small hill. It takes much more energy to rebend the leg to kick, thereby

Figure 2.2   The perfectly balanced glide position of Thomas Wassburg.

moving the body up and down, than it takes to balance it on a flexed one, which is immediately ready for the next kick. Contrast this to the skier in Figure 2.3, whose posture is in a state of overflexion. Each stride will be very powerful, but it is likely that this skier will run out of gas in a hurry. This skier would find it difficult to relax during the glide phase and would spend great energy on every kick.

Many intermediate positions exist between the two extremes, all of which are effective for tourer and racer alike. The racer is more likely to bend over farther than the tourer because of his greater emphasis on speed and forward momentum. But both must be in a physically sound position, balanced on the ski. So what should be observed from the side view?

In the glide position side view, the skier's center of gravity should be in a balanced position so the muscles do not have to work to keep him or her on top of his or her ski. The leg that hangs behind is balanced by the arm and head in front. An experienced coach can just look and feel that a position is wrong, but the neophyte needs something on which to focus. The leg in the glide phase should be in a slightly flexed state. The foot should be directly under or slightly behind

Figure 2.3 A balanced yet tiring posture. Too bent over for most skiers, yet some would claim racers use this much flexion.

the knee, and both should be beneath the chest area. The front of the knee is usually under the junction of the neck and upper body. Figures 2.4a through 2.4e show four very acceptable positions. If the skier has to straighten his or her leg or move forward and back while gliding, the position of balance is faulty.

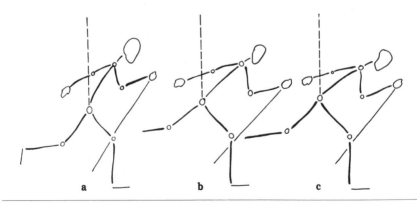

Figure 2.4(a), (b), (c) Acceptable racing postures.

Fig. 2.4 cont.

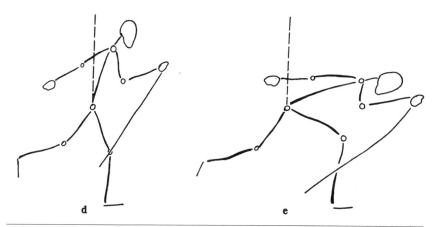

Figure 2.4 **(d)** Touring posture; **(e)** too bent—can be tiring.

Although the center of gravity does change slightly during the stride, any bouncing up and down during the glide phase is incorrect. The actual amount and timing of vertical movement in the diagonal stride will be covered in a later chapter.

If the skier is in a balanced position, he or she will be able to maintain the angles of the thigh to lower leg and thigh to body fairly well until the next kick is started. However, if the skier is sitting too far back as in Figure 2.5, the laws of physics take over. Unless

Figure 2.5 This skier has weight too far back and will have to immediately stand up to avoid falling back.

something is done, the skier will fall backward, the center of gravity not being forward enough. This is a position attained by many advanced skiers who have been taught to drive their knees forward but in the process have allowed their bodies to drop. These skiers will also have a pronounced up-and-down body motion during the glide. Just as skiers begin the glide, it is killed as they stand up to get balance. This imparts a force down to the snow that creates excess friction, causing the ski to slow down.

Common Errors in the Glide

As beginners progress in their skiing, they will experience slight variations in the glide error. These flaws were mentioned as common errors for the beginner in chapter 1. In that chapter they were treated as a lack of rhythm and abandon. They can be also approached as a function of balance on the glide ski. The first flaw is being afraid to place all the weight on the glide ski, tentatively shoving the ski forward like a person testing for cold water. The second is keeping the rear foot glued to the track rather than letting it follow through naturally. Some skiers raise their rear foot briefly from the track; however, because their weight is too far back, the ski will slap down early. These skiers must learn to commit their weight forward to the glide ski and find a balanced position. In both cases, the skier's body is too far behind the glide foot.

Again, short-step skiing is one of the best ways to learn to be on top of the glide ski in a relaxed manner. When the steps are small, so is the insecurity. After eliminating foot slap with short-step skiing, the stride may be increased to its normal length.

Several seasons ago, almost by accident, I discovered a way to get beginners onto their glide ski in a more confident manner. We were working on arm movements at the time, much like the material covered in chapter 1. The two students with whom I was working were stopping their poling motion before their arms reached their hips, rather than letting them follow through in a natural manner. When I got them to get their arms past their hips, a wonderful side effect happened. They both started throwing their body down on the track with abandon, their weight on their glide skis in a balanced position. The wonderful part was that one was 50 years old and the other was 10. Since then I have had the opportunity to work with quite a few beginners, and this method has worked quite well for most of them.

If you are having trouble getting on top of the glide ski, it would help to have someone check to see how far back your hands are going. You may even be able to detect this yourself. Another point to review at this time is your grip on the poles. Release the poles in the follow-through and regrip them only when they are again planted in the snow. This seemingly unimportant point can completely destroy your form by not allowing you to achieve relaxed motion and the abandon needed to balance on the glide ski; so release those poles. Control is in the thumb and forefinger. If you have trouble doing so, go back to Figure 1.5 in chapter 1 to see if your straps are adjusted properly.

The final variation of skiers who incorrectly ride the glide ski as viewed from the side, is that exhibited by many talented youngsters. They actually have their weight too far forward. Or, looking at it another way, their glide foot is too far back. As a result, they weight their toes which pressures the kick wax onto the snow, slowing them down. They are also in a weak position from which to move to the next stride (see Figure 2.6).

Figure 2.6 The position of many "talented youngsters." The knee should be under the chest.

Their arms and bodies are too far in front of the glide leg, but the extension of the legs in the rear is so good, and the diagonal is performed with such abandon that a very fluid stride is attained. To me these youngsters are jewels. They have always turned out to be very talented athletes and will learn very rapidly. They are typified by a smooth and rhythmic motion and, to the uninformed viewer, look perfect already. Thus, a checkpoint is needed to help identify these individuals and a method of correction is necessary for these already beautiful, but not powerful skiers.

These skiers can be helped by changing the basic posture of their body. They usually ski with an overly arched back (see Figure 2.7), whereas they should be skiing with a natural curvature of the spine (see Figure 2.8). This posture allows many nice things to happen.

Figure 2.7   An over arched back is a common source of back problems.

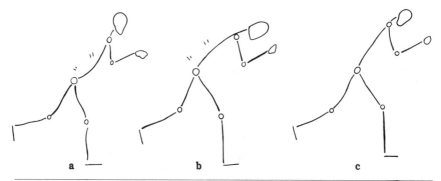

Figure 2.8 **(a)** Back pain; **(b)** corrective posture of the "C" position; and **(c)** natural back position.

First, it allows the legs to be farther forward, yet remain in a comfortable position. The arched back forces the legs behind the skier, whereas the natural back allows a comfortable position with the knee under the chest. It is the assimilation of this position that allows the talented youngster to step from the ranks of the pretty skier to the powerful one. The reasons will be discussed in more detail in future chapters. However, at this time, it will suffice to say that it allows the leg to be in a more powerful position of flexion with the weight of the skier over, rather than in front of, the gliding leg. When that gliding leg becomes the kicking leg, a more explosive kick results, and the skier will be able to more easily set the wax because the weight is on top of the glide ski.

Some instructors even go in the opposite direction and have the skiers round their back so that the spine assumes a *C* position (the opposite of arched). However, a close examination of the best skiers in the world shows that their backs are in the natural position, and that makes sense. Any artificial hunching of the back or shoulders will only create stiffness that will inhibit motion. The shoulders will be driving forward, but to artificially hunch them is a mistake; they should be in a natural relaxed position.

The teaching of the *C* position itself is usually not dangerous because most of the skiers wind up with straight backs. However, some skiers learn it so well that it becomes an inhibiting flaw. Skiers must attain the position in a relaxed manner, or they will find themselves crunched up, unable to kick powerfully, unable to naturally ride the glide ski, and generally limited to short-crunched strides. As athletes, skiers must never ever emphasize a position so much that the natural potential of full range muscle relaxation and explosion is lost. In the following chapters the ultimate step in learning to ski—that of uninhibited power skiing—will be further developed. For now, try to ski in a natural back position with the legs under the chest, but do so in a relaxed manner; then the power moves will be easier to master.

The natural back position also miraculously helps cure skiers' back problems. I have coached many people who have complained of a sore back while skiing but who do not normally have back problems. Almost all of these skiers have an arched back throughout the stride with their legs too far back to support their bodies. All the pressure is then on the lower back. Most of these skiers have seen their skiing-related back problems disappear when they changed their body posture. This is especially true during roller skiing where skiers have more difficulty relaxing and where the heaviness of some roller skis strains the lower back.

Being a former victim of lower back pain, I learned early that the over-arched back is one position that must be avoided in all activities. Extreme arching of the lower back places great strain on the back muscles and should be avoided, especially while skiing or in lifting. At no time should you start lifting with a rounded back and end with the back arched. In skiing, the straight back position (as shown in Figure 2.8) with the foot under the chest removes this strain through the natural support system of the glide leg. Contrast this to the skier in Figure 2.8a who actually has the body acting as a lever with the back muscles as the fulcrum, placed under much greater stress because of the mechanical effect of the lever. It is like trying to hold a long pole on the end—hard to do; but grab the pole in the middle, and it is much easier to hold. Likewise, the natural position with the leg under the chest has the same effect.

One of the problems in teaching the balanced glide position from a book is that the illustrations are two-dimensional, whereas the skier balances in a three-dimensional world. A skier can be perfectly balanced from a side view but not from a front view. He or she could have great difficulty staying on the ski and wonder where the problem is. That is why good coaches usually observe their skiers, not only from the side but also from the rear, by skiing behind the athlete. This is one of the best ways to check for lateral balance. Any premature falling off the ski is readily apparent. The skier should stay comfortably over the gliding ski until the next kick.

Many skiers move down the track with their hips and shoulders perfectly square and their heads moving in a straight line between the middle of the tracks. Several years ago this was believed to be proper technique. Analyses of the top international stars, however, as well as the forces of physics, show this to be an inefficient way to ski. First of all, the tracks are about 7 in. apart. To have perfect balance on the right and then on the left ski means that some side-to-side shift of the center of gravity is necessary (see Figure 2.9).

Figure 2.9   There is a slight side to side weight shift, due to the width of the tracks.

The top stars actually move their heads slightly from side to side as they stride down the track. This has the effect of slightly moving their center of mass from side to side. It is important not to exaggerate this movement to the degree that it becomes bending, that is, bending at the waist; instead, it is a subtle shifting of the entire mass of the body with the head being one of the indicators.

The second technique to help the skier balance perfectly on the glide ski is a subtle swiveling of the hips, which will be discussed in detail later. However, at this time, it is only necessary for the skier to know that the hips do not remain perfectly square to the tracks but that they swivel slightly to balance over the glide ski.

Are you confused with all this talk of subtle movements of the head from side to side, accompanied by a slight twisting of the hips? Stop, clear your mind, and realize that your only goal at this point is to learn to balance on the glide ski, and that trying to stay squarely in the middle of the track is not the way to do it. Allow a slight side-to-side movement to balance on the ski, but do not worry about how it happens. Just balance.

Drills for Developing a Balanced Glide

Three drills will help you learn this balance. The skier who never learns to ride the glide ski in an effortless fashion loses the biggest energy saver of skiing and its biggest pleasure. However, before you start working on these drills, remember: *Never try too hard to master these drills.* Trying too hard creates tension. Tension means that the wrong muscles are interfering or that the right ones are contracting excessively; instead, use one of three techniques to improve. First, get it straight in your mind, so there is no confusion as to what you are trying to accomplish; then keep it in the back of your mind as you work on it. Second, vividly imagine what you are trying to accomplish ahead of time and actually "feel" the motion. Watch good skiers to get the feel. Then *let* the feeling happen to you. Third, observe what you are doing, but in a nonevaluative manner. For instance, observe how long your weight is balanced on the ski. As you get better at being aware of what you are doing, your body will automatically adjust to riding the glide ski longer. If you fight it, the learning process will be delayed. The more advanced you become, the more you will be working on the rhythm and feel of your stride, trying to make the stride easier and more flowing. *That is why chapter 1 is not for beginners only.* It would be a good idea to go back to chapter 1 after each succeeding chapter, so you do not become bogged down mentally. You should never become inundated. If you do, just clear your mind and ski with rhythm.

Skiing without poles. Skiing without poles (or holding the poles in the middle) can be done on a section of track with a slight incline. Ski with rhythm but think about extending the time spent on each ski before the next kick. When you can do this until you have lost almost all of the glide, you have attained good balance.

Skiing with poles. The second drill is to ski up a slight incline using your poles. After all, that is how you will be skiing most of the time. Start short-step skiing, but then try to extend your glide before the next kick. One note of warning: *Plant the pole as soon as the hand swings forward.* During the glide phase before the pole is planted, the friction of the snow will cause you to slow down. So most of the glide phase should occur while the pole is pushing. If you wait too long to plant the pole, the ski will have slowed down. Then trying to use the arms will be more difficult, because of the loss of momentum. Planting the pole while the glide is faster makes it easier for the arms to keep you moving.

The benefit of planting the pole early is that it actually helps you on the glide ski (see Figure 2.10). The angle formed by the pole and your glide leg forms a triangle with the pole, helping to keep you from falling off the glide ski. In addition, you get the added bonus of a pole push while your momentum is still high, keeping you moving faster down the track.

 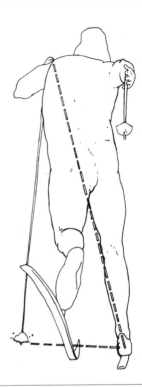

Figure 2.10   Triangle of support. Pushing the pole helps maintain balance.

Extended Glide Ski Drill.   The last drill is one that I thought was unique to our area until I heard Steve Gaskill speak at a Level 1 USSA clinic. He also has had good success with this drill. You pick a slight hill where it is easy to diagonal and ski as slowly as you can and *still keep your natural rhythm.* Try to extend your gliding time by doing two things: First, push on the pole to extend the glide; second, slightly delay the return of the rear leg. Skiers have more success if they just observe their foot motions on some runs and their poling motion on others. The goal in the back of the mind is to keep the weight on the glide ski until the next kick is started (at about when the feet are together) and to keep the momentum of the glide by pushing with poles until the kick. Take note, however: If your back is sore, stop this drill until your glide position improves. It usually means that you are not skiing with a straight back, with the foot being under the chest. Furthermore, do not lose your natural rhythm, but always ski fast enough to keep the flow.

I saw an interesting situation one day several winters ago. An experienced skier was helping one of my beginning racers on his second day of skiing. This beginner was very talented, and his only previous contact with ski technique was seeing an instructional videotape we had done on roller skiing. As with all beginners, his glide was not excessively long. But his poling rhythm was perfect, and he could move down the track with good speed and confidence. What was amusing was that the beginner had much better technique than the experienced skier. The instructor was trying to get the beginner to glide longer on the ski by delaying the pole plant. The result: *disaster*. The beginner lost all his natural rhythm and was falling off the glide ski more than before. By delaying his pole plant to get longer stride, three things were happening: (a) The naturalness of his skiing was gone; (b) the balancing effect of a correct pole plant was lost; and (c) he lost momentum. I suggested to the beginner that he plant his pole as soon as his hand came forward. He soon was back on the right track, skiing again with rhythm and extending his glide correctly, through his poling motion.

Main Concepts

1. In order to ski in an efficient and relaxed style, you must have a balanced glide position. You should not have to fight to maintain this position or be constantly losing balance.
2. This "ideal" glide position will vary from individual to individual but has some of the following aspects:

   - The skier looks natural and does not seem to have trouble keeping his balance.
   - The knee of the glide leg is somewhere under the chest and the foot under the knee.
   - There is some side-to-side head motion as the weight is shifted from ski to ski.

- The glide leg maintains a fairly constant angle until the next kick.
- Faster skiers tend to be more bent over than slower skiers and tourers, but not always so.

3. Totally commit your weight to the glide ski until the next kick.
4. Try to extend the glide while the pole is pushing, not by extending free glide. Work slowly to increase your glide, but never delay your pole plant to do so.
5. Always remember, the diagonal stride is a relaxed fluid motion where the opposite arms and legs work in unison. Abandoned skiing must be interspersed with the teachings of this chapter, as well as all of the following ones. At no time should the fluid motion of the ski stride be lost for any other technical gains because stiffer skiing is never a move forward. If in doubt, go back to chapter 1.

Efficient Skiing   3

A Closer Look at Basic Technique

I have often heard the criticism that racers are so busy sweating and training hard that they miss the real enjoyment of skiing, failing to smell the roses along the way. One of the main reasons for racing, however, is that the skier enjoys the sport immensely and wants to excel at it. The skier can also stretch the enjoyment well past the snowy months of winter by roller skiing during the other 9 months of the year. During a long-distance workout, a racer becomes synchronized to the terrain in a relaxed manner, truly is aware of nature, and is in tune with the inner workings of the body. It is a time for meditation, for working out one's personal problems, or for just feeling good as the skier's perspiration seems to have a cleansing effect on body and soul.

Floating over the snow, peaking on eskers, swooshing down kettles, and covering much ground, the racer sees more than the average tourer, who many times finds him- or herself trudging with a pack of fellow skiers on a well-used trail near a metropolitan area. Being in excellent condition allows the skier to effortlessly engage in a long-distance workout. The closer the average tourer can come to the efficient technique and over all condition of the elite racer, the more he or she will enjoy skiing (unless he or she is happy just walking on skis through the woods). The pain of exertion or the feeling of clumsiness will no longer hold him or her back. Therefore, anyone who truly loves skiing will be rewarded by improved technique, particularly in the diagonal stride.

I can recall my first impressions of the 1980 Olympic skiers. I was amazed at how different each skier looked from the other—from the locomotive style of Thomas Wassburg to the fluid grace of Nikolai

Zimyatov to the raw, lumbering power of Juha Mieto. Each of these skiers had a highly personalized style. As we pored over the tapes, however, we became equally astounded to discover that when performing certain basic movements and positions, these skiers were almost identical. Body types, pole lengths, and general physical mannerisms give these athletes a unique style; but the fundamentals remain constant. The following material is a presentation of these common elements of technique.

Fundamental Similarities Among the Experts

Body Motions

Because the diagonal is a continuous motion, I arbitrarily chose the beginning of the kick where the feet are together as a starting point. The purpose of the kick is to impart the most momentum to the body with the least effort. It must occur before the momentum of the previous stride has been lost. If it does not, additional force must be applied to overcome the body's inertia—not to mention the time lost as the body slows down. The top international racers do not show any noticeable slowdown between kicks.

At the point where the two feet are together, the postures of the top skiers in the world are remarkably similar. Their legs are flexed, hips balanced directly over their feet with the upper body at roughly a 45° angle to the ground. This posture varies slightly from skier to skier: Some of the most upright international stars are Bill Koch, Odvaar Braa, Lars Erik Eriksen, Evgeni Beliaev, and Yuri Burlakov; some of the most bent over are Thomas Eriksson, Alexandre Zavjalov, Thomas Wassberg, and Juha Mieto. The average tourer will be a little more upright and the average racer more bent over, simply because of the differences in speed. The general impression at this point is one of coiled power. Almost all of the weight is still on the kicking leg (see Figures 3.1 through 3.4, Position A).

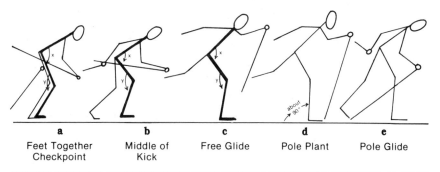

a	b	c	d	e
Feet Together Checkpoint	Middle of Kick	Free Glide	Pole Plant	Pole Glide

Figure 3.1 Body positions in the diagonal.

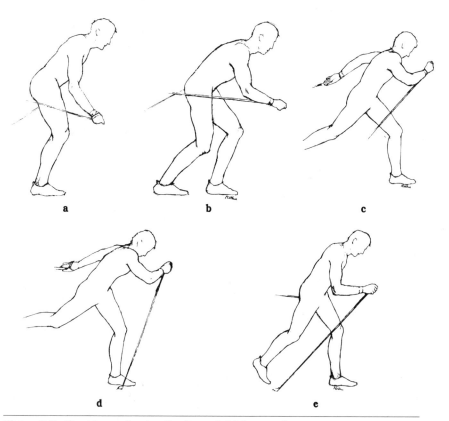

Figure 3.2 Zimyatov performing the diagonal: **(a)** feet together checkpoint; **(b)** middle of kick; **(c)** free glide; **(d)** pole plant; and **(e)** pole glide.

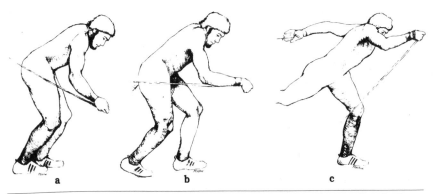

Figure 3.3 Mieto performing the diagonal: **(a)** feet together checkpoint; **(b)** middle of kick; and **(c)** free glide.

Figure 3.3 **(d)** Pole plant; and **(e)** pole glide.

Somewhere around Position *A* (feet together), the kicking ski has stopped moving (the glide has ended), and the leg is propelling the body forward (the kick has begun). The movement from Figure 3.1 *A* through Figure 3.1 *C* is the part of the kick that hurls the body forward with complete abandon. The entire darkened area of the skier in *B* and *C* of the figures is hurled forward as one piece. The force of the kicking leg is imparted directly to the mass of the entire body. At the end of this move, the skier is in free glide, beginning pole implantation.

If the skier really mastered the short-step skiing in chapter 1 and solidified it in chapter 2 while learning to ride the glide ski more effectively, he or she is probably throwing the body forward in the correct manner already. The skier then only needs some feed-

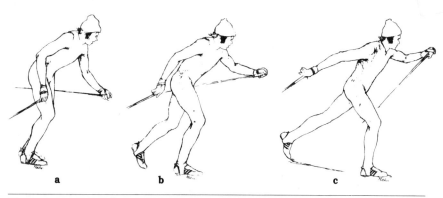

Figure 3.4 Koch performing the diagonal: **(a)** feet together checkpoint; **(b)** middle of kick; and **(c)** free glide.

Figure 3.4 **(d)** Pole plant; and **(e)** pole glide.

back to see if he or she is doing it properly. The skier should notice that by following the stepwise procedures as presented in this book, many errors made by the average beginner and intermediate can be avoided.

One of the most common errors found in skiers of all levels is that of slipping the leg, knee, and foot forward faster than the body. The telltale signal of this move is a dropping of the hips as the skier moves onto the glide ski. This imparts less overall momentum as the body lags and leaves the skier in a poor position for the next kick.

This is a critical checkpoint for the coach or observer. The body and forward leg must move together in a "one-piece" motion, thereby imparting the maximum momentum to the largest mass. The actual checkpoint is that Angles X and Y in the figures from Positions A through C remain fairly constant and the body mass does not drop. In fact, there is a slight rise in the body through these positions. Again this would all be mere conjecture except that all of the top skiers in the world ski in this manner. Note the illustrations of Mieto, Zimyatov, and Wassberg throughout these phases.

The above concepts are not entirely new, but because of weaknesses in communications, some have been misinterpreted, especially at the level of the beginning skier. *Ride a straight leg* is one of these. *Ride a firm leg* would be better; because observation of the world's best show the leg is definitely not straight. It is firm, however, in holding angles of the bent glide leg.

At this time, *head bob* must be mentioned. All the top skiers in the world move their heads up and down throughout the ski stride to some degree. Head bob results from the natural flexion of the trunk (coil) as the legs come together and the natural extension of the trunk in the explosive motion of the kick. The amount of "bob" varies anywhere from 1 or 2 inches to much more in some skiers. But as long as the hips do not drop and the drive is forward rather than up, the head bob is probably not excessive. One thing is sure: Absolutely no head bob may be pretty, but it results in a weak skiing motion that lacks the flexion and extension needed for a powerful stride. This topic will be more thoroughly discussed in the following chapters.

Arm Motions

Arm movement can be divided into two parts: the forward motion and the poling thrust. The arm must move forward in concert with the leg. There should be no independent forward arm acceleration. Any such acceleration would only cause an opposite and equal reaction, actually working to throw the skier backward. Aggressive arm action was in vogue several years ago, and many skiers learned it too well. They accelerated their arms faster than their legs and got way out of wack. Their arm swings actually carried them to a standing position on the glide ski. Their motions are typified by an exaggerated shoulder roll. It is important, therefore, to keep the arms and legs coordinated when going for more speed. (This will be detailed later in the chapter.) But if someone tells you to extend your arms way in front of your body and use them to carry you down the track, just smile, say you'll try and continue doing it your own way. The best skiers in the world definitely do not ski with over-extended arms pulling them down the track. Instead, they use a coordinated overall motion that is consistent with the laws of physics and that uses the strengths and natural workings of their entire body.

The poling phase is, however, a neglected motion for many competitors. Its purpose is not only to aid in balancing the skier, but more importantly, to propel the skier forward, thereby enhancing the momentum of the kick. The top skiers in the world, as different as they appear, actually have the following points in common:

1. The pole plant occurs quickly, even before the trailing leg starts forward. This quick pole plant assures a thrust before the glide has lost its momentum.
2. The arm is in a bent position when the pole is planted. Few of the top stars have their arms nearly straight before the pole plant—but only when the conditions are very fast. However, once the pole is planted, all have bent arms.

   The bent position of the arm ensures a stronger poling position. If the arm is too straight, in addition to a circular poling position, the lever arm is too long and the muscles are in a mechanically weak position. A person could use the large muscles of the upper back and still not exert much usable force.
3. The poling hand thrusts in a fairly straight line from the original pole plant position through the middle of the thigh area (see Figure 3.5a).

This direct line thrust in C guarantees that most of the poling energy expended helps maintain the glide phase. The skiers who plant with too straight an arm and use a semicircular movement are not getting a good return for their output (see Figure 3.5b). The only

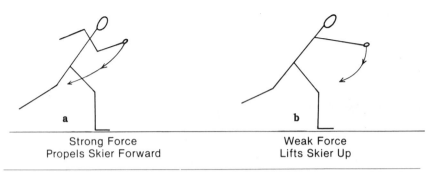

Strong Force   Weak Force
Propels Skier Forward   Lifts Skier Up

Figure 3.5   Poling phases. **(a)** Strong force propels a skier forward.
(b) Force applied at wrong time and with straight arms lifts a skier up.

way Skier B could use his poles more effectively is if
there were a wall behind him whereby he could get a
parallel push.

   With the bent arm and straight line movement of
the hand, the lats (latissimus dorsi), in conjunction
with the triceps, work from a mechanically stronger
position. This conclusion is not just a matter of theory
because the outstanding skiers from various countries
use this technique. (Note: Some top international stars
actually involve their stomach muscles to a large
degree; refer to chapter 6 for details.)

   This leads us to one of the most important and
useful checkpoints in the cross-country stride: *The
position of hands at midpoint* (feet-together position).
(See Position A of Figure 3.1 through 3.4). If the pole
has been planted immediately and has done its job
(i.e., it has continued the momentum of the glide), the
poling hand will be next to the thighs with the swinging arm in front of the body. Actually, any skier with
the proper arm and leg coordination will reach this
position, but any skier who does not, has not used the
poles powerfully. I have heard that some coaches teach
that this checkpoint will automatically be reached as
the skier learns to go faster. This is definitely not true.
The basic rhythm of the diagonal places the hand at
this checkpoint. Most beginners we teach reach this
position naturally. These lucky individuals only need
to learn to add power to their stroke.

   The advanced skiers who have these positions
reversed (that is, the poling hand is in front and the
swinging hand is at the hips) will find their job twice

as hard. They will have to not only learn how to use their poles effectively, but also will have to learn the natural rhythm of the ski stride. For them this rearrangement of rhythm is very difficult to learn because they have become so good at the wrong timing through many hours of practice. Skiers who have intentionally tried to extend their arms to the front will usually have this problem. They have delayed their pole plant while trying to achieve forward momentum through the use of their arms. Because this overextension of the arms has been popular for a number of years, many good skiers have this problem.

Once the correct rhythm is relearned, the effort pays off quickly. Instead of a stop-start motion, usually accompanied by the skier losing the angles of the glide leg by standing up, there is a movement that has little loss of momentum between strides. Admittedly, it can be a frustrating effort for the advanced skier, but it is well worth the effort. That is the reason for the warning note about pole plants in the first and second chapters. If the skier has learned to plant the pole in the correct rhythm of the diagonal immediately after the arm and leg have moved forward, he or she will never have to go through this relearning process. I am convinced of this after coaching many skiers of all abilities, many of them on roller skis. I have seen top competitors become frustrated as they watch rank beginners do, naturally, those things that are causing them difficulty.

To maintain momentum, the skier must plant the pole quickly before speed is lost, and a powerful direct thrust must occur. To reemphasize: The hand position at the midpoint is a key checkpoint that helps insure that this is happening. *The poling hand must be at the thighs, whereas the swinging hand should be a foot or so in front of the thighs.*

One area of confusion is how far back should the arms follow through? This varies among top skiers and from slow to fast conditions. If the hands reach the midthigh checkpoint successfully, the follow-through has probably not been excessive. Conversely, if the arm continues pushing to the thigh, any natural follow-through is enough: Fast snow—more follow-through; slow snow or hills—less follow-through. The varying of the arms in different conditions will be discussed in more detail in chapter 5.

A second area of poling confusion is, where should the pole tip be planted? First, this depends on the pole length (longer poles—farther back). Second, hill gradient and/or snow speed affect where the tip is planted (steeper hills or slower conditions—farther back).

One cause of this confusion was Dr. Charles Dillman's excellent biomechanical analysis, which was a real breakthrough for the American skiing scene. However, his reference to a forward and vertical pole plant has influenced many skiers into planting their poles too far forward, with the arm too straight and the pole too vertical. When the pole is vertical, any force will only lift the skier off the ski, not propel him or her forward, so these skiers cannot use their poles immediately and have to glide before their poling action can work for them. As a result, momentum was lost before the poling became effective. Those who did this forget that Dillman also recommends a powerful arm movement with a bent arm.

The top international stars on our tapes plant their poles near the toes of their boots (some even behind) in normal to fast conditions. On hills, the poles are farther back. I have seen films where the pole plant is farther forward, but the conditions were very fast. If a skier is experimenting with a forward vertical pole plant, it is important that the pole is planted as soon as the hand is forward and the poling hand reaches the feet-together checkpoint. Never plant the pole in front of the boot. No good has ever come from it, and many skiers have lost the basic rhythm of the diagonal, actually using their poles less efficiently than before.

One more excellent checkpoint tests the effectiveness of the pole glide phase and its transition to the next kick: In slow motion (videotape or polarvision), check the forward movement of the skier's upper body. The best international stars do not exhibit any stop-start motion at the transition to kick, whereas the poor skiers sometimes come almost to a dead stop between strides. They then have to overcome inertia to get their bodies moving again, whereas "a body in motion tends to remain in motion." If your body does not move steadily down the track, your poling motion has probably been ineffective. The most common cause of this is standing up or losing balance on the glide ski. Your poles can't work if you are not maintaining balance on the glide ski. Any stop-start movement takes more energy than a continuous one.

Glide Position

Therefore, it is appropriate to take a further look at the glide position. After all the discussion about dynamic flexion and powerful pole movement, it may seem strange that the success of the ski stride depends upon the one fairly static part: *riding the glide ski*. The whole purpose of the glide is to maintain the momentum of the kick and to encourage the "afterburner effect" of the pole on forward momentum. This has the delightful side effect of giving the legs a slight rest as the upper body does its part. The glide position has several key characteristics:

1. The leg remains constantly flexed (although there is a slight hitch near the end of the glide phase as the leg loads for the next kick). The angles established at Position A through C in Figures 3.1 through 3.4 remain fairly constant, especially the lower leg to thigh. This is not a rigid position, however, but one of dynamic balance as the skier's foot is constantly trying to extend the glide.
2. The weight is mainly on the heel with the lower leg (knee to ankle), nearly perpendicular to the ground. This keeps the ski tip light on the snow and snow contact with the wax pocket at a minimum. But remember that the body is centered over the ski, not behind it, with the knee under the chest.
3. All of the weight remains on the gliding ski (and thrusting pole) until the gliding leg loses contact with the snow after the kick.
4. Any standing up or upward motion imparts an opposite force downward onto the snow, thereby slowing the glide. Therefore, the top skiers ride a "quiet ski," their legs in a constant state of flex.

5.   The trailing leg and arm are completely relaxed
      and drift forward slowly while the skier is in free
      glide.

One of the common errors in the glide phase is
straightening the glide leg. This cuts off the glide,
forcing an earlier kick. In addition, standing up on the
glide ski introduces vertical body movement that is
fatiguing and leaves the leg in a weak position for the
next kick. The leg must then be rebent in order to
kick. It takes enough energy to propel the skier forward. Moving the entire center of gravity up and down
introduces wasted energy expenditure. The skier finds
him- or herself skiing as if he or she were climbing
nonexistent hills.

Proper Practice of Techniques

Spring and summer are excellent times to practice
the concepts of this chapter, especially because they
are harder to accomplish on roller skis. Once the skills
are mastered on roller skis, they will seem easier on
snow. However, in applying the lessons of this chapter,
it is important that the skier not lose sight of the
teachings of chapter 1—that of fluid motion. The goal
of any skier, racer or tourer, is to ski more efficiently.
If a skier is too wrapped up in technical details,
performance can actually decrease as the movement
becomes more stilted. Therefore, periods of relaxed
and uninhibited skiing have their place in the learning
process. The skier should be aware of what he or she
is doing but not bulldoze his or her muscles into doing
it. Too much intense mental direction only inhibits the
freedom of motion. Skiing with abandon so that
muscle groups do not oppose each other is the final
goal.

After teaching golf professionally for several years,
I was impressed by the fact that students had to
attempt to exaggerate certain movements to learn
them. As they became adept at the new movement,
however, they still tried to attain the feelings of the
original lesson even though the movement was easier

for them as they progressed. As a result, they exaggerated the feeling until it became a flaw. Many of the students would have to be corrected in reverse at the next lesson. I soon realized that some safety check or exercise had to be included with the original drill. The most common golf examples were those students whose swings were floppy and who had no constant left arm radius. At the next lesson, the student would be swinging very stiffly with an iron rod left arm. Fortunately, doing exercises of a free, continuous, back and forth swinging, interspersed with a motion emphasizing a firm left arm radius, allowed the golfers to achieve a happy medium.

Skiers who are making corrections need to be watched to prevent this same kind of "overcorrecting." Coaching and/or some type of buddy system is needed because each person feels things differently. While some people have an excellent awareness of what their body is doing, others are not so fortunate. A person can perform the same movement on 2 separate days, yet feel completely different and think that the movements were not the same. For this reason, feedback from a coach or other observer is important.

Even the top stars do not meet the coaching checkpoints all the time. Track irregularities, fatigue, and such cause variations in technique. In fact, most of the skiers viewed were noticeably stronger with their right pole than their left. Man is not a machine. However, the more ingrained good technique becomes, the more likely the skier will "hold technique" in trying situations and, in the end, ski faster, easier.

Main Concepts

1. There is flexion in the legs-together position with the weight entirely on the kicking leg.
2. The kick produces a one-piece motion of the body and forward leg (no independent forward leg slipping).
3. The pole plant is early enough to maintain momentum with a straight line thrust to the rear. The hand should stop moving forward as soon as

the leg does with pole plant following immediately. The arm should be in flexed position at the elbow to ensure a powerful thrust.

4. The skier glides with the weight on the heel (mainly) and ball of the foot and does not stand up on the glide ski.

5. The poling hand reaches the thigh area as the legs come together. The other hand is forward.

6. The upper body maintains momentum. It does not seem to slow noticeably at the transition from kick to glide.

7. The skier tries to increase the glide through the poling, not the free glide phase.

The Mark of the Elite Skier

4

Explosive and Supple Movement

Just what is the mark of an elite skier? Some would argue that elapsed racing time is the ultimate judgment, and I would have to agree. However, in terms of technique, it is a different matter. To choose just one area of technique that separates the elite from the rest of the pack would be very difficult. And, as in any oversimplification, it is. But I am convinced that there is one movement the elite skier makes that is almost never seen in the lower ranks of skiing, be it racing or touring. Surprisingly, it is not the powerful use of the poles. The elite skier certainly is far superior to the citizen racer in poling, but after viewing countless hours of world class, Junior Olympic, and good area racers, the major difference is something else: It is the powerful thrusting and twisting of the skier's body. (This is my opinion and anyone certainly has the right to disagree. But the material in this chapter is valid whether it's the most important, second most important, or whatever.) Even the best of the citizen racers looks dead in his or her movements when compared to the top world competitors. A large part of this is conditioning, but even for short distances, the citizen racer does not have the supple and explosive moves of the top international racer.

A note of caution to the reader: Before applying the principles of this chapter, you must have reached the point of having coordinated the arms and legs to the natural rhythm of the diagonal. You must be able to balance on the glide ski while poling. And above all *you must have ingrained the feeling of throwing your body forward in one piece.* If not—disaster—but more about this later.

Power in the Diagonal

We are now going to add the real power move to the diagonal. This power and position allows experts to stride up hills, still gliding, while lesser skiers with the same wax are resorting to herringboning or running in the softer snow outside the tracks in an attempt to make their wax work. Power and body position make this possible, allowing the expert to use natural strength in the most efficient manner.

Hip Rotation During Skiing

What is this well-kept secret of the stars? It is simply a supple spine and pelvic area, spurred on by an aggressive lower body drive (see Figure 4.1 a-d). As the expert skier hurls his or her body down the track, the pelvis rotates in two directions. The skier rotates

Figure 4.1(a) Blocked hips. The elite competitor had trouble with hills until he loosened up his lower body action.

Figure 4.1(b) Proper hip movement.

his or her hips around the axis of the spine and at the
same time, tucks the rear end of the gliding leg under
in an effort to get the leg and foot farther forward. This
double rotation is the elite athlete's response to his or
her natural drive for a longer stride. By rotating the
hips, the skier actually lengthens the stride. Because
the rotation brings the glide leg farther forward, it allows a greater release of stored energy in the muscles.

In the quest for a longer stride, riding the glide ski
is all important. Hip rotation actually helps the skier
balance by placing his or her weight more on top of
the glide ski. Without hip rotation, the skier would be
in a more upright position, taking shorter strides. This
is because blocked hips force the legs to be farther
back. Because the leg is farther back, the skier must
stand more erect at the waist to keep his or her weight
back over the kicking ski.

Does this hip movement contradict the one-piece
motion discussed in chapter 3? Not really. We are now

Figure 4.1(c)   A view of supple body motion.

only noting the suppleness of this athletic motion. As
the body is tossed forward in one piece, the lower area
rotates as the leg thrusts forward. One hip has rotated
farther forward and the other back as the hips swivel
slightly, resulting in the same center of gravity. There
is, however, a slight shift from side to side in response
to the width of the tracks. The distance between the
tracks and the effort to glide promotes this hip
rotation.

A runner needs little hip rotation to run in the
most efficient manner, with legs cycling continuously
and feet directly under him or her. The natural foot
placement allows a runner to comfortably run on a
painted line in the road. However, the skier, with his
or her foot placement farther apart because of the
tracks, finds hip rotation desirable, even mandatory,
for powerful skiing. The skier must do so to get his or
her weight over the ski without swaying from side to
side. Add to this the fact that the skier is pushing to

Figure 4.1(d)   Still another angle of body motion.

glide. While running, such attempts to lengthen the
stride cause the foot to get out in front and act as a
brake because the shoe does not glide. The runner
would get no return for his or her effort of hip rotation
with its accompanying explosive use of energy because
he or she gets no glide. This would only result in early
fatigue and impact-related injuries. By smoothly
cycling his or her legs with only a slight responsive
hip motion, the runner reduces impact forces with the
ground and uses less energy to move the body
forward. The skier, however, explodes and then rests,
alternating the use of the upper and lower body, each
stride a mini-fartlek. These are the differences that
make skiing a power-endurance sport and distance
running mainly an endurance one. Just look at the
contrasting body types of skiers and runners to see the
difference: The skiers are more muscular, the runners
much thinner.

This double hip rotation, along with a slight opposite twisting of the upper body, allows the skier to shift his or her weight more completely to the glide ski. This animal-like athletic movement allows a natural twisting of a supple spine. Without this hip rotation, the skier would have two choices. The first is straddling the track, that is, having his or her center of gravity constantly down the middle of the track, never committing to the glide ski. The second choice would be waddling from side to side. With the athletic twist, there is an aggressive motion to the glide ski with a maximum retention of forward momentum.

Hip rotation also allows the skier to get his or her foot and lower leg farther in front, helping to form the 90° angle of shin to ground with the weight on the heel. This keeps the kick wax off the snow, allowing a longer and faster glide. Any weighting of the toe drives the wax into contact with the snow, thereby slowing the skier down.

Hip rotation also enhances the poling motion, which in the top international stars starts while the hips are still rotating in the follow-through of each kick. Upon the first examination of the tapes of top world competitors, we were surprised to find they actually poled while their hips were still following through and the leg still traveling backward. This gave them more time to generate glide by using their poles.

A supple body also encourages a more relaxed way of skiing. The added range of motion allows more time to relax on the glide ski. The lower body works as the upper body relaxes. I am impressed every time I see the slow motion shots of Zimyatov in the 50 k at the 1980 Olympics. Some of this action takes place during Peter Grave's eloquent description of cross-country skiing. Zimyatov looks very much like a deer in motion, skiing so smoothly that it appears effortless. (And in the process Zimyatov was blowing away the entire field.) The only muscles working are those needed at the time; the others are relaxing and resting. All this is made possible by the perfect riding of the glide ski, which, in turn, is accomplished by the excellent lower body movement in conjunction with a complete weight transfer, accentuated by the fluid twisting of the hips, helping to make this all possible.

Contrast this to the average skier who has trouble getting up the hills. This skier usually doesn't set the wax well and is limited to short little steps. Proper hip and body motions are the key. Teaching students to unlock their bodies and to learn this supple hip movement has been by far the most effective part of our on-snow coaching. The results are very dramatic. Skiers who have had trouble with hills of any kind are able to move over them with power and abandon—and not just the talented skiers. Tourers of all abilities become much better skiers when they learn to unlock the potential of their bodies. Unfortunately, there are all sorts of problems in learning this on roller skis, so most of our instruction has been limited to snow for this topic. I will only say at this time that the average roller skier is constantly fighting to stop from using too long a kick on roller skis. It is the rare roller skier who can emphasize the pelvic twist without doing the splits and destroying the kick. On roller skis we just encourage a supple movement but do not dwell on the twisting of the hips and spine. Perhaps this will be one of our future breakthroughs. However, once the proper hip and spine motions are learned on snow, they are retained on roller skis. Many natural athletes learn the proper uninhibited motion on roller skis without any special prompting.

Before attempting this on snow, you need to prepare yourself mentally and physically. It is important to note that you are not learning anything that is unnatural. Because of mankind's greater ability to learn, the mind can override what for a lower animal can be a completely natural motion. Only the human species must sometimes be taught to stand and to walk normally. To the animals, this is pure instinct. A foal is barely born and it is running around the pasture. Compare this to the time it takes a human youngster to learn to walk, much less run. So for most abstract things, the mind makes the human far superior to the animals, but for simple movements the human is far behind even the lowest animal. That is why the slow motion shots of Zimyatov are so astounding. He has recaptured the grace of a deer in flight. I see his skiing at the 1980 Olympics as perfection because of its simplicity of motion, rather than its complexity.

The key to this type of movement lies in the mid-section. The largest and strongest muscles are located in the torso. Skiing stiffly or even walking incorrectly isolates the arms and legs and causes tension. A more natural motion would have the stomach, hips, and spine participating. Omitting them not only weakens the motion, but also creates tension as the athlete actually exerts unconscious muscular forces to stop the spine and hips from moving naturally. A skier may not feel this tension because it has become habit, but if the hips and spine do not twist, an unnatural force has been applied to stop them; this, in turn, creates tension and causes weaker motion.

To illustrate how the use of the torso increases the power of the arms, try the following exercise (see Figure 4.2). You will need a light weight for this; a

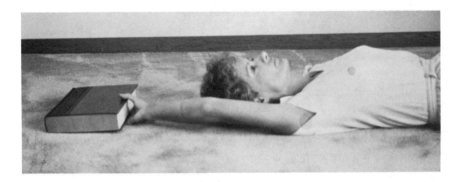

Figure 4.2(a) Start of motion with book on ground.

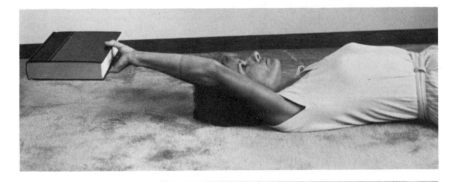

Figure 4.2(b) Use of arm only—book feels heavier.

Fig. 4.2 cont.

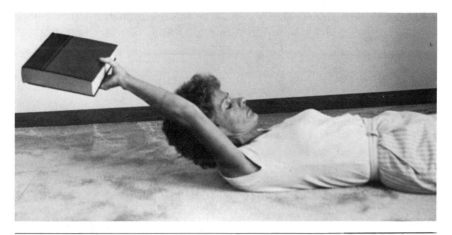

Figure 4.2(c)   Motion starts in midsection as head and chest are lifted, book feels lighter.

Figure 4.2   Demonstration of strength in actions initiated by the midsection.

couple of encyclopedias will do. Lie on the floor on your back with your arms stretched over head and the two encyclopedias in one hand. (One may be enough if you are not very strong, but if you are, you may need something heavier.) Now lift the books several inches off the ground with your arm straight. However, make sure that your shoulders do not lift off the ground. Remember how much strain was involved.

It would help to place the free hand behind your neck. Now repeat the above motion, but this time lift the book several inches off the ground by curling up at the midsection as in a sit-up. At the same time, make sure that your head is lifting by looking at your feet as you do this. As before, your arm should remain straight. All of the lifting should occur because of the stomach and none because of your shoulder joint. In other words, the arm should not change in relation to the body as it is lifted. Note how light the book feels now and how easily you lifted it. If it was easy for you to lift the book without involving the stomach muscles, then increase the weight until you feel a strain. If the weight was too heavy, decrease it.

This demonstration should convince you of the amount of strength waiting to be tapped in the midsection. Those who ski with a stiff body never can take advantage of the stronger muscles of the torso, whereas those who ski in an uninhibited manner will unlock all of the potential of their bodies. Once skiing properly, it will be similar to the lifting of the book— poling and kicking will seem much easier yet be much more forceful. You will certainly ski faster, easier.

Practicing with Power and Hip Rotation

Now that we have some concept of the proper movements of the body, it is time to head for the snow where we can begin to apply this suppleness that is inherent in all efficient movement. The best place to start, just as when having problems with the rhythm of the single stick in chapter 1, is a gradual hill where the diagonaling is easy. (Well, at least easier.) This way of moving is best learned on the hills where it has its most powerful application. The average skier will never be as dynamic as the world class skier but will still find this style of skiing a big improvement. It is always fun to be able to ski more easily up the hills than your companions do and to have your wax work when theirs does not. Unlocking your natural hip and back suppleness can do this for you.

Choose a hill that is gradual and increases in steepness as you near the top. Aggressiveness is the key to learning this move as an athletic motion, rather than a stilted effort. This is especially important on the hills where any tentativeness will cause you to stall. Even when first learning the aggressive lower body action, you must feel that it is easier to get up the hills. If it isn't, you are doing something wrong. Have an observer watch you and check you against the illus- trations. Even though we are emphasizing the lower body action, it is also important to remain aggressive with the upper body. Most of the spinal twisting comes from the hips, but there is a little opposing movement in the shoulders that causes slight twisting of the upper spine.

As you ski up the hill, push the forward ski and leg in front of you, slightly twisting your hips to get a bigger bite per stride. Do not overdo this or it will become a waddle. The proper use of a correctly organized muscular motion will allow the whole spinal column to participate. After a while, this will become so ingrained that it will happen naturally. When attempting to push the ski ahead, you must be careful not to leave the body behind. Hence the earlier note of warning: You must have mastered the concepts of chapter 3, that of throwing the whole body forward, before attempting this. Otherwise, you will just be sticking your foot in cold water, leaving your body behind, causing hip drop. and making it very difficult to get on top of the ski for the next stride. However, once you have learned the proper hip rotation, just concentrating on throwing or pushing your lead foot forward will cause the rest of the body to follow— especially if you remain aggressive in your poling action. Try to keep most of your weight on the heel of the foot as you extend forward. Feeling on top or over the heel is a good way to avoid just pushing the foot forward, leaving the body behind (see Figure 4.3).

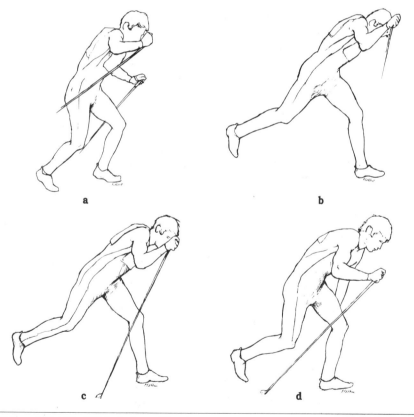

Figure 4.3(a)-(d) Hill technique of Zavalov.

Another note of caution when learning this new way of moving: *Plant the pole as soon as the hand is forward.* You must not lose the basic rhythm of the diagonal. Now it will really start to pay dividends. With the more effortless balancing on the glide ski and the greater power of proper hip movement, the pole glide phase will really start to develop. You will not have to force yourself to stay on the glide ski as you pole. The natural balance of the supple body, spurred on by hip rotation and the slight counterrotation of the upper body as the head moves toward the glide ski, will allow a longer period of time for a pole drive, making the hip-hand checkpoint easier to reach. In addition, you will have more momentum when the pole is planted because of a more efficient kicking motion.

The Gitchi Gami Games in 1982 were an excellent place to observe some of America's and Canada's top skiers. Because of the lack of snow, the 10 k course consisted of five loops around and up and down some of Telemark's Alpine slopes. Thus the skiers were in sight over much of the course. What was a grueling day for the competitors was an enjoyable one for the spectators. Craig Ward of the USST dominated the competition at these races. When Craig skied up the slope, traversing with a powerful diagonal, it looked as if he were in slow motion. Compared to some of the other competitors who had a much greater tempo, he seemed to be only touring. However, he quickly passed those who appeared to be going faster. His stride was just that much longer, each one taking a bigger bite out of the hills. Although average skiers cannot hope to match the stride of a Craig Ward, they can improve on their own stride to the degree their strength and overall conditioning will allow.

Another side benefit of this type of skiing with its dynamic hip motions is that of alleviating back problems. A dynamic hip rotation allows the front leg to be under the chest. This skier has little or no strain on the back as opposed to a skier who arches the back with the legs under the hips and has no hip rotation. All the strain of holding the body erect is placed on the muscles of the lower back. It is similar to a position of bending over to load something into the trunk of a car, a dangerous position for someone flirting with back problems. Loading heavy objects into the trunk of a car is hard on the back because the legs, due to the car's bumper, cannot get under the chest; therefore, the lower back takes all of the strain (see Figure 4.4).

Figure 4.4 Failure to keep leg under chest through supple hips. Places the same kind of strain on the back as lifting heavy objects from the trunk of a car.

We have had much success with skiers with back problems. Freeing the hips so the glide leg is under the chest is one of the main keys. This one adjustment immediately removes strain from the skier's back. The second part of the learning process is to not arch the back. It helps if the skier tries to assume the C position, formed by a slightly rounded lower back. This C position should be tried for only a short time because it can be easily overdone and become a flaw. It can also cause tightness by stopping the natural involvement of a supple spine. Any inhibition of the natural workings of the body should be avoided in the long run. The expert skier moves with essentially a straight back, the spine slightly bending and twisting in response to the movement of the entire body. The goal of any correction is to return the skier to a natural movement, not to a stilted and tight one. The dynamic movement of the hips helps to assure that this will happen.

You are now ready to better perform a drill introduced in chapter 2—delaying the return of the leg as you push yourself with your pole while gliding on one ski. Now that you have learned to ski with a supple body and complete weight transfer, this drill can really start to pay dividends. Find a slight incline suitable for fast diagonaling. As you stride out, delay the return of the rear leg as you emphasize the pole drive, trying to keep the glide ski moving. This is only a drill! Too much work on this can cause stilted and mechanical skiing. Intersperse some fast uninhibited skiing with this drill to protect yourself from becoming the "mechanical man." As you can see, a skier with an improper glide position, such as the skiers in Figure 4.4, will place undue strain on the back if he or she delays the return of the leg. If you feel your back is working overtime, discontinue this drill, for your glide posture is probably wrong. Correct your posture before trying this drill again. You cannot do this drill safely if your back is arched or if your glide leg is not forward in a position under your chest.

The preceding drill is also useful in eliminating *foot slap,* a slapping noise the ski makes as it is brought forward. Foot slap is the result of dropping the ski too early in the track. The foot should not come in contact with the ground until the two feet are together. The slap of the ski on snow is actually caused by the skier falling off the glide ski before he or she reaches the feet-together position. By deliberately delaying the recoil of the rear leg, the skier is forced to stay on the glide ski longer. If you have foot slap, your goal is to maintain your balance on the glide ski until you can place the ski in the track at the time when the feet are together. Once you can maintain good balance without falling off the glide ski early, the irritating noise of foot slap will disappear. Not only that, but you will be gliding longer and kicking better because more weight will be over the kicking leg as you set the wax.

This is as good a time as any to deal with the question, How far back or up should the rear leg go in a diagonal stride? The answer is simple: Any independent lifting of the rear leg is wrong as is any attempt to stop the rear leg from traveling its natural route. The first will strain the back; the second will prevent a long stride. Allow the leg to recoil naturally as the result of your kick. The top racers in the world vary considerably in how much their rear foot lifts, but all allow their foot and ski to recoil naturally.

As the hill steepens, attempt to keep your foot under your knee. Once the spine has become accustomed to reacting in a natural twisting motion, the hips will automatically follow the lead of the foot. You should always have the feeling of being on top, not behind the ski (see Figure 4.5). If you feel that your

Figure 4.5 A "first season" racer who has a natural hill technique and no trouble setting the wax. Notice how his weight is still over the ski half way through the kick.

weight is back, you may be skiing with blocked hips. If the foot alone goes forward, leaving the mass of the body behind, it will be very difficult to get back on top of the ski to set the wax for the next stride. But if the hips have been trained to pivot naturally, you will find your weight over the ski and in a favorable position to set the wax for the next stride. With the foot under the chest, you are able to bite off a bigger portion of the hill. Once you have trained your spine to react naturally, it is only a matter of observing how the ski is weighted as you go up a hill. This simple method of "just watching" yourself and allowing the natural movement to happen is much more successful than trying to "horse" yourself into some unnatural positions.

The skier in Figure 4.6a has not shoved his foot forward at all and will have much trouble getting up a hill because his feet are behind him. Any attempt to set the wax will result in a force that is directed more backwards than down, causing the ski to slip rather than grip the snow. The result is a skier whose wax never works as good as it should and one who resorts to babying it up the hills or using too sticky of a wax. Unfortunately, most skiers learn to ski in this manner.

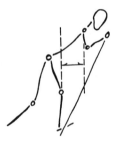

Figure 4.6(a)   Blocked hips. The skier's upper body is too far forward.

Contrast this to the skier in Figure 4.6b who has shoved his foot and leg forward but has blocked, not rotated his hips. He has the opposite problem. His foot is too far forward in relation to his body. As a result, this skier will also have trouble setting the wax because the body weight is not over the ski. This skier

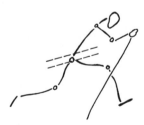

Figure 4.6(b)   Blocked hips. The skier's upper body is too far back and downward.

will feel very weak in his efforts to get up the hill. It takes a very strong person to haul him- or herself back on top of the ski and it becomes very fatiguing after a while. This usually happens in conjunction with straddling the tracks. If this happens, the weight is never over the ski in either direction. Not only must the weight be forward enough, but it also must move slightly from side to side. Remember, because the tracks are about 7 inches apart, there must be some side-to-side movement so the weight can get above the kicking foot.

Finally, compare the two previous skiers to the one in Figure 4.6c and especially Figures 4.3a-d. His foot is in front of his knee as the hill steepens, but his suppleness has allowed him to keep his weight over the ski, lower leg perpendicular to the hill. From this position it is fairly easy to set the wax. This is why the expert skier is able to stride up hills where lesser skiers resort to herringboning.

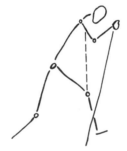

Figure 4.6(c) Good technique with the upper body on the top of ski.

This move does require a threshold level of strength and conditioning, however. If you are not as strong, you may have to adjust by taking smaller strides, but the same body motions should be used because the larger muscles of the body are brought into play. The new muscles involved are the *gluteals*, or rear end muscles. Just activating these larger muscles will make movement easier for the average skier. Extensive hill training and/or weight lifting will help develop the strength needed to get up a hill effectively.

As the slope steepens, funny things start to happen both in the lower and upper body. As the glide is lost, the skier's foot does not reach as far to the front and the action becomes more like running. Because the foot is extending less up the hill, there is less twisting of the hips. The foot is still under the knee, however, but the skier, realizing there is less glide, uses his energy more efficiently. At this time, trying to horse a long stride would either cause the skier to slow down and/or to use too much energy. Shorter and less demanding steps are needed. Of course, the tempo of these steps increases so momentum is maintained. Some skiers even break into a straight run if their wax is good enough. In fact, for short hills a skier might even bound into the air. This can be very tiring, but for short stretches may be the best way to crest a hill, especially if that's what is needed to make your wax work. Note that there is more than one way to get up a hill and the accomplished skier can adjust to conditions of track, wax job, and general overall physical condition and strength at the moment.

Arm Adjustment to Power

Although this chapter has dealt mainly with the natural actions of a torso that is responsive to the motion of the skier and that allows him or her to rely on the stronger muscles of the midsection, another topic arises naturally when the diagonal up a steeper hill is discussed. It is the way the arms adjust when the glide speed becomes less and less, finally reaching a culmination when the hill requires a tough herringbone. As the hill gets steeper, requiring more arm power and allowing less forward progress per stride, the advanced skier bends his or her arms more. This bent-arm position is more powerful than straighter arms. But because of the shortness of the distance between shoulder and hand, the skier will not be able to exert the force for as long a duration. However, as the stride shortens, a long application of force is not necessary. What is needed here is greater arm power over a shorter distance. The larger bend in the elbow gives the skier just that. As the hill gets steeper and the stride shortens, a more powerful, quicker application of arm force is needed.

For your own benefit, convince yourself that the arm is actually stronger in the bent position. Have a friend offer you some resistance with his or her own hands. Try moving his or her hands with a straight arm, then a bent one. You will soon be convinced of the power inherent in the bent position.

Another side effect of increasing steepness is the point of pole plant. In fast conditions the pole is planted near the toe of the boot. But when conditions are slower, the pole is planted farther back. This is because the length of stroke, again, is not as long. This brings us to a basic fundamental of the diagonal. As the conditions are faster, the arm is less bent. Because power is not a great requirement at this time and distance of force application is, a straighter arm is needed. Conversely, when the conditions are slower or the hill steeper, the arm is more effective in the bent position, and a shorter but more powerful stroke is needed. Muscles are stronger in the more contracted position. Just as when you flex your bicep, for instance, you are much stronger when the arm is in the most contracted position. Likewise, the upper back is also in a stronger power position when the lat muscle is partly contracted because of the pole being planted farther back. This premise is one of the basic tenets on which the Nautilus weightlifting machines are based. So just when the effort is greater as the hill steepens, an increased arm bend helps out in two ways: The stroke shortens, and the muscles are in a much stronger position just when they're needed.

As the hill steepens and the arms bend more, other adjustments are made. Glide length is lost and the stride rate increases. The steps become quicker as the skier instinctively feels the loss of glide. The main goal is to maintain forward momentum or speed. It takes more energy to start a body moving than to keep it moving. So the skier is continuously reaching up the hill with his or her lower leg and foot causing a slight rotation of the hips. As the glide disappears, the skier intuitively shortens his or her stride to keep his or her body moving—alway ready to take the glide when it's there, never totally submitting to just running up the hill.

In this chapter, you have learned about the importance of a supple lower body that allows the animal-like fluidity of a dynamic stride. This slight twisting of the hips not only allows a more complete weight transfer and longer pole glide, but also is extremely important in getting up a hill. It allows the foot to be in a better position to set the wax while keeping the weight over the ski. In addition, the arms start to work differently as the hill steepens. The stroke is shortened as the arm is bent more and the pole is planted farther back. Once learned, all a skier needs to do is try to keep his or her weight on the ski for the next kick.

Three Super Keys

To summarize and to simplify the material thus presented, let's reflect on what I call the three super keys to better skiing. Many skiers find that concentrating on these three super keys makes many of the other fundamentals fall in line.

1. The knee (foot) and the hand must arrive at the forward position together with the arm slightly bent. The pole must be planted immediately. This sets up the basic rhythm of the diagonal. The skier, no matter how advanced, must never lose sight of the goal of *a natural rhythmic motion* as described in chapter 1.
2. As the entire body is driven forward onto the glide ski, the hips rotate slightly and the head moves a little (a few inches) to the side of the glide ski. This allows a balanced position on the glide ski and a dynamic motion that utilizes a supple spine and the larger muscles of the torso.
3. The skier remains completely balanced on the glide ski until the beginning of the next kick, constantly trying to maintain his or her momentum with the poling motion. The glide is extended by the use of the pole rather than during free glide. The foot is still under the skier when the poling motion is finished and the next kick begun, the angles of the glide leg remaining fairly constant.

These three keys go a long way in allowing a skier to develop the stride of the champions. I have improved my coaching ability a great deal the last several years, not because of any new knowledge of the ski stroke, but because of finding better ways of getting through to skiers. I have found that there are certain movements that, if perfected, will also correct other things. By choosing different points of instruction, what used to take several weeks of work on the skier's part now sometimes only takes minutes. The fundamentals have not changed, only the method of presentation. The three super keys are a few of the shortcuts to better skiing. When applied properly, the other little things seem to take care of themselves; then the athlete only has to worry about going fast.

Advanced Arms

Some of the World Cup racers are using a poling technique that is slightly different than what has been the standard technique, which I believe is the way of the future. This method involves a more active use of the abdomen and upper back. It also requires more strength as the upper body involvement is increased. As we have seen, as the hill steepens, the skier's normal reaction is to bend his or her arms more and even saw off his or her stroke near the end. This means the skier will start to move his or her hand parallel to the snow rather than directly against the pole. This makes the stroke easier but loses the advantage of a direct pole push.

The emerging poling movement, however, as exhibited by Alexandre Zavjalov and Pall Gunner Mickelsplass among others, relies on a straight line poling motion at all times. To accomplish this, stronger muscles must be involved, hence, the use of the abdomen. These skiers are recognized by the active movement of their midsections. There is more bending and extending of the midsection during the poling motion, especially as the hill becomes steeper. These skiers initiate the poling motion by using the stronger muscles of the stomach, literally pulling and dropping the body down the length of the pole. It is like pulling on a bell rope attached to a very heavy object.

As the hill steepens, the arms may be bent a little more, but that is not the main compensation for the increased difficulty of the poling action. Instead, the path of the hand is shortened by removing some of the involvement of the arms. The stroke becomes mostly a movement of the abdominal and upper back muscles with little or no involvement of the arms. This shorter stroke is appropriate for the increased tempo used on the hills as the glide disappears. Then as the hill flattens, the straight line move of the hand is extended just past the hip, but with more arm involvement. At that time, the extreme folding and unfolding of the torso is reduced in a natural response to the reduced need to involve the stronger muscles.

In other words, as the hill gets steeper, the skier now reacts to it, not by bending the arms and sawing off the hand motion, but by involving the bigger muscles of the body. The skier can drag him- or herself up a hill when the wax is not so good. To do so, however, requires a more bent-over posture and may be too radical a change for some of the top skiers presently competing at a world class level. However, for the diagonal, it is the trend of the future. If you have a pulley to which you can attach a variable weight, place enough poundage on the pulley so that it is too hard for you to move by arm motion alone, but just barely. Then move the weight by holding the arm motionless in relation to the body and by pulling with your stomach muscles, bending at the waist. You will easily see the increased strength using this method.

One side effect of abdominal involvement is that once the skier folds at the waist during poling, he or she must then again extend during the kick. This has the effect of exerting an equal and opposite force that will help set the wax. Then as the slope decreases, this up-and-down motion will diminish slightly as the skier resorts to a fast diagonal, still maintaining the basic motion. Skiers who use their arms in this manner look very dynamic, particularly in slow motion. It is very conducive to the natural twisting and extending of the spine in a natural athletic movement. It is this un-inhibited and natural movement that makes the Norwegian men's team, in particular, such a delight to watch.

On the other end of the spectrum are the racers who have very strong legs in relation to their arms. They can benefit by racing with more of a leg and less of an arm involvement. Marja Liisa-Haemelainen dominated the 1984 Olympic games with a style that used minimal arm movement on the hills, especially while herringboning. This is not to say she has a weak upper body, but she definitely saved her arms on the diagonal and the hills. If you are racing a course with a long, tough uphill followed by a long stretch of doublepoling and skating, it may be wise to ease off on the arms up the hill if your wax is working; then blast away on the doublepole. This would be especially true for the citizen racer.

So, ultimately, how you race and ski will depend not only on your strengths and weaknesses, but also on such variables as course profile and how your wax is working. However, whatever your amount of involvement, increased arm strength will only help a skier. Practice sessions that emphasize abdomen and back involvement should be included in the workouts. But once the race starts, ski as efficiently as you can, and you will go faster, easier.

Main Concepts

1. A powerful ski stride is the result of an uninhibited motion using as much of the body's potential as possible. This is accomplished by allowing the body and spine to twist naturally.
2. Balance, as well as power, is enhanced by this uninhibited motion.

   - It encourages an athlete to be on top of his or her ski for the next kick.
   - This twisting allows the stronger muscles of the torso to participate more fully and demands a larger range of motion from the other

muscles. There is a more complete windup and follow-through.

3. The pole must, as always, be planted as soon as the hand is forward.
4. As the hills get steeper, the arms bend more. Some elite skiers respond by using their stomach muscles to a larger degree.
5. Remember and practice the three super keys to better skiing.

Tying It All Together for the Advanced Skier

5

You Can't Defy the Laws of Physics

Caution: This chapter is highly technical and can be dangerous to your skiing health. Use with moderation and combine with feedback from an informed observer and liberal doses of uninhibited rhythmic skiing.

This chapter is for the advanced diagonal skier or serious coach. However, skiers of all levels can benefit from reading this chapter if only to be able to become a better evaluator of technique. Much of the printed material about cross-country skiing is either out-of-date, incorrect, or defies the laws of physics. One reason is that the American public sees so little world class technique. The public can be told anything because it doesn't have models for comparison. Contrast this to football, baseball, basketball, and golf, for example, where there is so much television coverage of top performers that the average spectator can identify good technique. A little kid does not have to read a book on how to shoot a basketball. He or she merely turns on the weekly professional games to see the best shooters in the world perform. Unfortunately in the world of cross-country skiing, visual feedback from the top skiers is virtually nonexistent, so the written word assumes a greater significance. With nothing to check it against, the chance for misinterpretation runs rampant; furthermore, much of the material is just plain wrong.

Nothing can actually destroy the laws of physics. For instance, water cannot defy the law of gravity and flow uphill. But skiers continue, and in their attempt to ski fast, try to do impossible things that defy the physical laws. These individuals are doomed before they begin because the intended result is impossible. The forces of action and reaction and their compatriots of the world of physics are not to be trifled with.

Improving the average skier's ability to evaluate other printed material and instruction is one of the benefits of this chapter. There is some overlap between this chapter and the preceding ones as there must be. I would hate to think that the method of skiing presented here defies the laws of physics.

One thing that has impressed me after observing skiers of advanced abilities is that the elite become much more efficient in utilizing these natural laws. All of us must obey these laws, but the expert makes them work. In their quest for faster times, the top racers in the world, consciously or subconsciously, have learned to use the forces on the human body efficiently. Whether this comes naturally, from coaching, or from imitation of other successful skiers, I really don't know, but they're doing it. Some racers such as Odvar Braa, many times a world champion, have changed their diagonal style over the last few years and have developed a more powerful style following these natural laws.

Before continuing, one point must be reiterated. The goal of any racer is to ski fast in the most efficient manner. To complete this goal successfully, the skier must adhere to the two following concepts: First, a technique that is fast and powerful must not be too hard for the individual racer to maintain. It doesn't help to use a powerful technique if it lasts only for a kilometer or so unless you are trying to impress some other skier on the trail. Second, there is a threshold level of conditioning and strength in passing from level to level. Personal experience, however, has shown me that the average skier is well able to assimilate much of the technique of the top racers but on a lower level of execution.

Some of the more powerful movements will have to be modified by the unconditioned skier or the once-a-month tourer. These individuals may have to ski on straighter legs, use less powerful arm thrusts, and have less body compression than the top racers; but they, too, should follow the laws of physics, for any attempt to defy them is to ski using more energy. The tourer may herringbone when the racer is still gliding, may single stick when the racer is double poling or skating, may rest at the top of a hill when the racer is accelerating, and may stand more erect on the downhill when the racer is tucking tightly, but he or she must still make the basic laws of physics work. Otherwise, energy is wasted.

Applying the Laws of Physics

Exactly what are some of these laws of physics and how do they apply to skiing? Even the average tourer will find his or her skiing more enjoyable if he or she keeps in mind only one point of this chapter: *An object in motion tends to remain in motion. An object at rest tends to remain at rest.* In other words, it takes more energy to start something moving than to keep it moving—such as your body in the ski stride. This is called inertia. The main object of the skier is to maintain his or her forward momentum as much as possible. A stop-start motion requires more energy to get the skier moving again after slowing down between strides. That is, keep moving into the hills, off the downhills, around corners, and in the stride itself. Any time you stop and start, you use more energy. Proper pacing and course management are keys that will help anyone.

Because the cross-country stride is a continuous one, some place must be arbitrarily chosen as the starting point. I have chosen the feet-together position. It is at this point that the glide usually has stopped and the kick is beginning or has just begun. The goal of the skier is to kick effectively to maintain his or her forward momentum. If done properly, there will be no noticeable slowing down between strides with its accompanying demand of extra energy to bring the skier up to speed again (see Figure 5.1a-e).

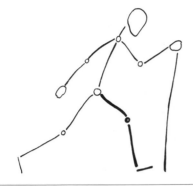

Figure 5.1(a) Pole plant.

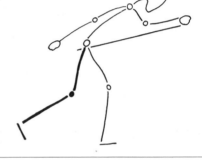

Figure 5.1(b) Slight hitch before preload.

Figure 5.1(c) Preload. Angle x decreases as does the angle behind the knee.

Figure 5.1(d) End of kick (fast conditions).

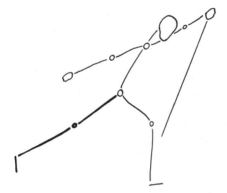

Figure 5.1(e) Free glide.

Figure 5.1 Phases of the cross-country stride.

At this point, the weight is completely on the kicking leg. There should be no straddling of the track, which causes less weight to be on the kicking leg, making it more difficult to set the wax and get a powerful kick. Again, straddling occurs when the skier does not shift his or her weight entirely to the kicking leg but rather has his or her center of gravity constantly down the middle of the two tracks. As stated before, the body mass does shift from side to side in order for the skier to balance completely on each ski.

Just before the kick, the glide leg slightly straightens in anticipation. Caution is necessary here because this move could easily become standing on the glide ski if emphasized too much. The straightening occurs at the end of the glide phase and is mainly subconscious in nature.

Preloading the Kick

As the kick begins, there is a slight flexing of this leg, a coiling which puts it in a more powerful position. This is analogous to the jumper's slight flexing of the legs in preparation for a standing long jump. The skier's upper body also coils or flexes slightly from the waist. There is a slight lowering of the hips with the flexing at the waist and cocking of the knee. Flexing more would put the skier in a more powerful position, but it would also be much more tiring, so the compromise situation results: slight coiling. The goal is not one long jump but a series of endurance strokes that must last for an entire race, whether it be for 5 or 50 kilometers.

From this position the skier explodes onto the glide ski. The last bit of stretching the quadriceps, gluteals, and calf in preparation for the kick is called preloading. It has been shown that a slight stretching of the muscles before contraction actually increases the power of the muscle by causing it to act like a spring. The muscle actually rebounds slightly, much like a rubber band. This is instinctive with most people until they let their minds take over. Witness little kids on the playground. They all know, subconsciously, that this preloading of the muscles is a good thing as they jump against the side of a building to see how high they can go. Each one performs a slight hitch in preparation for the jump. Likewise, the skier instinctively makes this little hitch before kicking. This springlike action will only work if the kick is quick and explosive. The preload and release happens fast, much like the stretch and release of a rubber band. If attempted too slowly, it will not happen.

Force equals mass times acceleration. Therefore, the quicker kick (faster acceleration) produces more force. More force means the wax is pressed harder against the snow with greater penetration of snow crystals into the wax. Thus, a quicker kick does a better job of setting the wax. In addition, this more forceful kick allows the accomplished skier to be on stiffer skis and therefore to drag his or her wax less during the glide phase. Some of the elite racers, including Bill Koch, exhibit this trait to the ultimate, looking almost effortless as they kick with a pure rebound off a quick preloading of the leg.

Action-Reaction:
The Upper Body During the Kick

As the skier straightens the kicking leg in a forceful manner, he or she also moves the upper body slightly up as it is hurled forward. Studies have shown that most of the force of the kick is directed downward and very little backward in comparison. This can be as much as three times the body weight. It is this downward force that sets the wax. The force of the leg pushing down is helped by the small but rapid rise of the upper body. As the upper body moves slightly upward, an opposite and equal reaction causes more pressure on the kicking ski, helping to set the wax. If done properly, this upward rise will be a reaction to the leg acting as a spring that was set by the preload. Be sure, however, that this rise happens during the kick, not the gliding phase. A slight uplift during the kick helps set the wax, but standing on the ski during the glide is an indication of either a weak kick or poor balance.

Head bob is something most skiers have been warned about many times, yet it was to our surprise to see that all of the international stars had some vertical head movement. This is good and something which is favorable to powerful skiing. As you have already seen, it is necessary to a powerful kick to have some kind of coiling of the body in preparation for this move. You will find out later on in this chapter that other good things happen during glide and poling because of this slight vertical movement.

Figure 5.2 shows the two paths of the shoulders and hips of Juha Mieto. Notice that the shoulders move more than the hips in a vertical direction. Mieto actually raises his shoulders more than his hips while keeping the angles of his hip to thigh and thigh to shin fairly constant. He does this by rotating his entire leg and body as he kicks (as discussed in the last chapter). Almost all international stars exhibit this characteristic. However, as the hill steepens, this path fluctuation is not as noticeable because the vertical movement of the body parallels the slope of the hill.

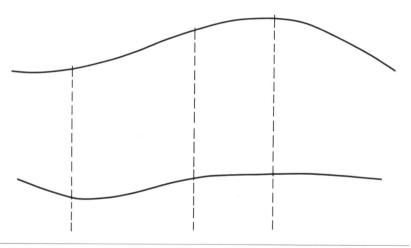

Figure 5.2 The path of Juha Mieto's shoulders and hips during the diagonal stride.

Center of Gravity at Midpoint

The feet-together or midpoint position is one of the best coaching checkpoints for the skier who is ready to step into the ranks of the elite (see Figure 5.3). Many times these skiers are dynamic, fluid, and very accomplished, but are not very powerful in their diagonal motion, especially when the hill gets steeper. Weight

Figure 5.3 This citizen racer has kept his weight over his kicking foot. Muscular dynamics and aerobic fitness, not technique, separate him from the elite racers.

lifting or strength improvement alone will not help this skier. Many times a faulty midposition is the problem.

For a skier to effectively use the coiling of muscles at the midpoint, the body must be in the proper position in relation to the feet, and the center of gravity must be over the kicking foot. The skier in Figure 5.4a has his mass too far forward, not over the kicking foot. Any straightening of the kicking leg will cause a force to be directed backward rather than down, making his wax set ineffective. This skier must resort to a soft motion rather than a powerful one because of his difficulty in setting the wax. From experience I have found that this position is the one most talented young skiers go through while learning, especially if they start around the ages of 13 to 17. For some reason, many who start at a younger age do not have this problem.

Every attempt must be made to have these skiers get their feet under them as the skier does in Figure 5.4b. Not only will their stride become more powerful,

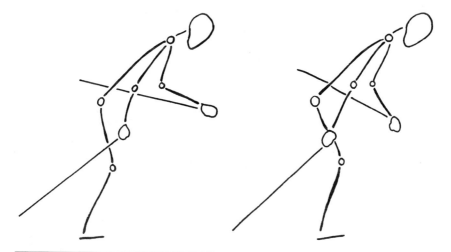

Figure 5.4(a) Bad—weight is too far forward making it difficult to set the wax.

Figure 5.4(b) Good—weight is over the kicking foot.

Figure 5.4 Body weight and the kicking foot.

but they will also avoid the back problems inherent in this position. The solution to this problem, surprisingly, is not found at the midpoint but in the position of the glide leg. Supple hips, with the glide foot being under the chest, is the first step in curing this problem. The second is to maintain the angle of the glide leg, keeping the foot in front with the weight on the heel. This is done, not by static holding, but by a feeling that the foot is always reaching for more glide. The maintenance of the foot position is dynamic, not static. If properly maintained, the skier will find himself at the midpoint with his feet under, rather than behind him.

Potential Energy and the Kick

The skier in Figure 5.4a has his weight above the kicking foot and is in a coiled position to set the wax properly and to have a powerful kick. But sometimes the skier is in the correct position of balance but does not have enough leg flexion. If the legs are too straight, a weak kick can also develop. To get a powerful kick the legs must be bent (a loading of the spring storing potential energy), in order for the muscles to work. The straight-legged skier cannot get any leg power into the kick as the leg is already extended and has nowhere to go.

Some skiers have to be convinced that skiing on a straight leg is not as efficient as skiing on a bent one. It does take a certain amount of strength to hold the state of flexion during the glide and kick; but it takes much more energy to raise and lower the body by straightening the leg and then rebending it at the midpoint. It is the equivalent of going up and down hills. You are raising and lowering your body unnecessarily when you do this.

Thus, it is important that the skier is in a coiled position at the midpoint with a slight flexing of the kicking leg taking place, but not enough to raise and lower the mass of the body very much. The main purpose of this move is the slight preloading that allows a more elastic use of the muscle. A vertical line drawn from the buttocks (see Figure 5.4b) should fall behind the heel of the kicking foot. This ensures that the force of the kick will be directed in a downward enough direction to set the wax. A special note is that the hip joint is actually above the arch of the foot, but it is much easier to see that the butt is a little behind the heel of the skier.

For the would-be Olympic hopeful or future world champion, an even more telling position is halfway through the kick. The kicking leg should still be in a state of flexion, and the skier's hips should not be too far forward, so a good amount of force can be imparted to the snow (see Figure 5.5a).

Imparting Momentum to the Entire Body

This brings us to the forward hurdle of the ski stride. The second half of the kick is a very telling place to observe the advanced skier. A good coach can look at a skier and just know that he or she is dropping the hips behind the body. The average person cannot perceive the problem as easily. The checkpoint is this: The hips should start to rise slightly during the second half of the kick (see Figure 5.5b). If they stay level or even go lower, the skier is guilty of dropping his or her hips. This means the momentum of the kick is not imparted to the entire body. In addition, the

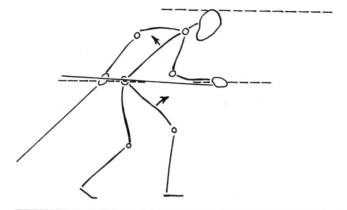

Figure 5.5(a) A powerful kick.

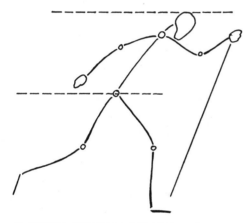

Figure 5.5(b) The hips rise slightly during the second half of the kick resulting in a balanced glide position.

Figure 5.5 The kick.

skier will later have to rise again, thereby standing on the glide ski, pressuring the ski against the snow and causing the glide to end prematurely.

This rise and fall of the hips, which is really dictated by the flexing and extending of the leg, is the key for many skiers who have trouble making their wax work. There must be a downward pressure to set the wax, and this cannot occur if there is no flexing and extending of the kicking leg (see Figures 5.2 and 5.5). Therefore, there must be some up-and-down motion of the body. Some day there may be a development in skis or waxing that will allow the skier to impart more force back and less down. If that ever happens, there will be major technique changes. But until that time, the skier must apply a downward pressure to set the wax and therefore have some up-and-down motion. It should be noted again that the steeper hills disguise this move because the upward motion of the body is parallel to the slope.

A good visualization that seems to take care of the problem of hip dropping and setting the wax at the same time is one used by Dick Taylor. His idea of up and over onto the glide ski is very effective in creating dynamic skiing. The skier visualizes a launching of the whole body onto the gliding leg. This has done two things for the skiers who have needed this: First, the hips are never left behind, and the entire momentum of the kick is maintained by the entire body; and second, this launching encourages a dynamic motion that involves a preloading of the leg and an explosive kick with its accompanying downward pressure.

As the body is thrown forward in one piece, there is a slight twisting of the hips and shoulders. The one-piece thrust imparts maximum momentum to the whole body. The hip twist allows the skier to balance more completely on the glide ski, allowing a greater flexion of the muscles. The width of the tracks also causes a slight side-to-side weight shift as evidenced by the slight horizontal movement of the head. (These points have already been covered in previous chapters but were presented here for continuity.)

One point must be examined before delving into the forces on the glide ski during this phase. A law of physics states, *any force in one direction will cause an equal force in the opposite direction.* This was the force that helped to set the wax as the leg extended and as the body slightly rose. The opposite and equal reaction actually set the wax. In a like manner, accelerating your arms and legs in a forward direction creates a force in the opposite direction, which is detrimental during the free glide phase when the kicking foot is off the ground. At this time there is no resistance to this backward force because the kick leg is off the ground, and the pole is not yet planted. This backward force causes a slowing of the glide; therefore, the arm and leg that are moving forward must not accelerate after the kicking foot leaves the ground. This does not mean that there is no forward drive of the arms, however. Once the kick is initiated (from the feet-together position), the maximum momentum is imparted to the entire mass, which includes the arms. An aggressive use of the arms during the kick can be very helpful in driving the whole body forward. Everything is moving forward, not just the arms. The body, containing most of the skier's mass, must not be left out as it is the major carrier of momentum. But once free glide is attained, the arm movement must be over. This means a crisp motion during the kick, which comes to an abrupt stop when the kick is over.

From viewing the tapes of the Norwegians, it is obvious that one of their major points of emphasis is just that. They accelerate their arms forward, which creates their overall tempo, but emphasize a stopping of the arms as soon as the kick is over. The result is a crisp stride with no unnecessary hand movement in the front. (It almost seems as if they are emphasizing low hands.) Some Americans got into trouble with this concept when they did not make their arm movements crisp, but let the arms accelerate after the free glide had started.

It can be dangerous to attempt to increase the forward drive by concentrating on driving the arms or knees forward, the danger being that the major mass of the body can be left behind. Some of the most difficult people to coach into efficient technique are those who have spent years perfecting their leg or arm drive. They have artificially disrupted their rhythm for such an extended period of time, moving their arms or legs fast but not in coordination with the whole body. For them proper timing becomes a major goal. What is frustrating to these experts is that almost any kid starting out has better timing, and it looks so easy. But they have done such a good job of learning their style of forward drive that it is now hard to unlearn.

Use of Poles in Conserving Momentum

You are now ready to look at the poling phase in a more sophisticated manner. Earlier, the problems encountered by skiers trying to get a forward pole plant were mentioned. In many cases, the basic rhythm of their diagonal was destroyed by extending too far to the front. This concept has always proved disastrous to the beginning skier and often so for the advanced skier. However, the pole must be forward enough to get the full range of motion.

In every way the elite skier is more dynamic than the average racer: The kick is more explosive, the glide longer. In addition, the elite skier maintains the momentum much better; in other words, he or she does not slow down between strides, and it is his or her poling action that is the momentum saver. Keep in mind that how the skier rides and maintains the glide ski is very important and can limit the extent to which he or she can use the poles. The effect of the glide position will be addressed later in this chapter; for now it is enough to know that the skier must be balanced on the glide ski properly.

To effectively use the poles in a strong motion, the angle of the pole to the ground is very important (see Figures 5.6a and 5.6b). Some advanced skiers try to

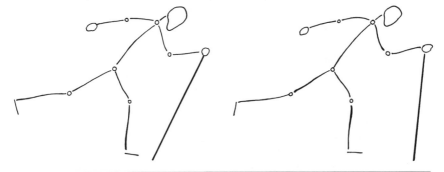

Figure 5.6(a) An effective pole angle.

Figure 5.6(b) The pole plant is too vertical making the skier ski past the pole before applying force.

Figure 5.6 Angle of the pole to the ground.

get their pole planted at a nearly vertical position as in Figure 5.6b. However, after working with many skiers of all abilities, I believe it is always a mistake to go for a bigger bite by trying to plant the pole farther forward. This attempt usually results in a loss of rhythm with the arms too straight and the poles planted too far forward. Simply put, if the pole is vertical when planted, the skier will have to wait until it is angled back to use it, for only then can a backward push be applied. A completely vertical pole plant can be attained only on very fast snow, and even then the skier should probably be double poling or skating if the conditions are that fast.

Whenever attempting to get more poling power by planting the pole farther forward, do not lose sight of the super key: *The hand stops moving forward when the knee stops moving forward.* In addition, the skier should not plant the pole in front of the boot.

Grip Pressures

The secret to efficient poling power is in how the pole is gripped. In chapter 1 you learned to release in the follow-through. How and when the pole is regripped is the key to good poling power. This sounds a little strange, and how can such a small thing be so important? Who cares about such little details? This little detail is much like the last bolt in a supporting structure: Without it, all comes tumbling down.

The skier should never really regrip his or her pole. Instead, the pole is gently caught in the fingers at the end of the forward arm swing and never really "gripped" by the whole hand. Pressure is then applied to the strap for poling. What does this do for the skier, and how is this happening? When the hand stops moving forward, the basket of the pole continues to swing. The elite skiers actually kick up the snow in a forward direction as the pole is planted. The pole is now in the near vertical position, but the arm and hand are in a slightly bent and powerful position, ready to push the skier forward. The basic rhythm of the diagonal has been maintained, and the pole is planted near the toe of the boot—exactly where depends on the length of the pole, the speed of the snow, and/or the steepness of the terrain.

Almost all skiers, other than the experts, grasp their poles too early; some never even let go. This is the result of an insecurity, and the most obvious result is a lack of freedom in skiing. Learning to free yourself of the death grip on your poles will allow you to ski more comfortably.

The skier who grips the pole too early must delay his or her pole plant as he or she lifts the hand to plant the pole. This wasted time causes the skier to slow down during free glide, making the poling motion more difficult and less efficient. The goal of the skier is to get that pole in early in the nearly vertical position. Once the hand is forward, the free-swinging basket enters the snow much faster than if it were lifted and thrust downward by a gripping hand.

The importance of the seemingly little detail of hand pressure on the pole cannot be emphasized enough. But super key Number 1 (hand-knee together), when used in conjunction with a free-swinging basket does wonders for the skier. By not regripping the pole, but lightly cradling it in the fingers and applying power to the straps, the skier will not only increase the poling power, but will also ski in a more relaxed manner. In doing so he or she will remove the unnecessary upward hand movement and get a quicker pole plant. He or she can then maintain glide while the momentum is still high by simply applying pressure to the poles. In fact, once the hand is forward, any upward lift only delays the pole plant. This hitch is always wrong and should be corrected. It is not a matter of style. By lifting the hand, a delay in poling develops, and during this time the skier loses momentum because of friction with the snow. Planting the pole immediately will allow the poling hand to reach the thigh easily by the time the skier reaches the feet-together position (checkpoint from chapter 3). (*Note:* Sometimes a skier is in correct coordination and reaches the feet-together position with the poling hand at the side, but the glide ski has stopped moving earlier. This skier has not been able to maintain the glide and has been forced to kick early. This observation is hard to see without videotape. If you have access to tape at a camp or clinic, make sure that your ski is still moving during the entire poling phase.)

Ride a Light Glide Ski

Now let's look at the forces on the glide ski. You already know that the kick exerts tremendous force on

the kicking ski, thus engaging the wax. Now the glide
ski demands attention. After all the emphasis on the
total commitment to the gliding ski, it may seem
strange to hear that experts really do not totally
weight the glide ski, but rather *ride a light glide ski.*

How is this accomplished and why is this not a
contradiction to commitment to the glide ski? First of
all, when the skier hurls him- or herself forward, the
mass of the body is slightly raised as the skier extends
out of the prekick coiling. Note the path of the mass of
the body during this phase in Figures 5.2 and 5.5. A
quick and powerful kick raises the body mass slightly
as the skier is hurled forward. During free glide this
soaring effect keeps the weight from being completely
on the glide ski. Then when the weight of the skier
would be descending onto the ski, causing friction and
slowing the skier down, the poling arm comes to the
rescue. Its initial move in planting the pole has the
effect of not only propelling the skier forward but also
pushing the skier up slightly, keeping him light on the
glide ski.

About one-third to one-half of the way through the
poling motion, the skier starts to compress (lower) the
body onto the pole as he or she propels him- or herself
forward. This compression is not excessive and will
cause about 1 to 4 inches of head bob. Compression
does three things: It (a) gets more power onto the
poling motion, (b) starts to get the skier into the state
of flexion getting ready for the next kick, and (c) helps
to keep the skier light on the glide ski. This causes
less friction on the snow in a kind of down unweighting. It's the old opposite reaction again. If the body is
lowered, there is an unweighting force in the up direction. Try this on a bathroom scale. Stand erect and
then quickly bend your knees. Notice how your weight
appears lighter. This is the same effect a downward
compression has on the forces of the glide ski. (*Note:*
Even though the body does not compress until one-
third of the poling is completed, the skier feels as if
this happens immediately.)

A stronger poling motion pays dividends in more
ways than one. It not only drives you forward by using
upper body muscles, but also keeps you lighter on the
glide ski. So for the good guys, "When is the weight
transferred completely to the glide ski?" The truthful

answer is not until the next kick. Trying to feel that the glide ski is light on the snow is an excellent drill. This drill will keep you in a naturally balanced position on the ski and will get you more on top of your poles, therefore, getting a more powerful pole thrust by helping with the larger abdominal muscles.

It is also worthy to note that the poling arm has another effect as already mentioned in chapter 2, Figure 2.10, and that is balance. This effect is largely subconscious and a spinoff from a powerful poling technique. The best skiers in the world do not have their poles directly perpendicular to the snow when viewed from in front or behind. Instead, these skiers are angled slightly in toward their shoulders, forming nature's stable geometric figure, the triangle. The three sides of this triangle are the glide leg and side of the body to the neck, the pole and poling arm, and, finally, the ground. The pole exerts some side pressure, actually pushing the skier onto the glide ski. This is not, however, a conscious pressure by the skier. Holding the hands too wide does not allow a skier to form this angle with the pole. The hands should be directly in front of the shoulder.

Some skiers have no compression in the poling phase, or they compress all at once during the kick and not at all during the poling phase. These are weaker styles of skiing and, although a very few of the top international skiers do ski this way, even they could improve by learning to compress on the pole at the correct time. The skiers with no compression during poling lose out in two ways: First, they do not get the gravitational effect of the body being lowered on the poles and miss out on the use of the stomach muscles to help with poling; and second, they are not in the coiled position at the midpoint, thereby losing much of the explosiveness of the kick as the body extends again, powering the skier forward and setting the wax. Skiers who ski this way look a little stiff.

Many good beginners do not have natural compression although they are fluid. These talented beginners, usually youngsters, could be helped by consciously trying to compress the body onto the pole during the poling phase. They should try to do this as soon as the pole is planted, although the actual compression will not occur immediately. Skiers have better success if they try to compress on the poles as soon as they are able. This is usually mastered in a short time and only needs to be reviewed once in a while to make it permanent. Special care should be taken so that this compression remains slight and is not overdone, otherwise, it can become energy wasting in itself. Another item of warning: This move is only for skiers who have achieved the basic rhythm and coordination. Beginners should concentrate on the material in the preceding chapters, mastering that before correcting any lack of compression. Rhythm, riding the glide ski, and projecting the whole body forward to a position of balance are more important.

Weight Distribution on the Glide Ski

Once gliding, it is extremely important to exert as little force as possible in any direction on the ski; in other words, as advocated at USST sponsored clinics, *Ride a quiet ski.* This is because a skier wants to get as much out of the glide as possible, and any forces transmitted to the snow will cause a drag and slow the skier down. I, however, would change this to *Ride a light ski,* as the skier must not be static in his or her effort to increase the glide. We have already seen how the correct movements of the body and pole keep the skier light on his or her ski.

At this time the skier should keep as much weight on the heel as possible, for any weighting of the toe will drive the wax pocket into contact with the snow. This slowing down is readily apparent to the skier. In order to keep the weight on the heel, the skier feels almost as if he or she is reaching forward with the foot during the glide. The best skiers in the world do move their foot slightly forward in relation to their knee while they are gliding. At the same time, the upper body is involved in dynamic poling; therefore, riding the glide ski like a rock or stone is not the answer.

For the advanced skier, riding the heel of the foot during glide while poling forward may be the most important technique on which to work. Not only does it keep the wax off the snow, but it also sets up the next kick. Concentrating on this one concept on roller skis virtually guarantees a well-timed kick. It is almost impossible to kick late if the kick is started from the heel because the foot must be relatively forward to even have any significant weight on the heel.

More importantly, on snow, a kick started from the heel is much more powerful than one initiated from the ball of the foot. It actually extends the time a forward and downward force can be applied during the kicking phase. A weaker skier will kick only from the ball of the foot with the chance that much of the force will be directed backward, encouraging a slip of the wax. By starting the kick with the heel, the advanced skier will exert a force with both the heel and the toe. In addition, the skier's stride will be longer because the foot will be farther in front when he or she starts to kick. But to have this powerful kick, the skier must develop a balanced glide position on the heel: The two are intertwined and inseparable. Without a balanced glide position, an efficient powerful kick is impossible. So for the expert (I can't emphasize this concept enough) always *strive to marry the kick and glide by keeping the weight on the heel during the glide and initiating the kick off the heel.* The skier should, at the same time, be trying to maintain all of his or her body momentum by use of a poling motion that allows him or her to feel light on the skis with the upper body feeling "over" the poles. So if you're a Junior Olympic or even an Olympic hopeful, that's the ticket. Once this technique is mastered, it is honed as the skier develops more power through training and maturation.

Glide Error—Standing Up

We have thus seen that a proper glide is the entry point to a powerful kick. The most common error that occurs during the glide phase is standing up. This is detectable by observing two areas of the body: The leg and the waist. If the skier straightens the knee or stands up at the waist while gliding, the laws of physics crop up again to hinder performance—the equal and opposite reaction again. If either of these joints, hip or knee, is abruptly straightened during the glide, a force equal and opposite is transmitted to the snow, causing friction and slowing the glide. (*Note:*

There is a slight rising just before and in anticipation of the kick.)

The slowing down that is due to standing up is not as obvious to the skier as that of pressuring the toe. It is easy to see, however, with slow motion replay on videotape or polarvision. By observing the sliding ski against a background, the actual slowing of the ski is apparent. Upon standing, the ski comes to a halt, cutting the pole glide short. This skier is usually characterized by a stop-start motion. As his or her ability improves, the actual slowing down is harder to detect; but if there is any standing up during the glide, the skier must be slowing down due to the opposite forces on the snow—those laws of physics again.

This is not the same as the slight rise that occurs during the properly executed kick. Any downward forces are favorable at this time because they help to set the wax. It also should be noted that some of the best skiers do have a *slight and gradual* rise while they are poling. This slight straightening of the leg does not cause a downward pressure on the ski because it is the result of poling pressure. It seems to be a compromise between efficient poling power and riding the glide ski longer in a more relaxed or energy efficient position. Undoubtedly, some of the poling power for these skiers is wasted in raising the body, but it is also easier and more energy efficient to ride on a straighter leg. Which is more important? As of now, I'm not sure, but some talented competitors ski this way. However, the majority of the international athletes ski on a fairly constant glide leg that does not straighten during the poling motion. These elite skiers probably don't even realize the rise they may have.

Drill—Developing Glide

Any skier can learn to balance longer and more dynamically on the glide ski. Start on a steeper hill where the glide is a minimum and then gradually work to the flats and eventually even to the slight downhills. You may not race these sections with the diagonal, but this is just training. Again, the reason for starting on a hill and working to the flats is the balance factor. As your balance gets better, you can handle the faster conditions. You are constantly trying to lengthen the gliding time without losing your natural rhythm. It helps to think a little about delaying the return of the rear leg, which will give the skier time to develop poling power. This delay is slight and actually causes the skier to perform in a slightly different rhythm, a rhythm that helps facilitate pole glide.

Remember to get the pole in the ground as soon as possible. When the knee/foot is forward, so should be the hand—not after. This drill can be dangerous because of the possible loss of the natural timing of the diagonal. So occasionally check your hand and knee; they should arrive forward together. When you can do this drill on a slight downhill, you have arrived. Have a friend check to see that you are not standing up and that your glide leg is fairly constant until the flexing of the leg for the next kick at the midposition (feet together).

Static Versus Dynamic Balance

Let's now examine the body position on the glide ski in more detail. Static balance and dynamic balance are not the same. In fact, static and dynamic balance are controlled by two different parts of the inner ear. So it is virtually useless to spend time balancing on one leg in the living room. To improve this skill you must be practicing while moving.

Because you are in motion, your hips will be a little behind the normal static balance point. The reason? Friction against the snow. This force tends to stop you and has the ability to throw you forward. The extreme case is when your ski gets stuck on a leaf or ices up, which happened to Thomas Wassburg during the 1980 Olympic relay. In the final leg, he was skiing behind Mieto, fighting for a third-place medal. As they came up and over a hill, his ski iced up. The result—Wassburg flat on his face—hopes of a medal gone. To a lesser degree, the friction of ski to snow during normal glide tends to throw a skier forward. This causes the skier to adjust by positioning his or her mass slightly farther back than in the standing balance position.

In addition, you are poling at the same time. If you were perfectly balanced before poling, the force of the pole would throw you a little forward and off balance. The skier's subconscious solution—a balance point that is slightly farther back. Do not make this more complicated than necessary, for this is mainly a sub-conscious adjustment. It does deserve mention because photos of the top stars show them in positions that at times look as if they would fall behind the ski. If the skier, however, can ride the glide ski in a position of balance, has a strong and well-timed poling motion (good pole glide), and is in an athletic coil for the next kick, the balance point has taken care of itself.

By holding the glide ski in a fairly constant state of flexion with the weight mostly on the heel, one additional benefit is uncovered. The foot will be in the proper position for the next kick. It will be under rather than behind the body. It is then ready to set the wax because the body is coiled above the foot and only needs the slight hitch of preloading for a powerful and efficient kick.

If, however, the skier stands up too early, his or her glide position should be checked. If off balance, he or she will be forced to stand up to regain balance. It's amazing how one flaw such as standing up on the ski can cause a chain reaction of bad results: That is, the skier has cut the glide, lost the poling power, and is in a too far forward position to get a good powerful kick (set wax).

If the average citizen racer just learned to relax so that muscle did not fight muscle and learned to balance on the glide ski, his or her time would drop immensely. Also, the average tourer would have a much more enjoyable tour, expend less energy, and be more in harmony with nature.

An overwhelming majority of citizen skiers I have observed have the flaw of standing up on the glide ski. No real reason exists for this. A little work could easily correct it. The only difference between the accom-plished tourer, citizen racer, and top competitor should be the amount of dynamic motion involved in the kick. It is always a flaw to abruptly stand up, no matter the starting point, whether you are a tourer or a racer. The laws of physics will take over as you expend needless energy.

Main Concepts

The points presented in this chapter are important for a thorough understanding of cross-country skiing; however, most top competitors are probably not aware of them and need not be. I protect my skiers from much of this type of detailed analysis by choosing a significant point and then attempting to communicate to them effectively. Under no circumstance should you decide to go out and master two or three of the main concepts of this chapter. Work on one or two points at a time with the assistance of a coach or knowledgeable observer. Above all, *always ski with the fluid abandon described in chapter 1 and get the pole in the ground immediately.* Do not let too much analysis destroy your freedom of movement.

This chapter should probably have the surgeon general's warning: Taken in too big of doses, the following material can be dangerous to your skiing health.

1. An object in motion tends to stay in motion. So keep momentum within your stride and everywhere else you can on a course.
2. The entire weight should be on the kicking leg, and the kick should be preceded by a slight hitch called the preload. The kick itself should be a quick motion so that the advantage of preload is not lost.
3. During the recoil of the kick, there is a slight body rise as the wax is set. This is really part of freeing the body in its natural animal-like responses as described in chapter 4.
4. When the feet are together at the midpoint, the mass of the body should be above, not in front of the kicking foot. The buttocks will appear to be a little behind the heel of the kicking foot.
5. The amount of flexion in the leg during glide and the preload is a compromise of power versus endurance. This is an individual thing with each skier. Too much flexion can tire a racer or tourer before the day is over.
6. Halfway through the kick the leg is still flexed, ready to unleash its explosion.

7. The hips and upper body rise during the second half of the kick. If they do not, a less explosive kick is the result.

8. There is no independent forward arm motion during the free glide as it would only cause a backward force.

9. The pole is never really gripped in the ski stride. It is cradled at pole plant and released in the follow-through. Pressure is applied mainly to the straps.

10. The advanced skier is light on his or her glide ski because of the slight upward loft of the torso and then because of the downward poling pressure. It is good to practice feeling light on the snow.

11. The weight kept mainly on the heel accomplishes three things: The wax contact is minimal with the snow; the body is over the foot at the midpoint; and the kick can receive a force not only from the toe but also the heel.

12. Standing up on the glide ski is the sure way to ski with a stop-and-start motion, wasting much energy.

Above all—Ski fluidly and don't get bogged down with the above points.

The Double Pole and Skate

6

Modern Power Skiing

Assuming the diagonal is dead, some skiers will probably skip ahead to this chapter. However, for the vast majority of skiers, the diagonal is still the basic stroke of cross-country skiing. In fact, I feel sorry for those who have abandoned the single stick and its contribution to the enjoyment and to the variety of skiing.

Regardless, even for the traditionalists, it is hard not to add the skate to the arsenal. Because the skate is much faster in many situations (I'll use it while racing as often as I can), our youngsters practice it extensively. As a result, when we coach we place more importance on the analysis of the double pole and skate than the diagonal.

Furthermore, quite an evolution in the technique of the double pole as well as the skate has taken place in recent years, which cannot be ignored. To ignore is to fall behind; therefore, these changes will be covered in this chapter. Those of you who will do nothing but skate will find everything you need in this chapter.

Even before the advent of extensive skating, diagonaling was used much less than 50% of the distance on a tour or in a race. Why, then, five chapters on the diagonal and only two on the rest? Simply stated, the coordination of the diagonal is much more difficult than the coordination of any of the other strokes. There are just more ways for the diagonal to go wrong, and once fouled up, these mistakes are harder to correct.

Once a person has achieved the basic balance on skis, the double pole is a simple motion and is easy to learn. The kick double pole is a combination of the kick of the diagonal and of the poling motion of the double pole. The skate is also relatively easy to master as compared to the diagonal, although it is more difficult than the strict double pole.

One note, however, before we begin. Some skiers have trouble deciding which stroke to use while skiing or racing a course, but this is not really a difficult decision. Consider your diagonal as a starting point. It is more energy efficient than the double pole or kick double pole. When the conditions are too fast for the single stick, another stroke must be used. As speed increases, the general order is to kick double pole to double pole to tuck. However, the extensive use of the skate has changed this somewhat. The skate may be used under a variety of conditions and depends a great deal on the strength and mastery of the individual. A few skiers can skate all of the uphill sections and double pole or tuck the rest. (They are in the minority, but each season their number grows.)

The Double Pole: An Overview

A fluid and powerful double pole is the foundation of modern power skiing. Once mastered, it may easily be transferred to the skate. However, skiers without an efficient and powerful double pole rarely become good skaters. The double pole at world class level has changed considerably over the last few years. The basic difference is the fluidity and acceleration involved in the stroke, which has become less mechanical and has evolved into more of a whipping motion. A few years ago, skiers double poled with a more rigid arm-body system, the body and arms locked together in one motion. Any sign of a collapse (increased bending at the elbows) during the stroke was forbidden. Now all top skiers collapse to some degree, and this is called preload. This preload (stretching of muscles) and release are responsible for the whipping motion of the double pole. The arms and body are not stiffly locked together; they move at the same time, but not in rigid cohesion. The body must rise and fall rhythmically while the arms move fluidly. Slow motion sequences of

world class double polers show a remarkable resem-
blance to graceful birds in flight.

The skier begins and ends the double pole in a
balanced position with the weight mainly on the heels.
This enhances the gliding aspect of the double pole:
The body is upright and relaxed; the hips are directly
over the feet (see Figure 6.1).

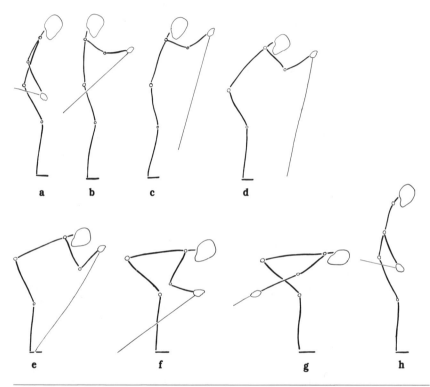

a   b   c   d

e   f   g   h

Figure 6.1   Double pole sequence. Especially note pole plant to
preload in (**d**) and (**e**), and full compression as exhibited in (**f**) and (**g**).

To start the stroke, the skier swings his or her
hands forward and up until they are about level with
the top of the head, the arms comfortably bent at the
elbow. As the hands approach head level, the elbows
are bent at a 90° angle, and the body drops down and
forward much like a falling leaf. These two actions
assure that the body is committed to the poles (commonly called compression).

As the poles are planted about a foot in front of the
ski boot, there is a slight give to the arms (see Figure
6.2): That is, the arms bend slightly more at the el-

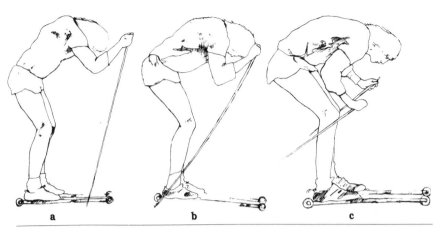

a   b   c

Figure 6.2 Double pole as executed by Joe Dernovsek. **(a)** At pole plant **(b)** after preload—note pole alignment with forearm. **(c)** Triceps are about to be unleashed after the lats and stomach have initiated the power stroke.

bows. This decrease in the angle of the elbows accomplishes several things. First, the initial shock of the pole plant is absorbed by the slight give of the muscles, and in doing so, a preloading occurs. The triceps are slightly stretched in preparation for the force they will exert in the double pole. The lats are also slightly stretched at pole plant. As seen earlier, this slight stretching or preloading increases the power of the muscles. From this point, the muscles recoil as the hands are whipped to the rear, propelling the skier forward.

Preload and recoil allow a longer power move than if the body and arms moved together rapidly. Because the hands are still in front of the head after preload and before the power is applied, a longer and more effective stroke ensues (see Figure 6.3). Skiers who lock their arm movement to their body look as if they take a half double pole, thus never getting the advantage of a full range of motion.

A longer range of motion is also encouraged by holding the hands higher before planting the poles. Traditional wisdom has the hands at shoulder height; however, a longer range of motion is allowed by holding the top of the hands level with the top of the head. Because the actual power of the double pole is not applied until after preload, a longer power stroke is

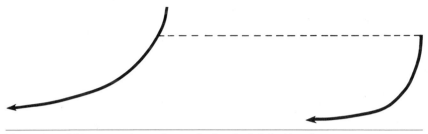

Figure 6.3 **(a)** Longer and straighter path of preloaded double pole vs. **(b)** shorter and rounder path of an overly rigid system.

ensured by having the hands higher to begin with. In addition, the use of longer poles (5 to 20 cm) also allows a higher hand position.

The vigor with which the double pole is executed depends on the skier's state of fatigue. The execution can be fast and whipping or can have a flowing grace, but it is never mechanical and stilted. The power is applied during the double pole by a smooth sequential motion, which emphasizes, first, the muscles of the abdomen, then the abdominals with the lats, and finally the triceps. Using the bigger muscles first and the smaller ones later is more efficient and less tiring.

The stomach muscles initiate movement by bending the body at the waist. The stomach muscles are particularly active during preload where they force the muscles of the upper back and arms to stretch. Rebounding from this stretch, the upper back muscles (lats) jump in as they drive the elbows back to the waist (see Figure 6.2). During this phase the elbows do not straighten much, which indicates that the triceps have not yet come into play. The final contribution comes from the triceps as the arm is straightened. All the muscles work through the entire stroke! As the stomach is powering the first part, the lats and triceps must be resisting while they are being stretched, or a complete collapse would result. Thus, the skier may feel that all of the muscles are working at once. As in all athletic motions, different skiers experience this feeling differently, even when they are executing almost identically.

As the skier finishes the stroke, the skier should find him- or herself with his or her weight on the heels and the body near parallel. The legs have bent and straightened very little during this sequence. For the weight to be on the heels, the skier must have had a slight shooting forward of the feet during the double pole. This shooting-through is not an artificial movement of pushing the feet forward, but it is the natural reaction to bending initiated at the abdomen. It is like having a hinge in the middle of your body. The nice side effect is that the weight ends up on the heels, facilitating glide, as it keeps the kick wax off the snow. Meanwhile, the body ending at or near parallel helps ensure that the bigger muscles of the abdomen and upper back have come into play.

The relaxed follow-through of the poling motion should carry the skier back into an upright position (see Figure 6.4). The skier now finds him- or herself

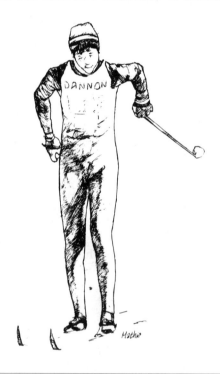

Figure 6.4   Racer during resting phase of the double pole.

back in the same position from which he or she started. A relaxation should occur at this point, the length of which depends upon the conditions. Those who maintain a rapid turnover at this point are wasting much energy by not using their momentum to its fullest. If the skier is out on the course and the conditions are fast, there will be a very noticeable pause between strokes. If the conditions are a little slow or if the skier is sprinting, the resting position at the top will disappear altogether. Then turnover will be all important. At this time, many skiers do not even raise their body anywhere near vertical. I mention this only so that the reader can differentiate between the normal double pole and the one most often seen on television—that of sprinting to the finish. The normal double pole does have a very noticeable pause for rest at the upright position.

The Three Stages in an Effective Double Pole

Before we begin the actual learning process, three basic goals are in order: (a) The motion must be fluid; (b) the big muscles are used first, the smaller ones later; and (c) the power stroke should be as long as possible, utilizing the above two points.

Stage 1—Compression: Moving the Body From Vertical to Parallel. In addition to involving the stomach muscles and body weight in the double pole, compression allows the skier to get his or her hands forward while keeping the elbows bent for power, thereby encouraging a longer stroke. Compression is the first goal of the beginning double poler.

Most beginners fear a large movement of their body. Their balance is usually precarious, so they use both poles in a weak thrust only through the use of their arms. To have a powerful double pole requires a strong move of the torso from vertical to parallel. This allows the mass of the body to be a factor and, more importantly, encourages the strong stomach muscles to initiate the poling position.

How this body drop is accomplished is important. The hips must move back as the shoulders move forward and down. This keeps the body in a balanced position over the feet. *This is a grossly overlooked principle.* In fact, the opposite is taught. Why move the hip back? Health is the first reason—those old back problems again. If you have ever hurt your back while double poling, you probably were skiing with rigid hips. Locked hips put the body in that precarious position where a great strain is placed on the lower back.

Fluid hips that have moved back as the shoulders move forward offer support to the lower back. (This same principle was discussed earlier in chapter 4 on the back and on the single stick.) Practice this motion fluidly without poles in front of a mirror or a window. The hips and shoulders should begin moving simultaneously.

Many advanced skiers have improved the power of their double pole dramatically by freeing their hips. This also prevents the skier from driving the ski tips into the snow. One note of warning, however: The hips move back, not down; it is not a bending movement at the knees. For the beginner learning compression, it is important to have fluid hips. The natural balance attained will enable the body to compress, making it easier to parallel. In addition, back problems will be avoided.

Stage 2—Fluidity and Abandon: The Prerequisites of Athletic Motion.   Most beginners and many older skiers have a very stiff double pole. Fluid hips help tremendously in loosening up the tight skier, so Stages 1 and 2 are interrelated. Practicing the double pole without poles in front of a mirror is a big help; again check to see that the hips move fluidly back as the body moves forward. Don't worry too much about power at this time. In Stage 3 the proper sequencing of the muscles will be shown that will allow you to use all of your potential; but this cannot happen until a fluid motion is attained with a decent amount of body compression.

Slight downhills are good places to learn fluidity. The strength requirements are not as great, and the skier can concentrate on balance and abandon. The checkpoints to look for are the body reaching parallel and the arms following through behind the skier and not stopping at the waist. Again the best checkpoint is the objective observer, for almost anyone can tell if you are moving stiffly or fluidly. Once some abandon is attained, you are ready for Stage 3; however, the quest for fluidity will always be a skier's goal.

Stage 3—Power Sequencing, or Big Muscles Before Small.   The most effective sequencing of muscles is stomach to lats to triceps. The bigger muscles whip and preload the smaller muscles into play, each increasing its natural strength by the supercharged start and stretch—the rebound of preload. The result is a quick and powerful snapping motion. (If you are unable to attain a whipping motion because the conditions are too slow or you are fatigued, you should probably be skating or kick double poling instead.) Before this can happen, however, each muscle must be in its proper position to be utilized maximally. The stomach is rather easy to observe. If the upper body continues to hinge during the entire stroke, the stomach has been active. If the torso does not continue to move during the entire stroke, look for the stiff hips discussed in Stage 1. Surprisingly, this is often the culprit.

In Stage 3, the utilization of the lats is the main objective. Very few skiers use the lats powerfully through their entire range of motion. It helps to visualize the power portion of the double pole. Before reading any farther, look closely at Figure 6.2. Positions *b* and *c* are the microcosm of all efficient double poles. The three positions take us from pole plant to preload to hands near legs. Don't be misled by superficial differences you see in various skiing stars, such as the angle of the arms at initial pole plant and the amount of compression. All powerful double poles go through this sequence. When the power is applied, this is it. The stomach has remained active throughout the sequence, but the main movement comes from the lats. They have been placed in a position where they can work isolated from the triceps. The main drive of the triceps will be observed after the last picture of this sequence and will be automatic if the microcosm is accomplished. Take the time to absorb this sequence. Use the following checkpoints:

1. *At pole plant* (see Figure 6.5), the body is at a 45° angle to the ground. The upper arms are 90° to the body, and the elbows are also bent 90°. In addition, the hips have moved back as the shoulders moved forward. At this time, the lats are being slightly stretched before exploding into action. The forward lean of the upper body also encourages a longer power stroke with a more direct push to the rear.

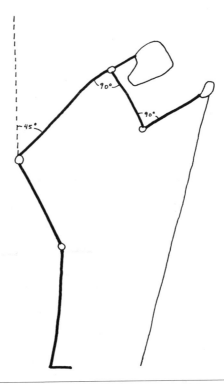

Figure 6.5 Pole plant checkpoint. The body is at 45 degrees at pole plant with the upper arms at 90 degrees to the torso and the elbows bent at 90 degrees.

2.   *After preload* (see Figure 6.2b), the hands are still in front of the forehead, ensuring a full power stroke. If you cannot attain this position, your poles may be too short.

The elbow has increased its bend and the pole has moved closer to the forearm. *This is the critical power position.* The pole must be close to the forearm. (We call this closeness of pole to forearm the Marty Hall checkpoint because we picked it up from Marty.) This is the main benefit of preload, even though the stretching of muscles is important. Once this forearm-pole alignment is reached, the skier can "let 'er rip" with confidence, knowing that the biggest muscles are doing their thing.

As the elbows begin their drive to the waist, the triceps remain fairly inactive (see Figure 6.2c). The lats are powering, stretching, and preloading the triceps.

This can be visualized in two ways. One way is to observe that the bend at the elbows remains constant during the first part of the power stroke; therefore, the lats have to be taking the major share of the load. The second way is to observe the closeness of the pole to the forearm. If the pole remains close to the forearm, the lats have to be working, pulling from the elbow. If the pole moves away too quickly, the triceps have been used too early. The pole should be close to the forearm during the beginning of the microcosm of the power stroke and should remain there initially. Then gradually the pole moves away as the triceps enter in, providing the final whip.

A brief reminder: The power is applied to the straps rather than the poles. To effectively use the straps, the hand must face a little forward so the thumbpad (the fat part of the lower thumb) can exert pressure.

This power move is best learned on an uphill where a weak stroke will be of no avail. Concentrate on keeping the pole close to the forearm, leading with the elbows and keeping the angle of the elbows constant. The steeper the hill, the more you will need the stomach and lat involvement. Of course, the whip of the triceps will not be a factor in these conditions.

Just before the launching of the triceps (see Figure 6.2c), the elbows are driven to the waist and the stretched triceps will now whip into the final portion of the double pole.

A final comment about the microcosm of the double pole: In trying conditions, especially in the uphill skate or kick double pole, the preload and whip of the triceps may disappear, but the microcosm remains. The main power of the double pole will be the stomach involvement and the driving at the elbows through the use of the lats. In the future, in my opinion, the best racers will be strong enough to maintain a preload and whip through most of the course, even the uphills. As it is now, the winners on the World Cup circuit do so for more segments of the course than the also rans.

Common Double Pole Errors

The beginner's most common double pole error is the failure of the body to move to, or near, parallel (see Figure 6.6). This is called a lack of compression. It places most of the work on the triceps, as the double pole then consists mainly of straightening the elbow joint. This is not a very dynamic motion. The body must bend at the waist for the powerful muscles of the stomach and upper back to contribute. Bending at the

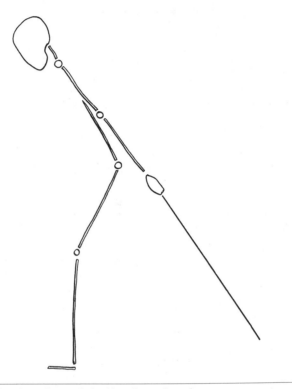

Figure 6.6 The weak double pole resulting from no compression.

waist also gives the lats a longer range of movement. Failure to compress results in your tiring more quickly and in slowing down prematurely because you are relying on the smaller muscles of your upper arms. Most beginners quickly attain compression once they know what they are trying to accomplish. Simply make sure that the chest moves down during the entire stroke and that your hips also move slightly to the rear. At first, it may seem as if you will fall flat on your face, but it only takes a little time on skis to gain the confidence needed to make such a huge move with the body.

The second common error is compressing well below parallel. The cure is usually simple. Rather than trying to inhibit or curtail movement, which would decrease power, a positive correction is used: The Stage 1 checkpoint of mobile hips. Most people who let their body drop too much can correct this immediately by allowing their hips to move backward. However, if you still drop your body too far, you may be collapsing—the next common error.

Collapsing the body completely to parallel before the hands have exerted any force is the one real danger of preload (see Figure 6.7). If preload is exag-

Figure 6.7   A complete collapse, well past preload. A weak effort will result. Note: Some world class skiers have their bodies parallel before applying power, but all angles of their arms are less than 90 degrees. Their arms are considerably bent, not straight.

gerated, it becomes a collapse: That is, the body reaches parallel before the hands have done any work. In that case, the body has dropped to parallel without propelling you forward, which is a tremendous waste of energy. There is a fine line between preload and collapse. The preload should be complete with the body still above parallel. However, if in doubt, use the following guideline: If the pole moves toward the forearm during the microcosm of the power stroke after pre-load, a collapse has occurred. The pole should momentarily hold its position and then gradually move away from the forearm as the triceps enter in. Some very powerful double polers have exaggerated preloads that closely resemble a collapse (e.g., Wassburg and Svan of Sweden), but they use their lats to drive their elbows to their sides. Their poles remain close to their forearms during the first part of the stroke.

The next error, in vogue several years ago, was that of jumping onto the toes before each double pole. However, this technique was discarded as skiers realized the return was not worth the effort. Likewise, any unnecessary bending of the knees only wastes energy. The legs are not a rigid system, but they do not bend appreciably either. Any excessive up-and-down motion is wasteful. It is like placing hills on the course when they are not even there.

The next error stems from the skier's overexuberance. In an enthusiasm to have a powerful stroke, the skier tries to get a running start and develops too much momentum before planting the poles into the snow. At first, this running start may appear to be a good thing—why not get a power boost in that manner? What happens is that the skier develops too much power for his or her strength, and the result is a stall as the poles are planted. Rather than a smooth stroke, this skier looks rather jerky. Too much energy is exerted at the wrong time and is wasted as the skier's motion stalls before his or her stroke is powered. This skier is mainly driving the poles into the ground, which will only lift him or her up, not propel him or her forward. The most pressure should be exerted on the poles after they are in the ground, and then the energy of the stroke will be used to propel the skier forward.

From the angle of the poles, it is easy to see that excessive force too early in the stroke will only lift the skier up, not propel him or her forward (see Figure 6.8). Thus, it is important to accelerate throughout the double pole. The force will be greatest when the poling motion is most directly pushing backward. If you look at the path of the double pole, you can see that the hands move down as well as back during the first part of the stroke. The last part of the stroke is more direct, with the hands pushing almost straight back. As the skier accelerates, he or she exerts more force, which results in an efficient use of energy. One added note: The use of longer poles allows them to be angled back, from the beginning of the double pole. Therefore longer poles allow effective force to be generated earlier in the stroke.

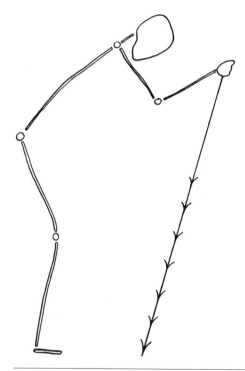

Figure 6.8   Too much force at initial pole plant will only lift the skier up.

The Kick Double Pole

Once the conditions slow down so that the double pole is too difficult, the skier instinctively breaks into the kick double pole. This stroke (see Figure 6.9) takes more energy but has the added benefit of the legs propelling the skier. With the advent of the skate, some areas that were formerly kick double pole or

Figure 6.9 This sequence is an artist's reproduction from fuzzy video tapes of the final sprint of Odvar Braa in the 1982 World Championship Relays at Oslo. This classic battle of the kick double pole, just after Braa broke and received a new pole, ended in a dead heat with Alexander Zavjalov.

even double pole sections are now being skated. This is something that each skier will have to decide, depending on his or her strength and ability with the different strokes.

The kick is initiated much like the kick of the single stick. As in the diagonal, the foot should be under the chest as the skier gets ready to kick so that the weight is over the ski. If the foot is allowed to drift behind the hips before the kick is started, it will be too late. The force will then be applied too much in a backward motion for a good wax purchase on the snow. The kick double pole is a good way for late kickers to learn to kick with the foot under the body. After getting the correct feeling, they can apply it to the single stick.

The timing of the kick double pole is basically a 1-2 rhythm. The foot kicks and moves back at the same time as the arms swing forward. The body opens up as if it were hinged at the waist. Then the poling motion and leg return occur as the hinge closes. *Note to beginners:* Spend most of the first several weeks using the 1-2 timing of the kick double pole. 1 (open), 2 (close): that is 1—kicking leg moves back at same time arms move forward and then 2—double pole.

As in the normal double pole, the arms should be in a naturally bent position. If they are too straight, they will have to be rebent, and a collapse can occur during this time. The skier's body should be in a good riding position on the ski. The leg, as in the single stick, is under the chest with the weight on the heel. The body slightly rocks up and forward before the poles are planted. The trail leg is relaxed with no attempt made to accelerate it forward, remembering that any such acceleration causes a backward force. The trail leg drifts forward naturally as the body hinge closes.

When the torso rocks forward onto the glide leg, care must be taken so that the glide leg does not straighten. Completely straightening the leg is a waste of vertical motion (climbing hills again when they are not even there), whereas the slight rocking forward is conducive to a powerful double pole rhythm and does not take much additional effort. Any effort is more than paid back by an abandoned and powerful effort in the poling.

The poling power should be applied with little or no delay. Any undue hesitation will only result in a loss of momentum because the friction of the snow is constantly slowing down the skis. The exact timing depends on the speed of the snow. The poling part of the kick double pole uses the same muscles as the regular double pole and therefore will feel quite similar.

At the end of the stroke, the body is again parallel to the ground and the weight is on the heels of the feet. There is one slight modification, however, in the foot movement of the kick double pole. The most efficient way to kick double pole is to alternate feet: The left one will kick in one stroke and the right one in the next. This allows the skier to alternate muscle groups and to be more rested. It is more effective to kick when the foot kicking is a little farther in front of the other foot. This allows a bigger bite and a longer stride. It also allows the weight to be better placed to set the wax.

Advanced note: In order for the kicking foot to be in front of the other foot, it must get there at some point. Obvious, isn't it? But it matters how it gets there. If it is shoved forward just before the kick, we get that old bugaboo, the opposite and equal reaction. Any acceleration forward of a body part during the glide will cause a force in the opposite direction, thus slowing the skier. So when the kicking leg comes forward, it must never catch up with the gliding leg. That means the gliding leg must move forward smoothly during the poling motion. Then the gliding leg becomes the kicking leg and already is in position for the next kick.

After the poling motion, the skier naturally rises, as in the double pole, and prepares to initiate the next stroke. The amount of rest in between depends on the speed of the snow, the skier's condition, and the amount of fatigue. The next kick should be initiated before any considerable slowing takes place. Under most circumstances, there is no deliberate rest. The skier allows the natural rhythm of the stroke to dictate when to kick next.

Many of the same errors that occurred in the double pole also crop up in the kick double pole. Lack of compression, completely collapsing, raising and lowering the hips, and jumping onto the toes are all flaws to avoid. Ideally the skier will have the same motion in both double poles and will also feel the same throughout the motion, the only difference being the preceding kick. In practice, however, the double pole motion of the kick double pole is a little less vigorous with a little less preload. The reason? The kick double pole is an energy demanding stroke and compromises have to be made sometimes. For some, however, this is debatable because the expert skier now uses the skate where he or she once kick double poled. Indeed, it is not the diagonal that is dead for many skiers, but the kick double pole. For the average skier, though, it's a nice weapon to have in the arsenal and adds to the diversity of skiing.

The Skate

The skate, the newest entry to world class skiing, has always existed for those who have done any skiing on lakes, snowmobile trails, or other areas where tracks have not been set and the snow is packed. Skiers have also used it for years on parts of the course where accelerating around a corner was best helped by skating. Mass start citizen races have long witnessed the use of the skate as skiers tried to clear themselves of the field. But this maneuver is not quite the same as the one which first emerged at the level of classified and world cup skiing.

Bill Koch was the first to introduce the marathon skate to the World Cup circuit. Until that time, this skate was more or less relegated to the flatter marathon circuits. The fact that Bill Koch was able to use it on the hillier courses took the competition by surprise. Bill became the first World Cup champion from the United States. One of the initial reactions of the Scandinavians was very predictable: Ban the skate. A compromise was the result, with the skate being banned for only the last 200 meters of international competition.

Interestingly, the Norwegians and Swedes led the protest, yet it was a Norwegian, Ove Aunli, who was the first Olympic competitor to be disqualified for skating. Ironically, it would have been Norway's best male performance in those 1984 Winter Games. It was also a Swede, Gunde Svan, who dominated the World Cup and Olympics in 1984. His coaches credit his efficient skating technique for much of his success. Then in 1985, Annette Boee of Norway dominated the women's World Championships, skating the entire course.

For the 1985-86 season, world class skiers can expect two types of races: classical, or traditional, races where no skating will be allowed, and races where any stroke may be used. To add to the confusion, the rules in local races will probably fluctuate considerably. But it is obvious that there is quite a move to save the diagonal at an international level. Some predict that the classical races will disappear in a few years while others predict the opposite. Despite the controversy, one thing is clear: If you want to compete successfully at any level, you must master a proficient skating technique. It's been my experience that the average skier also enjoys learning and using this new technique. Through evolution on the World Cup circuit, an efficient and powerful form, well within the reach of the average skier, has emerged.

The marathon skate is used on a different part of the course than the traditional skate. In the traditional skate, both skis are angled out, as in ice skating. This motion is performed where there are no tracks. The skier skates from one ski to another, poling on every other stroke. This is a very fast technique and is still best where there are no tracks. However, the marathon skate requires tracks, creating the basic difference between the two skating methods. In using the marathon skate, the skier skates with only one ski at a time, while simultaneously performing a double pole with the upper body; the other ski remains in the track. The result—a powerful stroke that combines the pushing power of the legs with a thrust from the upper body.

Stage 1—Marathon Skating: Elementary Timing and Motion

Several years ago at a clinic, some skiers asked me if I thought the skate was a factor in our local races. I replied, "Not yet." Some juniors were proficient skaters, but the masters still had not caught on. My comment was that I was happy to see the older skiers, my competitors, skating because it usually spelled one thing—a fall. Since then, this situation has changed drastically. Juniors now skate extensively, and the Geritol bunch have just recently learned the skating coordination.

When first learning to marathon skate, you must concern yourself with proper timing. If you plant the poles incorrectly, you can find yourself sprawled on the trail. Sprawling is a direct result of planting the poles between the skis; therefore, initiate the poling motion just outside, and slightly before, the skate begins. Plant the poles as to engage the snow anywhere from the boot area to about a foot in front of the bindings. This will also vary with the length of the poles. Then you can simultaneously double pole and push off with the skating leg.

Once you master timing, your next goal is weight transfer. To initiate the weight transfer, your feet should be together at the beginning of the skate, with all of your weight on the ski in the track. The trails of the skis will actually cross, but because one of the skis is in the track and therefore lower, they will not touch. After you plant the poles and start the double pole, you should forcefully push your foot to the side with a slight push to the rear. (The slower the conditions, the more the push to the rear.) During the push-off, the weight is, for a moment, completely on the skating leg and then quickly transferred back to the gliding ski. To get a powerful thrust, the weight should be transferred in a rhythmic and snappy fashion—explosively.

The next stage in learning to skate is compressing your upper body. Without compression, a weak arm stroke results. At first, fear is again the enemy. But once you gain confidence, the upper body part of the skate should more closely resemble the normal double pole, but with slightly less compression. The beginning skater usually combines a very poor weight transfer with almost no upper body compression. As a result the beginning skater assumes a squatting position. By squatting, the skier not only fails to compress the body but also has a very poor weight transfer (to the skating ski and then completely back to the gliding ski, which remains in the track). The weight stays basically in one position in relation to the skis, and the skier uses a weak push of the leg. If the skier has a good push-off with the skating leg, the angle of the ski will not allow a bowlegged appearance. The ski will then be set on edge for a good bite, and as force is applied, the leg is in more of the knock-kneed position. In addition, a compression of the upper body encourages a dynamic motion of weight transfer. Squatting also causes excessive leg bending that should be stemmed before it becomes a bad habit. The skating motion does not require much leg bending but involves more of a lateral push. Too much bending at the knees is very tiring.

The best overall checkpoint for both weight transfer and compression of the upper body is by observing the motion of the head. The head of a good skater will actually travel in a circle as the skater transfers the weight from the gliding ski to the skating ski and back again (see Figures 6.10-6.11).

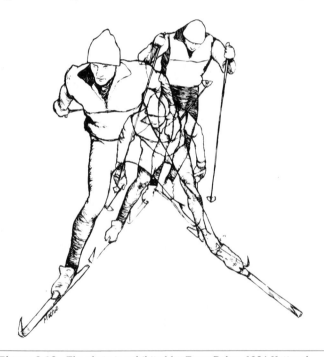

Figure 6.10   The skate is exhibited by Terry Daley, 1984 National Collegiate Ski Association Champion. In winning that title, Terry skated the entire course.

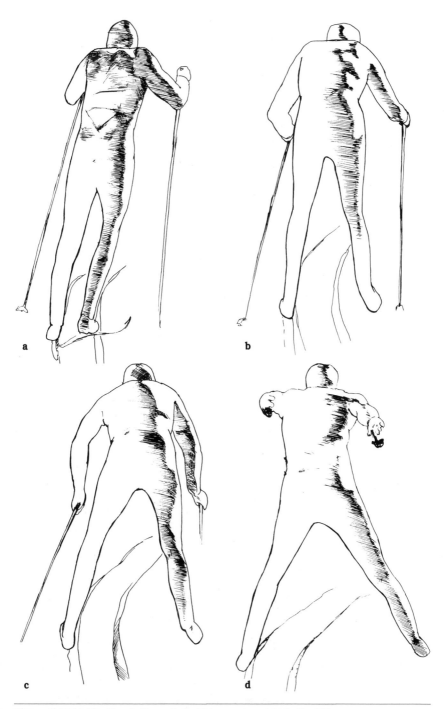

a

b

c

d

Figure 6.11(a)-(d)　Gunde Svan skating his way to a gold in the 50k at the World Championships, Seefeld, 1985.

At the conclusion of the skate, the body moves down, but is not quite parallel to the ground. The arms are extended to the rear and the pushing leg is also extended to the side and rear (see Figure 6.12). At

Figure 6.12   The ideal follow-through as exhibited by a top Birkebeiner finisher. Note the posted glide leg.

this time the head is circling back over the gliding leg. The vertical motion of the head is caused by the compression of the double pole, the horizontal motion by the weight transfer. The extension of the arms and leg, follow-through, is one indication of a complete abandon during the stroke. As in all strokes, this should be typified by a total relaxation of power, no muscle opposing another. This total lack of inhibition is seen in the follow-through.

Thus, the beginner has four basic goals when learning to skate: (a) timing the pole plant and push off, (b) transferring the weight from the gliding ski to the skating ski and back again, (c) compressing the upper body in powering the arm stroke, and (d) avoiding excessive leg bending.

Stage 2—Advanced Skating Techniques

Posting the Glide Leg.   The marathon skate should not be an extremely exhausting stroke. If it were, how could all those "older guys" on the World Loppett circuit do it continuously for 50 k to 100 k? On the flats, unless you're really hammering it, the skate should seem even easier than the double pole. To accomplish this, your glide leg should not get overly tired. If it does, you are not *posting* the leg correctly. The glide leg should not be consciously bent much during the skate but should feel as if it remains rather straight. In fact, the pushing or skating leg should not bend and unbend to any great degree either. Any excess bending of either leg is energy depleting, tiring you needlessly.

Observe Figure 6.13 of Gunde Svan skating. It appears that his gliding leg is bent to a considerable

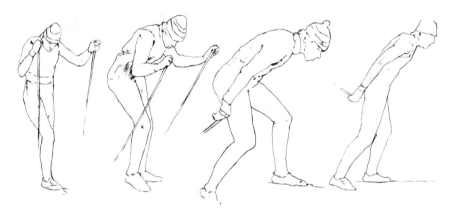

Figure 6.13   Gunde Svan again in the Seefeld 50k.

degree. And it is; so why doesn't his leg get tired? The reason is simple: all of this weight is on the skating leg. But why must the glide leg bend this way if the skier is not conscious of it? Again, the answer is simple. As the skater pushes off with the skating foot, the foot travels backward in relation to the body. In order for the skating ski to bear the entire body weight for an effective push-off, the hips must move to the rear. Sound familiar? It is the same move as seen in the double pole, which actually helps the skier maintain a balanced powerful position over the glide ski, and which is also easy on the lower back. However, at this time, the glide leg carries no weight, and the skier should have the sensation that he *could* lift the glide ski out of the track if he wished. In fact, in his next move, he almost does just that as his glide foot shoots forward and his weight is quickly and dynamically transferred back to the heel of the glide foot.

At the time of the weight transfer to the glide ski, the body also rises. If it continued to drop, it would be fighting the lofting motion of the skating leg's push-off. Therefore, the skate has a smaller compression than the normal double pole. This lofting motion from the push-off and double pole allows the glide leg to straighten from the momentum of the push-off without using extra effort from the glide leg itself.

The skier should ride the glide ski between strokes as long as the ski does not slow down to any great degree. This glide should feel effortless, with all of the weight on the posted glide leg. In faster conditions, the glide will be longer; in slower conditions, the glide will be shorter and the turnover faster. An effective drill to become a fast skater is to skate downhill. Getting the gliding foot forward and transferring the weight to the gliding heel is a big help. If balance can be maintained in those conditions, it will be easy elsewhere, for being able to skate where others lose their balance is a great advantage.

Rotating the Body.   At this time, it is appropriate to delve a little deeper into weight transfer and also to introduce a new concept—the parallel pole push. In the diagonal stride, we saw that a complete weight transfer allowed the skier to be more dynamic in his or her motions, flexing and extending his or her muscles more completely with more abandon. The same principle applies here.

The quick and complete weight transfer of the skate is facilitated by a rotation of the upper body. The body is first rotated to face in the direction of the skating ski. For example, if the right ski is initiating the skate, the body is faced in that direction, to the right of the direction of travel (see Figures 6.10-6.11). Then, as the weight is transferred back to the gliding ski (the left one in this example), the upper body is rotated to the left, now facing the direction of travel on the gliding ski.

This rotation does some favorable things for the skater. First it allows the weight to be momentarily over the skating or pushing ski. Second, it then allows all of the body's momentum to be transferred to the gliding ski in a dynamic body rotation. Before presenting another interesting side effect, an important principle must first be introduced: *The poling motion of the skate should always be directly parallel to the path the body is travelling/facing.* Because the body actually changes the direction it faces and temporarily travels in the skate, some interesting things happen. At the beginning of the skate, when the body is facing in the direction of the skating ski, the initial push is in that direction. The poles are angled to push slightly at an angle to the track. Then as the body is rotated over the glide ski, the actual angle of the push stays parallel to the body. Sounds complicated, doesn't it? It's not. If the skier only makes sure that the initial push is parallel to the skating ski, the rest takes care of itself.

The arms and lats are in a much stronger position when double poling if they push parallel to the direction the body is facing; so the skier naturally compensates as the body rotates over the skating ski. Although the original push is in the direction of the skating ski, it ends up in the direction of the gliding ski and helps push the skier on top of the gliding leg.

Besides placing the muscles in a stronger position, there is another reason to push parallel to the direction of travel (in the skate, slightly side to side). This parallel push is more efficient as can be seen by applying the laws of physics, which can be simply explained in nonphysics terms as follows: Although you travel slightly from side to side while skating, the only motion that counts in a race is in a forward direction. So, although skating is faster, there is some loss because of the sideways direction of travel. If you pole parallel to the temporary direction of travel, all of your energy will be directed into propelling your body along the direction of your ski. However, if you push parallel to the track, directly back, you will lose one more time mathematically. Because your body is really moving a little to the side, only a portion of the push will propel you in the direction of your temporary side-to-side motion. This loss is in addition to the loss from the body not traveling directly down the track. Therefore, you should *always pole parallel to the direction your body travels.*

Another positive element to rotating the body is that it saves a skier's hips. As you skate, the foot and hip move behind your body because of the angle of the ski. However, if the body is facing in the direction of the skating ski, no undue strain will be placed on the ball-and-socket joint of the hip. The hip bearing the pushing pressure will only have to move in a lateral direction. However, if the body is kept facing forward, the hip socket will not only have to accommodate a sideways motion, but also a twisting to the back. The effect is almost like ripping the hip joint out of its socket. If your hip is sore, check the direction your body is facing as you begin to skate. In addition, in the off-season, be sure to skate with the lightest two-wheeled roller skis available, especially if you are light to begin with; otherwise, serious injury could result.

Upper Body Compression—Double Pole Portion.
The same principles that applied to the double pole are valid for the skate. In practicality, however, preload and whip are minimized except in sprint conditions or when the skiers are fresh. It should be noted, however, that the top finishers of a World Cup skating race can be predicted by observing the amount of whip they exhibit throughout the course. It should also, again, be noted that the body compresses less in the skate than the full double pole.

The things on which to concentrate to ensure a powerful double pole portion of the skate are as follows: The body should be leaning forward to about 45° as the poles are planted. The stroke should be long with the hands still forward before the power is applied. The forearms should be close to the poles when the lats and stomach interact and control most of the motion. The feeling and motion is almost identical to a Nautilus Torso Pullover machine, if you've ever used one. This has been one of our most successful visualizations in getting skiers to properly use their arms in the skate and double pole. This seems to help skiers keep their triceps out of the stroke until the stronger stomach and lats have done their job.

Rhythm, Fluidity, and Abandon.   Fluidity and rhythm are main ingredients to successful, efficient skating (see Figure 6.14). The upper body flows up and

Figure 6.14   Youngsters pick up skating easily as shown by 10-year-old Brian Fish of Rhinelander, WI.

down in a constant wavelike motion as the arms flow back in a whipping, relaxed thrust. This is accompanied by a snappy weight transfer back to the posted glide leg. A good checkpoint for quick weight transfer is to observe the motion of the head. The head, which makes a circular motion during the skate, should start back toward the glide leg halfway through the push-off portion of the skate. If it doesn't, the skate will be sluggish.

Rotating the body, as described above, helps enormously in creating a skate with fluidity and abandon. But ending the glide with the two feet together is the posture that helps greatly in encouraging abandon. I

recall the "away we go" technique in memory of
Jackie Gleason's "And away we go" routine where he
would pick up one leg and propel himself off the stage.
An efficient skater does the same thing (see Figure
6.15). This leg position, along with a body facing in

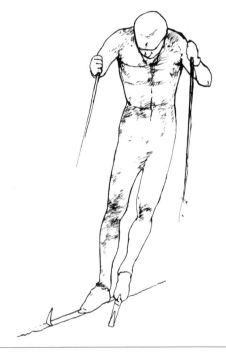

Figure 6.15 Pall Gunner Mickelsplass, of Norway, initiating the
skate with abandon from the "away we go" position. (Seefeld
15k.—1985)

line with the skating leg, creates an atmosphere of
abandon. The skier "away we goes" onto the skating
ski with a dynamic weight transfer. This encourages a
snappy and efficient skate and requires excellent
balance. The "away we go" move almost places the
skating ski on the outside edge before the skating begins. I say *almost* because the ski is really flat but
almost looks as if the outside edge (as in speedskating)
is first engaged. This ensures that the entire bottom of
the ski can be active as it pushes toward the inside
edge.

Changes During Slower Conditions (or Hills)

As the conditions slow and/or hills are encountered, two things happen. First, the tempo of the skate increases with less glide time between strokes. A slower tempo allows too much slowing down between strokes and an accompanying loss of momentum. It takes more energy to accelerate again than it does to keep the speed fairly constant.

Second, as a result of the increased tempo, the downward movement of the upper body is shortened. There is less compression, or bending forward at the waist. At first, this would seem incorrect, sacrificing the power of the larger body muscles just when they are needed the most. But upon further thought, it becomes apparent why less compression works better. The smaller body motion allows a quicker turnover. Therefore less stalling occurs between strokes, and momentum is maintained. It is similar to quickening the diagonal on the steeper hills.

In these conditions most of the upper body work is done with the stomach and lats. The triceps are kept inactive because they are weaker and because the stroke is shorter and quicker. The triceps are left out because they would be the last to come into play—now there is no time for them. You can see that the triceps are not used by observing the constant angle of the elbow of world class skiers as they skate up steeper inclines. The arm is slightly bent and kept that way throughout the stroke. This principle will be used later in discussing the V-skate.

V-Skate

V-skating is actually an older form than the marathon skate, but in all the recent publicity, it has taken a back seat to the marathon skate. However, that has changed recently. V-skating has always been used at the start of mass start races and in open, untracked sections. Today, it is the marathon skater's primary weapon in negotiating a hill, and many even think it will eventually replace the marathon skate on the rest of the course.

The major advantage of the V-skate is that both skis are used to propel the skier forward. In the marathon skate, one ski remains in the track, but in the V-skate, both are angled out and can be used for propulsion. One main use for the V-skate is on the hills. Often a skier will stall out during the glide time on the marathon skate because both arms and one ski push at once. The next cycle does not start until the arms and skating ski can be recycled. Because one ski is always working, the V-skate is more efficient on the hills (the old momentum story again). It's harder to speed up an object than to keep it at a speed; therefore, stop-start is an energy waster, and the V-skate is more efficient on the hills.

As with the marathon skate, the faster a skier is moving, the more the skating skis line up parallel to the track. The slower the conditions, the more they angle out to get more push. The various types of V-skating will be described in more detail in the next few sections.

Double Pole V-Skate Up a Hill

Once a hill becomes too steep, a skier must switch from a quick-tempo marathon skate to a V-skate. Now both skis are angled out and are used in a skating motion push-off to propel the skier forward. With this technique, stalling out on the hills is avoided and momentum maintained. The rhythm of the pole plant revolves around this theme, avoiding the stall (see Figure 6.16).

The V-skate up a hill has the same basic rhythm of pole plant as the marathon skate, except the turnover is greater and the compression is less (not enough time for a huge compression). Some of our skiers call it the "marathon hop." The pole push has two functions: (a) To increase the glide time on the first skating ski and (b) to help the first skating ski push the skier onto the second ski, which is now angled out. The ski that has received the weight transfer is then used to skate back to the other side. In the marathon skate, you could have picked up the glide ski momentarily during

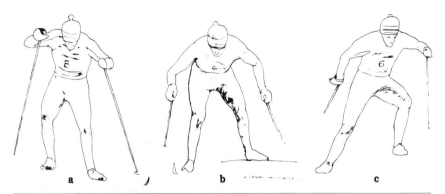

Figure 6.16(a)-(c)   Maurilio DeZolt, of Italy, double pole V-skating up a hill in the relays at Seefeld.

the weight transfer, but in the power V-skate you actually do it and angle it out as you push onto it. What was the glide ski in the marathon skate is now angled out and can be used to propel you forward.

In initiating the power V-skate, the body faces the ski that is angled out at the beginning of each stroke. The body is then rotated over to face the direction of the second ski as the weight is transferred to that ski. (The circling head is an indicator.) The poles actually change their angle of push to help accomplish this weight shift to the second ski. When the weight is transferred back to the original ski, another cycle is begun.

Most beginning skaters are too stiff, especially in the hips. A fluid midsection, with some side to side hip motion, facilitates weight transfer and glide. Actually, the skis should be kept as flat as possible to encourage glide. Most skiers edge their skis too much while V-skating. Extreme edging is only a factor when the hill gets steeper—what would have been a herringbone hill.

Maurillio DeZolt of Italy demonstrates the power V-skate up a hill in Figure 6.16. But in this sequence, you can see that in order for DeZolt to push in the direction he is moving, he must rotate his body from the direction of the right ski to that of his left. For his poles to push first in the direction of the right ski and then in the direction of the left, they must be pivoted in the snow. Look closer at Figure 6.17 and see how his poles push right and then left (most easily seen by

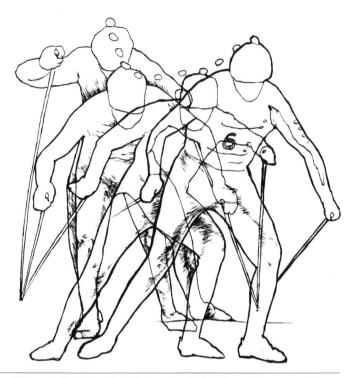

Figure 6.17 Maurilio DeZolt, again. Notice the rotation around the right pole. The force is always in the direction of travel.

observing his right pole in this sequence). This way he is always pushing in the direction he is traveling (the way the body is facing). All through this motion, both arms are used in poling.

The trend with many top skiers is to use a syncopated pole plant on the hills. The marathon skate rhythm with an early pole plant is maintained; however, both poles are not planted simultaneously. If the skier is initiating the skate with the right ski, the left pole is planted first, just as or slightly before the right ski hits the snow. The left pole pushes the skier temporarily onto the right ski, but the stronger pole push comes when the right pole is planted a fraction of a second later. This pole push increases the glide time of the first skating ski and also pushes the skier onto the gliding left leg. This is a 1-2 rhythm, the spacing of which varies some between skiers. On steep uphills, the amount of body compression is minimal; however, some skiers use a little more than others. Again, a quick tempo is the key to success.

Annette Boee, the 1985 World Champion at several events, uses a syncopated pole plant when V-skating up a hill (see Figure 6.18). Boee's left pole is planted slightly before her right pole. The left pole pushes her onto her right ski, but the main poling thrust comes from the right pole. Spend some time looking at these figures to see the differences between the two styles. The differences are subtle at first glance and to the casual observer, there may be very little difference. Why then, do so many of the top skiers use the syncopated motion other than that they obviously think it is faster?

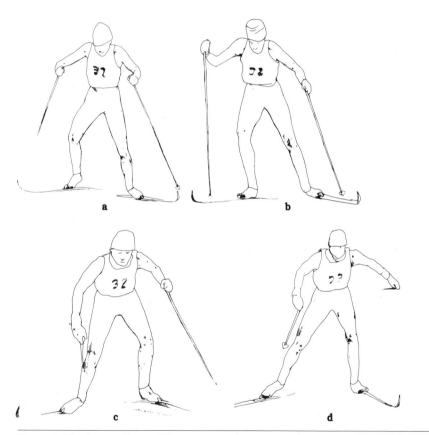

Figure 6.18 Annette Boee, of Norway, using the syncopated timing to V-skate a hill. She swept the gold at the Seefeld World Championships (1985).

In both simultaneous and syncopated pole plants, the two arms do not work equally. There is definitely a strong and a weak side. Try this drill and find out for yourself. V-skate on snow or on roller skis, pushing only onto the left ski from the right. You will see that the left arm gives almost no push, but the right has considerable power. You will discover that even when you pole with both arms onto an angled out ski, the opposite arm works much more than the one on the same side. For this reason, the syncopated skater uses both arms to push onto his or her diagonal ski; but to do so, the pole plants must be syncopated.

The real bonus is that the second poling arm is placed in an even stronger poling position. This stronger poling motion results from increased stomach and lat involvement and a squaring off of the body to the line of travel. In addition, the body is able to add a twisting motion, which adds to the power. One observation is that the body is able to compress more onto the pole.

Thus, the first poling push of the syncopated skate is not nearly as strong as the second, which has been powered by a rotating compressing body aligned mainly for that side. The rotating muscles are now able to add their contribution to give more drive. In addition, this vigorous rotation helps immensely in the weight transfer onto the glide ski. This is especially important on a steeper hill, as it prevents stalling out on the second skating ski.

How close is the timing between the two pole plants? The action can be separated only slightly to be effective. If the two pole plants are not close enough together, a single compression cannot power both arms. The motion then becomes a single pole V-skate, which is a slower style (discussed later). If the *1-2* timing of the pole plants is close enough together, one compression is able to power both pole plants. However, most of the force is directed onto the second pole. The skier will feel more powerful with the second poling arm—almost as if he were a giant swinging a big hammer.

In both uphill V-skates, the arms should maintain a fairly constant angle at the elbow. This forces the tricep to be fairly inactive because the uphill is tough going and the triceps are just too weak. The lats and stomach are much stronger. By maintaining the constant bend at the elbow, the lats are required to work. Bending forward at the waist during the stroke indicates the stomach muscles are working.

Open Field or Mass Start Double V-Skate

In this section the difference in pole plants between the uphill double pole skate and the open field, or mass start double pole skate will be clarified. The open skate is easy to learn and is very instinctive. It is used in faster conditions, so the poles are planted later in the stroke. In this skate, the skier glides on the first skating ski for a short period of time before planting the poles. For example, the skier glides on the right ski and then plants the poles (see Figure 6.19). The skier simultaneously pushes off with the poles and right leg onto the left ski, much like the uphill V-skate. The skier then glides on this ski and pushes off onto the right ski again, using only the left ski (without the use of poles). When you practice this move, remember to have the body facing the direction of the gliding ski and the poles pushing along the temporary direction of

Figure 6.19 Free skating may be practiced on roller skis. Note that the poles are planted after the first ski has glided.

travel. If the conditions are very fast, this angle may not be sizable.

In the uphill skate, the poles must be planted sooner than on the flats in order to prevent stalling. A few top skiers use the open field skate rhythm on the hills, planting their poles after gliding on the first ski. However, observation has shown they are in a definite stop-start pattern. These skiers would be better off by planting their poles earlier before their momentum was lost.

In reality, the only difference in pole plant timing is caused by the speed of the skier. The poles are used when the skier feels he or she would stall. Then they help to slightly increase the glide on the first ski and then help push the skier onto the second skating ski. It just happens later in the faster conditions of the open field V-skate than on the uphills.

Some top competitors feel that the V-skate will replace the marathon skate on the flats just as it has on the hills. Many even feel that poling on each skate, rather than every other one, will eventually become the dominant stroke throughout the entire move. These competitors are presently experimenting with this in mind.

Single Pole V-Skate Up a Hill

The single pole skate uses a poling motion that is similar to the diagonal stride where each pole is used individually. The timing of this poling motion varies between the top skiers, from passgang (same arm and leg working together) to normal diagonal rhythm. However, for the most efficient timing, the poling motion should be initiated just as the opposite glide ski touches the snow (see Figure 6.20). For example, the right pole pushes the skier onto the left glide ski as the right leg pushes off. The right pole is planted just as the glide (left) ski touches the snow. This pole plant is earlier than it is in the regular diagonal stride where it is planted after the weight is on the glide ski.

The complete cycle has a *1-2* motion with the poles and legs pushing off together. It helps immensely to keep the weight on the heels and to have fluid hips which slide from side to side. Using this technique,

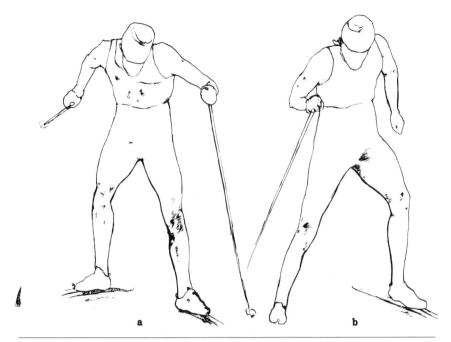

a   b

Figure 6.20(a)-(b) Ove Aunli, of Norway, exhibiting the single stick V-skate in the 15k at Seefeld (1985).

even the steepest hills can be skated if the weight is transferred completely.

Order of Progression of Various Uphill Skates

For most skiers, the double pole V-skate is faster than the single stick V-skate; however, it is more energy consuming on steeper hills. When a hill gets steeper, some top skiers will sometimes change from the double pole V-skate to the single stick V-skate. Others seem to prefer one or the other for the entire hill. I do recommend that each skier tries both styles. To determine which stroke is the best for you, time various sections of a course. Compare both methods to your level of exertion and/or heart rate; then make a decision based on practicality of speed versus energy. And for the tourer—have fun with both.

When and where you skate on a course, or even which skate you will use, will depend on three factors: your strength, the steepness of the hill, and the speed and firmness of the snow. Two good examples come to mind. The 1983 Birkebeiner was skied on very fast and icy tracks. The leaders of this race actually skated most of the course. This caused some of our local skiers to hypothesize that the diagonal was truly dead. Yet a month later, in the last World Cup race in Canada, the winners did not skate at all except for a very few stretches—the reason being slow, soft snow on a hilly course.

It takes strength to skate extensively. Otherwise, the small gain in speed will not be worth the amount of energy expended and the ensuing oxygen debt. This means you must be in shape. Because different muscles are used, skating must be practiced. Fortunately, this can be done in the summer on roller skis. The serious skier will be well advised to get a pair of two-wheelers or the skate boots that have been developed for cross-country skiing. The motion used is very similar to that used on snow.

Therefore, each individual will have to decide when the skate is faster but not too tiring, when to use it to accelerate over a hill, and how to use it around corners (see Figure 6.21). Course management is something all skiers must adapt to their particular strengths and weaknesses. The skate only adds one more variable; however, it is a complicated variable to the beginning skater because it has so much overlap with the double pole, kick double pole, and even the fast diagonal. To some advanced skiers, the skate does the opposite: It removes some of the variables. These skiers may skate the entire course and not have to worry about such mundane things as the kick double pole, the diagonal, and the kick wax of the day.

You can do timed intervals over various terrain and snow conditions to see which strokes are faster and then judge for yourself. Skate the interval once; then ski it again, using the double pole or kick double pole. These intervals will help you get a handle on which stroke is faster for you and which requires the most energy.

The skate opens up a new dimension in getting around the course. It is a challenge. It is also exciting to learn the various new skills that have evolved with the skate, even for the veterans who have been skiing for years. Turns are the most obvious areas that are conducive to the correct use of the skate. Skillful

Figure 6.21 Free skating, without using poles can help keep momentum into a hill.

execution here can gain much time. When rounding corners, use the outside leg to push yourself. That way the force will be directed more in the direction of travel and will be more efficient. This means if you are turning right, the left leg should be used to skate, and the right one should be in the track. Before you turn, you should be in the inside track if possible. Any time you can shorten the course in this manner, do so.

If the snow to the outside of the tracks is not packed very wide, but there are two sets of tracks, you will find yourself in the position of only being able to skate with the ski that is next to the packed area between the two sets of tracks. The soft, outside snow will easily catch the ski tip, and it's the old snow-in-the-face routine again. At this time, you may choose to switch tracks every 8 to 10 strokes or let the rhythm of the curves dictate when to switch lanes. Switching lanes is something at which to become adept, for it is a necessary skill and should become second nature for every skier.

The skate is especially helpful in gaining momentum over the tops of hills. It is important to go over the tops hard. To a racer, the importance is not so much the time gained on the downhills as it is the speed carried onto the flats. The actual time gained on the downhill section will not be very much, but the distance and speed carried out to the flats will be significant. The skier should, therefore, make every effort to push off the top of hills as much as possible and learn to take the downhills in an aerodynamic tuck. I had this lesson drilled into my head the hard way during the Central Division Championships in 1982. As I topped a hill, I took the usual kick double pole. At the same time, a skier who had been next to me for much of the race used several aggressive kick double poles, followed by a strong double pole. As we hit the flat, I started to double pole, and he flew out of sight, still in a tuck. Later in that same race, I gradually overtook another skier and pulled near him at the top of a hill. I used the aggressive tactics I had just witnessed and had 40 yards on this racer before I began double poling. The new breed of racer would have used a skate at the top of those hills to even greater advantage. The additional rest time picked up the bottom of the hills more than makes up for the extra effort at the top, to say nothing of the gain in time. That's what racing is all about.

The skate is very handy to use on the uphills. There are some short uphills that usually have to be run or even herringboned (which can be skated over easily if the skier has enough momentum). These hills alone will allow a skier to pick up quite a bit of time on a course that has many short ups and downs. In addition, these tactics make the course more fun to tour. It's a challenge to see if you can skate up a hill that you once had to herringbone.

Maintaining momentum is the key. The skate or kick double pole will allow the skier to keep his or her speed into the hill. Then, assuming the skier will not skate the entire hill, the diagonal should start with no noticeable slowing down of the body as the incline steepens. As the skier is unable to maintain his or her glide, he or she will break into more of a running technique. Comparisons of world class athletes on the uphills show that their diagonal technique at this time is almost identical to hill striding with poles in the summer.

Sooner or later the hill will become so steep that most skiers are forced to break into a herringbone. But before abandoning oneself to the full herringbone, which is a slow maneuver, one last technique may be used by the skier with kick wax. Jumping out of the track into the softer snow may allow a skier to run rather than herringbone. If the hill is short, the skier may even resort to a bounding motion for a few steps. Any motion up rather than forward is wasted effort, but a semibound, if used only for a couple of steps, may get the skier over a short hill with the fastest time-to-energy ratio. In normal circumstances, however, the skier will finally break into a herringbone.

Why the reluctance to full herringbone? It is tiring and slow. But we haven't succumbed yet. Before full herringbone, the skier can use a partial herringbone. Only one ski is angled out to grip the snow because the wax is not quite working, or both skis may be angled slightly. As the hill gets steeper, the angle between the skis increases until a full herringbone is achieved. An expert doing the herringbone looks quite different than a novice doing the same movement. The expert will stride forward, biting off large parts of the hill with each stride (see Figure 6.22 and 6.23). The arms are used aggressively—for power rather than for balance. The tips of the skis will be only as far apart as needed. The farther apart the skis, the slower the going. The beginner, on the other hand, will waddle up the hills with the legs bowed way out and the arms only supporting in case of a fall or a slip backward.

The angling in of the knees is very important. Because the wax is no longer working, the edge will have a greater grip, and the skier will not have to assume a wide stance. As a result, the skier will be able to attain a much greater speed up the hill.

The beginner's most common mistake in the herringbone is to have the weight too far forward. This usually happens when the skier looks at the ground in front of him or her; then the feet are too far back, and

Figure 6.22   Racing herringbone—front view.

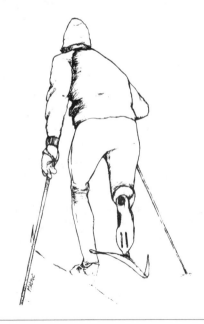

Figure 6.23   Racing herringbone—rear view.

the skier finds himself falling and slipping back. The weight should be back on the heels, and the gaze should be up the hill. Otherwise, it's face first into the snow again. Another caution for the beginner is to avoid catching the tips of the skis in the snow. This is especially dangerous when moving up the hill near the edge of the soft, outside snow. Practice will certainly make perfect and an occasional trip to the local down-hill slopes during the season can alleviate many deficiencies.

In fact, practice on all the techniques of this chap-ter will give you much satisfaction. These techniques offer different alternatives for handling a course and, therefore, expand the horizons for both tourer and racer alike. Their mastery can save you much energy, helping you to ski faster, easier.

Main Concepts

Double Pole

1.   The modern double pole is a fluid whipping mo-tion rather than a rigid one. There is acceleration through the whole stroke.
2.   There is a preload, or slight give, at pole plant that encourages a stretch-and-rebound effect in the muscles, thereby promoting an accelerating motion.
3.   The body moves from vertical to parallel during the stroke. The poles are planted when the body is at 45° to the ground.
4.   The slight collapse of preload and the forward body position of compression allow a longer and more direct push.
5.   The pole should be aligned near the forearm, im-mediately after preload and before the power pull of the lats. The large muscles of the stomach and back initiate the application of power. The smaller and weaker triceps participate later as the elbows reach the legs.
6.   The stroke begins and ends in the upright posi-tion, the duration of which depends on the con-ditions.

The Kick Double Pole

1. The kick double pole is performed in a *1* (open) *2* (close) rhythm.
2. The kick portion starts when the kicking foot is under the chest, not behind the hips.
3. The double pole portion should be very familiar to the skier's normal double pole.

The Marathon Skate

1. The marathon skate with one ski in the track is a fluid motion.
2. The pole plant occurs just before the skating leg pushes out. Nonetheless, the leg push and power move of the double pole portion occur simultaneously.
3. The upper body movement is very similar to the skier's normal double pole, only with less compression.
4. Neither the pushing nor gliding leg is bent very much during the stroke. An excellent visualization is to think of the gliding leg as a post.
5. The push-out of the skating leg is accompanied by a quick and definite weight transfer, out and back. This is identified by a circling of the head that shows both side-to-side movement as well as the up-and-down movement of compression.
6. There is a slight twist of the torso outside and back that helps facilitate the weight transfer and puts the body in a more powerful position.

The Open Field or Mass Start V-Skate

1. The open field V-skate is used in fast conditions with no tracks.
2. The pole plant is timed differently than the marathon skate. The poles are planted later in the cycle after the first skating ski has glided. Its purpose is to enhance the glide in these faster conditions. (In slower conditions, the timing reverts to that of the marathon skate.)
3. There is a slight twist to the torso so that the skier is always facing the gliding ski.

4.   As in all strokes, fluidity is of the utmost importance.
5.   Some racers are now poling on each skating ski, rather than every other one.

Double Pole V-Skate up a Hill

1.   The double pole V-skate up a hill has the basic pole plant timing of the marathon skate. Here, the poles are used earlier in order to prevent stalling (as compared to the V-skate in faster conditions).
2.   The turnover rate is faster and therefore less body compression is used—this again to prevent stalling.
3.   The syncopated *1-2* pole plant is more efficient because it allows the skier to place his or her muscles in a stronger position.

The Single Pole V-Skate up a Hill

1.   This stroke in conjunction with the double pole V-skate has replaced the herringbone at elite levels.
2.   It occurs in a *1-2* rhythm, with pole and opposite ski hitting the ground at approximately the same time.

The Herringbone

1.   This stroke is the uphill mainstay of the tourer. The only more certain way to get up a hill is to sidestep with the skis perpendicular to the line of travel or to remove the skis and walk.
2.   However, the best rule of thumb for fast skiing is: Don't herringbone unless you have to. For racing, it is the slowest way up a hill.
3.   The narrower herringbone with big strides is faster than the one with a wide separation of ski tips.
4.   The arms are a source of power in the racing herringbone.
5.   The head must be up and the weight back in a balanced position to avoid falling forward into the snow.

Handling the Downhills

7

or "Quick, Move the Trees"

Handling the downhills means something completely different for the expert than for the novice. The expert is usually looking for ways to increase and maintain speed, whereas the beginner is looking for ways to slow down. But in each case, the fundamentals remain the same: a balanced position that will allow reaction without falling. The expert will use this balance to enhance momentum, the novice to check it. In both cases, a positive mental attitude is of the utmost importance. "Sure," I can hear you say. "You need confidence to handle the downhills, but you only get confidence from conquering the downhills—the old Catch-22." Developing an aggressive attitude requires some time, but it will come.

Downhill Posture— A Balanced Position

One of the first keys is to fool your mind by taking the proper stance, which has a certain aggressiveness about it. At first, bend slightly at the waist and knees with the hands to the front. *Feel aggressive.* The legs must feel light and lively with the weight centered above the feet. The skis should not feel like they are glued to the ground (see Figures 7.1 and 7.2).

The biggest mistake a beginner makes (usually out of fear) on the downhills is leaning back. An aggressive posture can cure this by placing the body forward and fooling your mind. Before you know it, you will actu-

Figure 7.1 Aggressive stance, hands forward and lively legs as demonstrated on a very fast and bumpy downhill.

Figure 7.2 The correct downhill stance may be practiced and is important while roller skiing.

ally have the confidence to handle the tougher hills.
When encountering a hill, get into your aggressive
flex, keep your hands forward, your legs light, and go
for it. The tracks will keep you heading in the right
direction. If you do not panic and stand up or lean
back, you should make it to the bottom of the hill. If
there are any bumps along the way, the light and
lively legs will absorb the shock. The same rules apply
for the expert, except that you will probably be in a
tuck with your legs lively and hands forward.

Sooner or later the hill will get too steep, or there
will be a turn that is too treacherous. Sitting back is
the easiest way to bail out. It's much softer landing on
your fanny than running into a huge, unyielding oak.
Serious damage can result from high speed collisions
with trees and rocks. I vividly remember witnessing a
skier's back breaking from a collision with a rock. It
sounded as if someone hit a tree with a baseball bat.
About a year ago, one of my former chemistry students died after colliding into a tree while Alpine skiing. So believe me, it's no sin to sit down when the
speed gets too great for you to handle. As you get better, the number of sitzmarks you make will gradually
decrease, especially with a little mental and physical
practice.

Several years ago I was teaching a group of three
young girls who could not make it down any of the
faster hills. We stopped for a little pep talk. All I said
was for them to flex their legs slightly, keeping their
hands in front of them, under no circumstance standing up or letting their weight shift back (see Figure
7.3). After a few runs they were brimming with confidence, no longer having any trouble with any of the
hills. The next week they were joined by a young boy
who, although a novice skier, was a very good all-
around athlete. They informed me that this young
man was having trouble with the hills and they
couldn't understand why. Ah, the short memories of
youth. Just a week ago they themselves were poised
like frightened birds at the top of each hill, but now
they were seasoned veterans.

Once you are able to go down a fairly steep hill in
the tracks, it is time to learn how to control your speed
and to increase your ability to turn when there are no

Figure 7.3 Leaning back and allowing the hands to drift backwards is dangerous on both snow and roller skis.

tracks. According to Dr. Jim Stray-Gunderson, a friend of ours, the Norwegian ski trails have tracks that are wider on the downhills. Many fast and challenging turns that would normally be left untracked are very safe and exciting when groomed with the variable width track setter. But currently in America, the tougher downhills usually do not have tracks. They have either been wiped out by skiers edging through the turns, or they deliberately have been left smooth. This allows the skier to choose his or her own path. In fact, trying to hold the track around turns at excessive speeds will only result in being thrown out of the tracks by the buildup of centrifugal force.

The key to handling untracked downhills is again in the total posture, emphasizing a lively lower body. The skier must be bent at the waist and knees and should have a feeling of lightness below the waist. The skier must always keep his or her hands forward and display an aggressive attitude.

The lively legs are very important for several reasons. One of the most terrifying things for a beginner to encounter is a downhill that has been rutted out. Frozen or rigid legs will cause the skis to get stuck in any rut along the way. Lively legs allow the skier to transfer his or her weight quickly off the ski that is in the rut, lift it out, and continue on a straight path.

Lively legs are also the key to the basic concept of most turns and methods of checking speed. The cross-country skier does not have a rigid boot and binding system to control his or her skis. As a result, finesse and touch must replace brute force. The better Alpine skiers have this finesse, but the average recreational Alpiner does not because he or she has been relying too heavily on groomed slopes and a rigid boot and binding system. As a result, some of the cross-country skiers who have had the most difficulty on the downhills are newly converted Alpine skiers. Once accustomed to the difference, they become very good. But until then . . . look out! Some of the most difficult experiences I've had in the last several years of instructing have been with Alpine racers who can't adjust to the helplessness they feel on those skinny skis with the flabby bindings. Those who have survived a whole season have done very well, however.

The Snowplow

The use of the ankle and knee to control the amount of edging is the key to mastery of cross-country equipment. In order to turn or slow down, one or both skis must be set on edge. Rolling the ankle to the inside and moving the knee to the knock-kneed position will edge the ski. If both skis are edged and the heels pushed out, a basic snowplow results. To slow down to a stop, the skis are edged radically and the heels pushed out drastically. The more you want to slow down, the farther apart the heels should be. To stop, the ski edges are really dug into the snow. Don't expect miracles however; some hills are just too fast for quick stops with a snowplow.

Practicing the snowplow is an excellent place to start learning how to control speed. The skier can then progress to the elementary turns. Pick out a gradual slope for practice. Snowplow down the hill, trying to slow down, and speed up by varying the amount of edging pressure on the skis. Change both ankle-knee pressure and heel spread. One of the first things a beginning skier will notice is that a snowplow will not bring you to a very quick stop. So for now, sitting down is still the quickest and safest method, especially if you're out of control.

The Snowplow Turn

After you are able to control your speed, then learn the snowplow turn. Start with the snowplow. If you wish to turn left, the ski pointed in that direction must be weighted, that is, the right ski. To do so the upper body must be shifted in that direction. This is the basic premise of all turns. The ski that is heading in the intended direction must be weighted and edged. As you weight and edge the right ski, you will turn left (see Figure 7.4). Then weight and edge the left ski to

Figure 7.4 Snowplow turn to the left. The right ski is edged and weighted.

turn right. Intersperse this with some slowing and speeding up and you have the tools to navigate a trail safely (if you remember to sit down when it gets too rough). So practice playing around with the snowplow turn, as it is the basic ingredient for downhill ability on cross-country skis (see Figure 7.5). Once mastered, you can graduate to more advanced turns.

Figure 7.5 Sequence of snowplow turn to the right. This turn was initiated by a normal snowplow to slow down, and then weight was transferred to the turning (outside) ski as it was edged.

The Stem Turn

The most widely used cross-country turn for the average skier is the stem turn. If you wish to turn left, the tail of the right ski is pushed out and edged by the use of the ankle and knee. If the legs are leaden instead of lively, this move is not possible. It helps to transfer the weight momentarily to the inside ski, in this case the left, to allow the skier to easily move the right ski to the stemmed position. The weight is then shifted to the outside ski, in this case the right. Because this ski is already pointed in the proper direction, the skier will then turn left. Increased stemming and edging will result in a more drastic turn, but will also slow the skier down proportionately. If the skier keeps the stem throughout the turn, it is the snowplow turn, in this case, the half-plow, actually. But if the inside foot is allowed to slide over until it is next to the outside foot, a stem turn results.

Because cross-country skis have little or no side-cut—a curve in the base of the ski that promotes turning when edged—some skidding will be part of most turns. That is, the edge of the ski will not carve a line in the snow but rather slide sideways a little. The better skiers will skid appreciably less. Any skidding tends to slow you down because some of your energy of travel is lost in a direction that is not along the intended path.

Choosing the Turn to Use

In summary, the basic turn for the average cross-country skier in fast conditions is the half-plow or the stem turn. The skier will generally stick to the tracks whenever possible, but when he or she feels he or she will be thrown from the tracks, the outside ski will be stemmed, edged, and weighted. If a slowing down is required, this stemming motion becomes the half snowplow. This is achieved by really edging and weighting the outside ski. Better skiers can check their speed very quickly in this manner. But then better skiers are not usually looking for ways to check their speed; normally they're trying to increase it.

The average skier is usually the one looking for ways to slow down in these situations. Then the half-plow becomes the full-plow. In these situations there will probably be no tracks with which to contend because they will have long been wiped out by other skiers or not set at all. The amount of edging, stemming, and torquing required for these sections will determine how much of a slowing action will be achieved. These moves should be practiced on a slight downhill until the skier feels confident about controlling his or her speed. Until that happens, stay off the expert trails. Not only are you endangering yourself, but you could ruin the skiing for others.

Body Posture During a Turn

When practicing turning on a downhill, it is important to keep the hands low and to the front, almost as if you are reaching forward. This forward reach will keep you aggressive and will help you avoid the most common error of beginners, that of sitting back and standing up. It also helps to think of the knees pressing forward in an aggressive flex through a turn. Together the aggressive use of the hands and knees eliminate the common flaw of sitting back.

Another common error of many skiers is to stiffen the entire body. When this happens, the entire side more or less forms a straight line. If a skier does this, the amount of edging and weighting is limited. If he or she edges, using whole body lean, not much weight can be transferred to the outside ski, or he or she will tip over. If a lot of weight is on the outside ski, it cannot be edged very much. The solution to this dilemma? Hinge sideways at the waist. The whole lower body will set the ski on edge, while the upper body leans out slightly over the outside ski, thus weighting it. In other words, both halves of the body react independently as two separate segments. Independent use of the upper and lower body gives the skier more control and places parallel skiing within reach.

Maintaining and Increasing Speed on the Downhills

There are some other ways to handle a downhill in which increased speed is the goal. Most racing turns occur while in a tucked (crouched) position (see Figure 7.6). A tuck is easy to master and can be very restful.

Figure 7.6(a) Upright or resting tuck. May be used when tired or in fast conditions.

Figure 7.6(b) Resting tuck.

Figure 7.6(c)   Normal racing tuck.

Figure 7.6(d)   Deep tuck. Only practical for very fast conditions or into a strong head wind.

Figure 7.6   Several types of tucks.

The idea behind tucking is to decrease the wind resistance on the downhill sections of the course, allowing greater speed. Several years ago, the "in thing" about tucks was that they had to be aerodynamic. The super egg tuck was it. However, although the tight egg may be a little faster, it is sure a lot more tiring. Most citizen racers never really used the tight egg, and, for once, the international racing community seems to be moving toward the citizen racer rather than the opposite.

When Steve Gaskill spoke at a Level 1 clinic, I was pleased to hear him say that the crucial thing was to have the back parallel to the ground and that at the slower speeds of cross-country skiing, there was almost no measurable difference between the variable tucks. So the tuck with the elbows resting on the knees or thighs is adequate (see Figure 7.7). There is no real

Figure 7.7　Normal racing tuck.

need to get so low that there is a strain on the legs and back. One note, however: If a downhill is very fast and/or into a fair-sized wind, the alert racer would use a tighter tuck because of its greater reward in those conditions.

When the course starts to curve or has bumps, the skier wants to be able to stay loose and be ready for anything. Again, the two fundamentals for beginners also apply here. When bumps occur, the skier should simply absorb them with a light flexing of the legs. The purpose is to keep the body moving in a straight line down the hill. Any bouncing up and down of the entire body, while it may be exciting to do, does nothing but slow down the racer. The shortest distance between two points is a straight line. In addition, any air caught in the chest and the impact of wax on the snow will both have slowing effects.

The Skate Turn

The fastest turn for the racer is the skate or step turn. Rather than slow you down, this turn actually increases your speed. So to the racer it is the best way to negotiate a corner. There are actually two versions of this turn. The first is for slower conditions. Here the skate is similar to the marathon skate as described earlier. That is, the poles are used to push off simultaneous to or just before the skating motion. Acceleration is important, and getting the weight on the gliding leg as the skate is started is the key. Otherwise, the skier can find him- or herself straddling the track, caught in no man's land. It helps immensely to try to lead the skate with the inside knee, flexing forward at the ankle. Correct skating allows the expert skier to pick up considerable speed as he or she drives around the turn.

The second skate is for the faster conditions (see Figure 7.8). Here the skier keeps his or her hands well

Figure 7.8 Skate turn in fast conditions. Some elite racers would be skating from a deep tuck on this turn with hands further forward.

forward and in the direction of the turn. There is no poling motion, for the hands are used for balance. Sometimes several skates are needed to negotiate a difficult turn. Again, the key is to transfer the weight completely to the inside (glide) ski by leading with the inside knee, emphasizing a forward ankle flex. This turn is not as easy as it may appear, so some practice is needed. Some of the most beautiful and exciting footage of cross-country skiing is of Bill Koch skating around corners in the Rossignol film, *Cross-Country Experience.*

Cross-country skiing, however, is not as easy as Bill makes it appear. In a race in Minocqua several years ago, I attempted my imitation of Bill skating a corner. The result would have been humorous had it not been so close to disaster. My ski tip caught in the snow as I attempted to execute from the bowlegged, semisquat position. I missed losing an eye by about a quarter of an inch, falling onto the only short stub of a sawed-off sapling on the entire trail. Bleeding profusely, my first thought was that I may have gouged out my eye. But once ascertaining that it was only a gash above the eye itself, I finished the race. The eye did get me much attention, but it was the kind I really didn't want.

This experience taught me several things, however: First, it is harder to skate turn when tired than when fresh; second, watch those ski tips in the soft snow; and finally, the bowlegged method with very little weight transfer is not effective or reliable. On this skate turn, the fundamental of lively legs with the knee and ankle angling the ski against the snow is important. Then a complete weight transfer to the inside ski with the hands in front is a must. I consider myself lucky to have learned that lesson so cheaply, especially when the price was almost an eye.

Sometimes just riding a turn out in the tracks can be difficult. This is especially true if you are tall or have wide hips. (The small skier has a distinct advantage in this respect.) Because the tracks are a constant width, they are relatively farther apart for the smaller skier. As a result, the base as defined by the feet is proportionately wider and gives the smaller skier more lateral stability. Add to this wide hips, and it is difficult to keep the mass of the body within the out-side ski. Again, the variable width track setter would remove this problem by setting wider tracks on the downhills.

However, given the narrow tracks, there are two styles of executing an in-track turn. The first entails keeping the hands to the inside, leaning in that direc-tion while keeping pressure on the outside ski. The knees should be angulated in, the skis riding on the walls of the tracks if necessary. If things are getting out of control, the skier can lift the outside ski from the track, stemming the ski to regain control. This is a last-ditch effort, used after control is slipping away, but is preferable to picking oneself out of the bushes.

I must admit that the above method has not al-ways worked for me although some racers swear by it. The old Marty Hall "reverse shoulder" seems to be the best for riding out a fast turn in the tracks. To do this, keep the hands over the outside ski with the effect of moving the outside shoulder back. This keeps a lot of weight on the outside ski. In addition, angle the legs to the inside of the curve, again hinging at the waist. This allows you to ride the sidewalls of the track. If you start to fly out of the track, because of the cen-trifugal force, a small skating motion can bring you back; or you could resort to the slower but maybe safer method of stemming the outside ski.

Turns in Untracked Areas

Negotiating the fast turns in untracked sections of downhills gives a skier much leeway, not only in the type of turn to use but also in its path. Many times on a tough corner, the best route is to the inside. The rest of the turn may be rutted and icy. Then any effort at control falls short and the skier will slide where all others have gone, sweeping too wide and losing much time. Getting to the outside before the turn, skating to the inside, and using the existing powder may be the fastest and easiest path.

If the conditions are too fast for a skate, the skier can resort to a snowplow, stem, or parallel turn (see Figure 7.9). The difference between the smooth curve

Figure 7.9 Parallel turns with racing equipment. This skier flexes in anticipation of up unweighting, then edges and weights the outside ski in the middle of the picture. The actual unweighting occurred between the top and middle picture.

of the expert's parallel turn and the crude pushing stem of the beginner is often a matter of proper unweighting. The expert subtly unweights his or her ski and moves the outside ski with little or no weight on it to the proper line. This happens very fast and will be a parallel turn if both feet move together during the unweighting. The key, again, is lively legs and aggressive action. Some of our kids who were once Alpine racers can come down a slope parallel turning, actually wedeling, like a downhiller. You would have to see their boots and skis to know they were not on Alpine skis.

The unweighting can be the result of either up or down motion. At high speeds in a tuck, down unweighting usually prevails. The skier generally lets his or her body drop slightly, by bending the knees, which causes the opposite reaction and lifts weight off the skis momentarily. Simultaneously, he or she slightly raises his or her lively knees to release the skis and move them in the direction desired. As the weight is applied again, the skier uses the ankles and knees to make the edges bite just the right amount. The goal is to maintain speed by not going into a wild skid or edging too much and slowing down.

At the slower speeds and especially the tighter turns, up unweighting may be used. The preference is the skier's own and will become instinctive as he or she begins to turn subconsciously. In this case, the skier does a down, up, down motion, changing edges and angles after the up motion. The up could very well become a jump in extreme cases.

But in both turns, down or up unweighting, the lower body must be light and lively and be independent of the upper body. The key is to set the edges with the ankles and knees angled in. The entire leg should be angled in when doing this with the upper body bent at the waist, tilted slightly over the outside ski. Beware of stiffening up the hips, which usually locks the skier in a rigid position, causing the predominant factor to be a skid rather than a carve. If the legs are kept lively and independent, they may make the adjustments needed on the turn. In addition, the knees must be kept forward, flexing the ankles in an aggressive position with the hands forward and low.

Practicing the hockey stop is a good way to learn to unweight the skis and release the edges as required in the parallel turn. The skier comes to a stop very similar to an ice skater by skidding and edging with both skis, ending parallel to the path of motion. Both down and up unweighting may be used. In fact, this is the best way for the better skier to stop and is certainly more dignified than the sitzmark.

Telemark Turns

Cross-country race courses do not generally demand the turning skill of slalom gates, but there are some exceptions. Several winters ago I met a Canadian skier who was citizen racing in our state. He was a former Alpine racer who had also raced telemark style. Fooling around on the downhill practice area at Winter Park in Minoqua turned out to be very enlightening. I had never seen a skier able to control himself as well as this young telemarking Canadian did on his light racing skis and bindings. His up unweighting was as drastic as the top slalom racers in the world. His turns were carved and his speed was extraordinary. His diagonal style was fair and needed refinement, but his downhill technique was something else. He did something that I had never seen on a ski trail: He telemarked his way through the toughest and steepest snake turn on the trail with ease, never diminishing his speed at any time, on a hard and skidded out surface. I have skied with many good skiers but have never seen anything close to the way he took that turn.

It got me thinking. Why not telemark on a racing course? I realize that most courses do not have the proper situations, but for fast hairpin curves, it is just better than any other turn. Because cross-country skis do not have sidecut, any drastic turning must involve an amount of skidding and therefore loss of time. (See Figure 7.10). The action of the skis in the telemark, however, form sidecut by liking the two skis as one. The beauty of it is that the skier can dial his or her own sidecut, simply changing the angle of the skis.

Because of the rarity of its use, I would not recommend it as a major item of work, but the telemark does have its place on some ski trails. Here are some random thoughts on the matter: The trail must not be tracked through the turns, and don't telemark if you can skate—in other words, the turn must be sharp. Some of the more primitive courses, usually converted hiking trails, have ideal terrain for telemarking. It is fun to use the telemark, and it can be a welcome respite from normal skiing.

Figure 7.10 Telemark sequence. The skis angled against each other supply the turning power.

The racing telemark is not quite the same as I have seen written up in the various how-to manuals. In the first place, the unweighting is very drastic. It looks a lot like Phil or Steve Mahre during a slalom run. There is a huge upward motion during which the skier changes the angles of the skis and switches his or her forward foot. Second, the feet are much closer together than generally pictured, the boots being only 12 to 20 inches apart. Finally, the hands are not held in a very high position. They are in the forward balanced position as in other normal skiing turns, but a little more to the sides for lateral stability. I will not go into further detail here on the telemark except to say that lively legs are again the key. Weight must be transferred to the front ski—something most beginners are unable to do. Both legs are bent and the rear knee is not dropped to the ground as in the traditional telemark. Varying snow conditions require a lesser or greater amount of weight on the rear leg. The tougher the conditions (where the skis can't skid much), the more weight on the rear ski. Only by practice will the skier get the balance needed to perform this move efficiently.

For the trail skier the telemark is only a specialty turn, the main brunt of the situations requiring snow plow, stem, parallel, or skate. Again, nothing can replace practice because no one is really going to move the trees, and skillful downhill technique is one of the sure ways to go faster, easier.

Main Concepts

Given a good boot and binding system, there is nothing mystical about controlling speed and direction on cross-country skis.

1. A balanced stance with light and lively legs is important.
2. The posture should be aggressive both physically and mentally. Never sit back unless you want to go down. Keep the hands forward at all times.
3. The easiest way for a beginner to control speed on a steep downhill is to sit down.
4. Other methods of turning and slowing down depend on three things: (a) edging, (b) stemming, and (c) weighting.

   The more you edge, stem, and weight the more you will turn. Weighting the ski, facing in the correct direction, will turn you in that direction. This is true for the snowplow, stem, and parallel turns, and as the skier progresses one method naturally leads into the other.
5. In order to turn easily, light and lively legs combined with aggressive unweighting are mandatory. This is to free and set the angle of the outside ski and its edge.
6. Stiffening up and leaning back are the two most common errors of skiers who have trouble negotiating turns and downhills.
7. The skate or step turn is the fastest way to negotiate a corner and is therefore the racer's turn, especially when done from a tuck.
8. The telemark is a fun way to turn and can be used on extremely tight turns in softer snow. I would suggest a book that specializes in cross-country downhill for a more thorough presentation.

Roller Skiing   *8*

The Summer Alternative for Those Who Love to Ski

In our area some winters have a limited amount of skiable days in a season. If a skier wishes to excel or just loves the kick and glide of the sport, the only solution is roller skiing. The winter of 1982-83 had only 7 to 9 skiable days, plus a few in March when the season was already over. Yet it was also the most successful year for ski racers from the Milwaukee-Chicago area. The reason—roller skiing combined with weekend trips to the snow.

These skiers honed their techniques on roller skis and applied them to snow. Much of this development came from local clinics using videotape and from the group workouts that were carried out during the off-season. It really was a good season, not only from the race results, but also for studying roller skiing. Being on snow, back to the pavement skis, then back to the snow again on a weekly basis allowed an excellent study of the differences and similarities between snow and roller skiing and this was during the heyday of the diagonal. Skating is even more specific on roller skis.

The fundamentals of roller skiing are basically the same as those for snow. If a person only wanted to be a roller ski racer, the technique would be different. However, I see roller skiing as an adjunct to skiing with the techniques mimicking snow as closely as possible. Our skiers make the transition to snow immediately, and luckily so, because some of the most important races for Central Division Junior Olympic selection are in the first 2 weeks of December. Because the technique is the same, the material from the earlier chapters may be directly applied to the roads as well as to snow.

Diagonaling on Roller Skis

Everyone feels strange when he or she first starts roller skiing. Even to the accomplished skier, the initial insecurity on roller skis can do strange things. However, after a short adjustment period, almost every roller skier I have seen uses a technique similar to his or her form on snow. Arms, legs, poling motions, and weight shifts are all the same. But a skier must first get to the point where he or she is at home on roller skis. Most younger skiers make that adaptation in a few weeks, while older skiers usually take longer, although some make the transition amazingly fast. Unfortunately, some accomplished skiers give up before the adjustment is made (see Figure 8.1).

Figure 8.1 Dynamic roller skiing.

During the summer of 1982, Sepp Sports of Madison sponsored a "Ski With The Best" roller ski series in which some top European skiers participated. Most of them were still not as comfortable on roller skis as they were on regular skis. Their movements were stilted and rather stiff looking. These talented

Europeans never really made a good adaptation to roller skis. Many Europeans claim that roller skiing is dangerous to their skills. Therefore, they never really try to master the diagonal, so they never will be good at it, and what little they do becomes dangerous to their snow skiing.

All it takes is a little patience and a knowledge of what you are trying to do. Many of the top skiers in the world are afraid of diagonaling on roller skis because of the fear of developing a late kick. With this negative attitude, it's no wonder that they never develop into competent roller skiers. Roller skiing is not that difficult, once you have desire. This is demonstrated by the number of skiers of all ages from the Milwaukee-Chicago area who are as comfortable on wheels as they are on snow. The difference between them and some of the top skiers in the world is that they have to roller ski if they want to be proficient on snow. The short season forces them to develop their technique on the roads. With basic technique problems taken care of in the summer and fall, they can then concentrate on going fast on the snow. There are other ways to train, but they are not as specific and, therefore, not as effective.

Many of the Europeans have been skiing since childhood and they feel they need no summer work on technique—hence, the poor roller skiing technique. However, no other exercise is as specific as roller skiing, and even the best in the world are not immune to the benefits of good training.

The chapter on equipment covers how to pick roller skis, poles, and clothing. Just one word of caution: Wear pads when you start skiing on the pavement. Kneepads, elbowpads, and even a helmet are a good idea. The best terrain on which to train is hilly and is most conducive to a spill. Also, avoid traffic and know your local ordinances. Most coaches suggest skiing on the right side of the road. This gives traffic more time to react to you, similar to riding on a bicycle.

I will now review the stages a skier goes through in the learning process as presented in the earlier chapters. But this time the specific problems encountered in roller skiing using the diagonal will be emphasized.

Stage 1: Rhythm

At this time, the most important concept is to get the arms and legs working in the proper coordination of the diagonal. As mentioned many times before, when the left hand arrives forward, so should the right knee (foot) and vice versa. Again, this happens in front of the skier so it may easily be seen by just looking down.

Many beginning skiers will passgang or semipassgang. These skiers bring the pole forward way too early, some actually in sequence with the wrong knee. This is the passgang. In the semipassgang, the hand arrives forward before the opposite knee, yet not in sequence with the knee on the same side. Most tourers in America ski in this fashion, using the poles mainly for balance. So be sure that your hand and opposite knee arrive forward at the same time. If you are confused, have a friend watch you. Just run or walk naturally to show your friend how the proper leg-arm action looks. The basic rhythm should be the same.

At this time, do only short strides with no attempt at glide (see Figure 8.2). Believe it or not, this is best accomplished on steeper hills. Ski up and then walk down. Because of the steepness of the hill, the glide will not be long, and the beginner will have better confidence and learn the proper rhythm much quicker. Any attempt to glide by the beginning roller skier usually results in mistiming the diagonal, disastrously. Roller skiing is many times more difficult than actual skiing and can cause much insecurity. If the skier tries to go too fast, too soon, he or she often loses the basic motion. This is because he or she starts using the poles for balance, much like a cane. The poles are mainly for propulsion, only slightly for balance.

In the beginning it is very important for the roller skier to plant his or her poles behind the boot. Many beginners will try to use the poles for balance by placing them way to the front of the toe. Planting them behind the foot makes the poles less available for balance.

If the short-step diagonal is difficult to master, the skier can practice skiing without poles, which encourages the proper coordination of the diagonal. Because

Figure 8.2 Short step skiing. Effective way to learn on roller skis as well as snow.

it is the same movement as walking, the skier can start to walk on the skis, gradually moving to short-step skiing without poles. Again, the checkpoint is that the opposite hand and knee arrive together at the front end of the diagonal. When the skier can get the proper coordination without poles, he or she should again try the short-step diagonal. Alternating 100 yards without the poles and 100 yards of the short-step diagonal with the poles is a drill that many successful beginning roller skiers have found to be the key to attaining proper coordination. But please, don't try gliding as of yet. There will be plenty of time for that later.

Stage 2: Throwing the Entire Body Forward

If the skier has done a good job on Stage 1, Stage 2 is already accomplished. This is where the skier, while diagonaling, starts learning to ride the glide ski as he or she tosses his or her body forward with complete abandon. Most beginners push their foot forward but leave their bodies behind, much like placing their feet in cold water. If the beginner sticks to the short-stride diagonal with the poles being planted behind the boot, the *foot-in-cold-water* flaw can be avoided. With short strides the weight is easily kept on top rather than behind the glide ski. It is the beginning roller skier trying to go too fast, too soon, who usually starts reaching with the foot and leaving the body behind. However, once you learn the natural rhythm of the stride, you can start to stride out and learn to glide properly.

You should start slowly and try to throw the body forward onto the glide ski. Have a friend watch and see if you are just pushing the foot forward, rather than having the whole body mass move onto the ski. The idea of hop and glide may not be a bad one at this time. But, be sure it is only temporary. Intersperse hopping from one ski to the other with a little glide in-between and normal short-step skiing until you get the idea. If you have trouble making the adaptation, you may want to go to hop and glide skiing alone for a short period of time (1 to 4 weeks).

One of our local skiers had a very late kick on snow. Her technique was the classic *foot-in-cold-water*. Try as she would, she could not get herself to move her whole body forward and would always resort to tentatively pushing only her foot forward, her body lagging behind. In addition, her arms were slightly out of rhythm. As a last resort I asked her to hop and glide. Her last month on roller skis was spent this way. She looked funny doing it but when snow arrived, presto! She was skiing beautifully—strong, with a well-timed kick and perfect arm coordination. Her first race was an outstanding success. She won her age group, was much improved over the last year, and beat some very good skiers in the process.

It is a terrifying experience for some people to commit totally to the glide ski, especially on their first roller skiing attempt. It does take time, but the period is greatly shortened when they realize what they are trying to do and when they get some occasional feedback from a coach, observer, or videotape.

At this time, posture should again be emphasized. Many skiers suffer from lower back pain when roller skiing, whereas they do not on snow. Two factors account for this. First, these skiers tighten up on the pavement skis, but if that is the only problem, it will go away as relaxation is learned. The second factor crops up when the skier tries to commit his or her weight to the glide ski. He or she only leans over the ski with an arched back, the glide foot under the hips rather than the chest. This position of lordosis is a great strain to the lower back.

These problems can be cured by changing the stance. The two key checkpoints are the curvature of the back and the relationship of the glide leg to the upper body. The back should not be arched but should be straight or slightly rounded. The arched position is the source of many back injuries. Correcting this will remove the strain from the lower back. Roller skiing as such is not the culprit in lower back pain. It is the poor position that some roller skiers get themselves into that causes the damage. In the days when I had back problems, both snow and road skiing helped immensely to loosen my back. The natural stretching and relaxing motion of the legs and arms is actually quite therapeutic for the lower back when done correctly.

Common Diagonal Problems

Once you have mastered the short-step diagonal, there are several things that should be noted. The following problems are flaws that are especially seen in roller skiing. First, check to see if the arms move freely past the hips. Many beginning roller skiers, because of insecurity, stop their hands at the hips. When the arm reaches the end of the poling motion, the pole should be released and not regripped until it is again planted. Then, as on snow, the pressure is applied mainly to the straps. The path of the poles is controlled by pressure between the thumb and forefinger, the hand only lightly gripping the pole during the power phase.

Lifting and walking with the skis is another common roller ski error. In the natural ski motion, the legs swing forward in a relaxed and leisurely manner. However, because of the insecurity of roller skiing where there are no tracks to keep the skis straight, some skiers lift and plant their feet, rather than allow the feet to swing slowly forward.

This lifting of the foot and clumping it down is called bicycling because the skier's leg action resembles the circular motion of the bicyclist rather than the low-swinging motion of the skier (see Figure 8.3—for this and other common errors). Many skiers who bicycle their legs also lift the ski and actually place it in front of the kicking foot, rather than swinging it in next to the foot on the ground. To correct this flaw, the skier must learn to relax. Sometimes it just takes time for the skier to develop the confidence to allow the leg to come forward in a relaxed manner. Being aware of the problem and keeping it in the back of the mind will usually be all that is necessary. (*Note:* A slight bicycle motion is not something to excessively

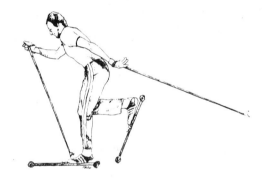

Figure 8.3(a) Extreme bicycling. To control this flaw, allow return leg to relax and swing forward naturally.

Figure 8.3(b) "Foot in cold water." Correct this by short step skiing, keeping the weight over the ski.

Figure 8.3(c) No compression on double pole.

Figure 8.3(d) Extreme collapse on double pole.

Figure 8.3(e) Jumping onto toes, a waste of energy.

Figure 8.3 Common roller ski errors.

worry about. The important thing is that the ski makes contact with the ground when the two feet are next to each other and that the motion is natural and relaxed.)

The other end of the spectrum is not lifting the ski but rather the *foot-glued-to-the-track* syndrome. The cure for this is twofold. First, the skier must learn to relax the trailing leg and allow the natural momentum of the kick to carry the roller ski off the ground. The skier should make no effort to actually lift the ski by muscular action, but rather should allow the natural reaction to the kick to carry the ski off the ground. At the same time, the skier should make an attempt to balance on the glide ski longer, allowing the trail foot to lift free off the ground. Also, he or she should stay completely on the gliding foot until the kick.

After the beginning roller skier finally allows the trail foot to follow through naturally, he or she will usually lose confidence and drop it right back into the ground. The trail ski should not completely reach the ground until the skier is in the feet-together position. If the foot hits behind the glide ski, the skier has dropped his or her ski early, and usually falls off the glide ski. This is very closely related to the foot-glued-to-the-track syndrome; learning to balance on the glide ski is the answer. Be careful not to overcompensate, however, and start to bicycle instead.

Some roller skiers try to drive the leg (knee) forward when they try to correct this flaw. The leg swing should be steady as any acceleration forward will create a force backward. Some skiers fall into this habit by trying to get knee drive and overdo it. Remember, knee drive and hand drive are all right if they are accompanied by enough body drive. No part should lag.

The Late Kick

The late kick is the infamous and feared villain of roller skiing. Actually, this reputation is undeserved. Few skiers have developed a late kick on roller skis. The many roller skiers who kick late, also did so on snow before ever roller skiing. Unfortunately, most people are unable to recognize a late kick.

What exactly is a late kick? First of all, the kicking leg is the one that the skier uses to push him- or herself forward. In a late kick the skier simply kicks too late in the stride. Simple enough. The kick should occur when the feet are together and even before in many instances, such as on steep hills.

How do you recognize this action? There are several indicators that may be used. The best is most easily seen in slow motion on polarvision or videotape. The key is to note where the leg flexes as it prepares to kick. The flexing should occur when the feet are together, or if the poling power is poor, a little before. Then much of the force of the kick will be directed downward and the skier will have little trouble setting the wax when the snow arrives. However, if the kick is late, the knee will flex after the kicking foot is behind the other one. In a few extreme cases the flex occurs when the legs are very far apart. This late flex is actually very efficient on roller skis but doesn't work on snow because roller skis need no downward force to. set the wax. All pressure may be exerted in a backward direction. When this is tried on snow, the result is slipping. If someone were just interested in roller ski races, this technique might deserve a try, but I doubt that many skiers would be willing to ruin their skiing for a few seconds of improvement in a roller ski race.

This late knee flex can actually be observed at regular skiing speed if the observer knows exactly what he or she is looking for. The observer should stand off to the side to get the best angle. Look only at the lower half of the skier and concentrate on the kicking leg. Note where it flexes. If the flex occurs after the feet are together, you have located the enemy—the infamous late kick. But an easier way to see it in everyday normal speed is to watch the follow-through of the foot to the rear. The late kicker usually has a very low foot carry to the rear, as most of his or her energy is directed backward. Even if the skier has a normally low foot carry, there should be a little natural rise at the end of the stroke. Those who late kick do not have this rise, and it looks as if their foot goes straight back.

Some late kickers appear to be running on their skis, usually hopping toward the sky. This is usually accompanied by a clumping of the ski in front of the kicking foot. The trailing foot is actually lifted and planted in front of the kicking foot rather than sliding in next to it (as described earlier in the chapter). Once the late kick is detected, what can be done to correct it?

For the beginning skier it can mean only a return to short-step skiing. Beginners have to get on top of the glide ski. Do not underestimate the power of this drill: Interspersed with some hop and glide work, it can do wonders for all kinds of errors.

For the more advanced skier, this problem can be resolved in two ways. First, the skier can make an effort to kick earlier when the feet are together or even before. The skier should do this when there is an observer present to achieve correct timing. The observer can tell the skier when the kick is timed properly. The skier can also use his or her own personal videotape, the shadow, to see if the knee is flexing at the right time; or he or she can make the effort to kick earlier and glance down once in a while to see just when the kick is being executed. This is a little less effective than an actual videotape or an informed observer, but it can produce results.

The best way to prevent the late kick is to concentrate on the glide ski. This ski should be kept in front of the hips during the glide and remain there until the kick is initiated. This is easily accomplished if the skier keeps his or her weight on the heel until the next kick. In fact, the skier should feel that he or she *is initiating his or her kick with the heel.* As previously stated, the advanced skier holds the glide longer, keeping his or her weight on the heel, and actually has a doubly effective kick using the heel as well as the toe.

It is almost always a mistake to try to roll the heel of the foot over the toe on roller skis or on snow. Some people mistakenly think this will give a stronger kick by emphasizing the toe-off, but it usually only encourages a skier to kick with no heel involvement and much too much backward pressure. This is especially true on roller skis. The rollover is a natural move, but emphasizing it usually destroys the kick, changing it to a weaker movement. On roller skis, it is a sure way to develop a late kick.

This brings us to the most insidious of roller ski induced problems—the nonkick. Here the skier does not kick at all but only pushes directly back on the roller skis. The skier looks smooth in this motion, which can be misleading because he or she looks so "good." The skier's head does not move up and down at all, and to the casual observer, this skier will look even better than the skier who is executing powerfully and properly. All the energy is directed back, none down—probably the most efficient way to ski on roller skis. But when the snow falls, the roof caves in on this skier. With no kick, the hills are impossible. The skier will feel weak and ineffectual. The problem is mainly improper technique and misdirection of force application rather than a lack of strength.

Luckily, this flaw is rare. The cure is flexing the glide leg at the knee in preparation to kick when the feet are together. But to be safe, the skier should try to flex the leg a little earlier, and then make an effort to kick down in an explosive manner. Another way of looking at it is that the good skier lofts his or her body "up" onto the glide ski, which can only happen if he or she has kicked down (that old opposite and equal reaction again). At first, the skier will tire rapidly because of the unusual output of energy. The skier must become convinced that he or she is getting a better workout because the skiing is more like being on snow. However, if the skier continues to tire rapidly after a week or so, he or she is probably overcorrecting. The most noticeable difference in this skier's appearance will be the development of some vertical head movement. When this happens, the skier is on the right track.

Stage 3: Poling Power

Once the skier has proper arm and leg movements and good balance with the body on top of the glide ski, he or she is ready for the third stage of development— poling power. The skier now learns to get the most out of his or her upper body by extending the time that the pole is in use. To do so, the skier must extend his or her ride on the glide ski, using the time to develop poling power (see Figure 8.4). The best checkpoint is

Figure 8.4 Good roller ski technique.

the position of the arms when the feet are together. When the feet are together, the poling hand should be at the thighs, and the hand swinging forward should be in front of the body. The skier tries to get the pole in the ground as quickly as possible without disrupting the natural rhythm of the diagonal. As soon as the knee is forward, so is the hand. The pole is planted when the free-swinging tip becomes almost vertical. The goal is to get the pole working while the speed or momentum of the skier is still high. Remember, the skier does nothing but slow down during the free-glide phase.

Working on this poling motion helps the skier learn to ride a balanced ski. This pole thrust should continue until the hand reaches the hip. It is very helpful to feel light on the ski while the poling is going on. This will encourage two things to happen: First, it will encourage a downward kick, which lofts a skier upward, second, it will encourage the skier to feel on top of the pole where he or she can effectively initiate poling with the stronger muscles of the torso. Then when the feet are together, the kick is initiated with the heel.

The most successful drill we have used for increasing poling power has been to slightly delay the return of the trailing ski. The skier delays the return of this leg until well into the poling motion. This delay is used to give the arm time to propel the skier on the glide ski. It is easier for many skiers to achieve the same delay by thinking of it as a supple follow-through, allowing the arm and leg to complete their intended path. It is actually this follow-through that carries the body into its natural motion, which involves a slight twist of the hips.

Many skiers find it more desirable to think of the delay as being one of the hips continuing its rotation, hesitating and then returning, rather than that of the foot. In any case, the delaying of the return movement of the trail leg is something that must be done in order to give the skier time to develop his or her poling power. All the top skiers exhibit this trait when viewed in slow motion.

This hesitated return of the leg has another beneficial side effect: It teaches the skier to ride the glide ski for a longer period of time. In fact, the basic rhythm of the skier is changed when the skier learns to ride the ski longer and does so through better poling motion. Instead of a *1-2* rhythm, it becomes *1-aah-2*. Or kick-kick becomes kick-pole-kick, remembering that the pole is planted during the pause. This delay is really like the pause of a pendulum as it finishes its arc. Most skiers are just not relaxed enough to benefit from it.

Double Poling on Roller Skis

Many experts around the world tell us to avoid the diagonal on roller skis so we can escape the horrors of a late kick. The risk of developing a late kick is rather minimal if you are careful. But double poling in both its forms is very valuable on roller skis and will be covered now, along with some other helpful skills that can be developed in the summer on the pavement (e.g., tuck, skate, corners, step turns, and safety on skis).

The technique of the double pole is rather straight forward and almost identical to that of the snow double pole. The hardness of the pavement, however, encourages insecurity. At first, most skiers do not compress (lower) their bodies as much on roller skis as on snow. This is easily corrected once a little confidence is gained. Again, the poles should be planted in front of the feet and the body forcefully committed onto the poles with the torso ending up approximately parallel to the ground. Most of the work is done by the abdomen, lats, and triceps, in that order, the details of which are covered in the previous chapter on double poling.

One flaw that almost all roller skiers fall into occasionally is the collapsing of the arms as the poles are planted. The hardness of the road causes considerable shock to be transmitted through the poles. However, the special shock absorber tips are very bouncy and difficult to handle and should be avoided unless the skier develops a sore elbow from shock. (Fortunately, none of our skiers have ever developed this problem.)

The timing of the applied force is very important. A small collapse occurs at the beginning of the pole plant. This slight flexing of the arms is a form of preloading. Stretching the contracted muscles allows a more powerful pole drive as the muscles release the stored energy of the stretch. But when too much of a running start is used (i.e., too much downward body speed is developed before the pole plant), the force is too much for the muscles to absorb readily. Then the motion will come to an abrupt halt before continuing. This stall is the most common flaw on roller skis. There definitely is a running start to the double pole and it causes the preloading of the arms. But if the skier tries to pound the poles into the blacktop, there is too much force for the muscles to absorb. The motion is stopped as the arms collapse. This is easy to detect, for the skier looks very mechanical and the stall is very apparent. However, the cure is easy. Remember where the power should be applied! The propelling force is applied once the poles are in the ground. All the skier has to do is plant the tips more gently and apply more force later.

Kick Double Poling on Roller Skis

The kick double pole is also essentially the same as on snow. It does have one particularly good application for roller skiing: It offers a unique way to defeat the late kick. If you remember, the late kick happens when the kicking leg flexes and pushes off after the glide foot passes the kicking foot. One possible way to correct this and, at the same time, get the feeling for what an earlier timed kick feels like utilizes the kick double pole.

The skier emphasizes the forward placement of the kicking foot. It is easier to keep the foot in front than in the diagonal. The kick is started while the foot is forward, under the chest. The skier only has to look down to see where the foot is actually kicking. It is easier to observe with the kick double pole than the diagonal. Short stretches of kick double poling alternated with diagonaling helps attain the correct feeling of the well-timed kick. This feeling is one of lofting the body over the glide ski and is much easier learned here than in the diagonal.

The kick double pole is actually a little tougher for the beginner to learn than the diagonal. Once mastered, however, it is much easier to control the timing of the kick. All the basic on snow tenets discussed before still hold and can be easily mastered during the off-season.

Skating on Roller Skis

Skating is also something that can be practiced on roller skis (see Figures 8.5a, b, and c). Here the type of

Figure 8.5(a)   Skating on three wheelers.

b

c

Figure 8.5(b) and (c)   Special roller skate ideal for kids of all ages.
These models are especially effective for quick tempo uphill V-skating.

roller ski chosen is more critical. The slower three-wheeled skis are the hardest to use, the fast three-wheelers are next, and the two-wheeled ones are the best. There is also a skate boot that has been adapted from the speed skaters that works very well. Some slight differences in technique exist among all these models and snow; however, the adjustment is quick once the skier is on snow. The main concern of the summer skater is that he or she learn the proper arm, leg, and body coordination and that he or she exercise the specific muscles. Because the skate technique on roller skis so closely resembles the technique on snow, very little must be added at this time. Be sure to refer to chapter 6 for the proper skating techniques, especially that of "posting" the glide leg and transferring the weight.

Evaluation of Roller Skis

If you are serious about your skiing and do not have snow for the majority of the time, roller skis are a must. No other training activity simulates the actual conditions of skiing as completely. The added benefit is that the chance of developing stress-type injuries is much lower than in running. Be careful, however, knee pads, elbow pads, and walking down steeper hills will keep you training when you might otherwise be hurt.

Roller skiing has gone through many phases in our country. At first, it was a novelty viewed with suspicion. Then it was cautiously accepted, but only as a double pole workout. This attitude seemed to come mainly from European influences and from a fear of ruining their technique. This fear was well-grounded with some of the early versions of roller skis, which were quite unwieldy. Soon, however, some of the top coaches in the United States endorsed roller skiing as the best way to train during the off-season. Marty Hall had some skiers maintain their ability, as measured by race times, very well while only training on roller skis during one snowless winter. The skiers performed as well in the later races as in the earlier ones. They did not have the same access to snow as did their U.S. Ski

Team rivals. John Caldwell has also long endorsed roller skiing as the single best way to train in the off-season.

Yet, on occasion, you hear voices with disquieting information. One study showed that you do not get as tough an aerobic workout on roller skis that you do on snow or by running. This may have been true for that study, but on the whole, it is false. Many variables must be considered, a major one being the terrain. Without hills, roller skiing will not be as good cardio-vascularly as skiing or running; with hills, it's a completely different story.

Another factor includes speed of skis. Contrary to popular opinion, fast skis give less of a workout, even on hilly terrain. I discovered this twice one spring. In each case I worked out with a far superior skier. In one instance, I had faster skis than my colleague. I felt that I was pushing it to keep up but was surprised that my pulse never got over 110, even on rolling terrain. (My normal pulse max in roller skiing is around 200.) The second time was with a skier who was also much faster than I and this time we both had faster skis. The workout was on extremely hilly terrain. Again, I had no trouble keeping up and was surprised to notice that a normally brutal course actually seemed easy on faster roller skis—and this despite the fact I was moving out with a better skier.

Too fast of a ski does two things: It makes the workout too easy, and it has a leveling effect on performance. This is easily seen in roller ski races when comparing skiers of different abilities. The gap narrows between the best and those below, especially when the course is fairly flat. One thing for sure, not everyone is on fast skis, even if the skis are the same model. There are tremendous differences in ski speed and any inferences from roller ski racing can be dangerous. The best measurement of winter carryover from roller skiing would be to race in rolling terrain on roller skis that are no faster than snow. Unfortunately, this situation is unlikely to occur in a race where competitive desire places skiers on skis that are too fast to be good for training but that allow the racer to win. This is now being carried to extremes where the extremely fast skate boots are dominating the top finishing positions.

Although I compete relatively better in roller ski races than on snow, I know they are not good measurements of progress. But they are a great inspirational happening. Roller ski races give the skiers something to look forward to and help maintain the competitive spirit in the summer. They are fun, but they are different. Our skiers get their best indication of progress in the weekend workouts when the group, using their slower roller skis, gets together in very hilly terrain. These workouts sometimes get quite competitive and indicate progress much more effectively than a flat land roller ski race.

Selecting a Diagonal Roller Ski

What really matters is the effect of roller ski selection on the training results. The ideal ski, then, would be one that is as light as a racing ski and about as fast. Because of the greater kick, however, this ski would have a slightly slower rolling speed, yet would give about the same time over a measured distance. Such a ski is currently on the market, but it has the drawback of needing a great deal of maintenance. Most of the serious skiers use this particular model. Names of brands are not mentioned purposefully because models change so rapidly that it is out of place for a book to recommend the best brand. Other less fragile models are available, but they are heavier—some faster and some slower. Some of these faster three-wheelers also skate well. You can see that picking out a roller ski is a compromise. How serious are you? Do you want only one pair or can you afford one pair each for skating, normal workouts, and racing?

Bill Koch wants the slowest ski possible but has compromised for the lightest, slowest combination. The slowest ski is too heavy in Bill's opinion, which brings up an interesting point: The bigger skier can handle a heavier ski; the smaller skier must go for lightness. Our young girls have virtually no choice in picking out a roller ski for they cannot ski properly on the heavier models. Thinking of the younger girls brings an important point to mind. Bill Koch may like slower skis, but I am convinced that younger skiers need a ski that is about the speed of snow. Otherwise, it is too hard for them to ski, especially double pole. They easily get discouraged when it becomes more work and less fun. Bill is a horse in terms of cross-country skiing. Therefore, slower skis may be appropriate for someone of his ability, but not for everyone.

Fast but heavy skis may create little workout for a strong skier, but may completely devastate a weaker one. Each person has his or her individual situation to consider. In most cases, the light ski about the speed of snow is best. I am hopeful that a durable one will be marketed soon.

One other variable is the terrain. If it is very hilly, you may opt for slower and safer skis. If it is flat, you may choose a little faster pair, going for speed and power on your double pole. (Power is related to how fast you move the poles.)

Selecting a Skating Roller Ski

You might also consider the two-wheeled skis. Many new models are available and all skate quite well. Some are more unstable, some heavier, and some hard to control—but all work well. The only real solution is to try them out and see which work best for you. As of December 1985, I have skied on all of them, and my only fear is that the skate boots are a little wild in hilly terrain. So there is no real solution to the choice of skis. The answer will be a compromise.

Each skier will probably go through a new pair each year with at least one change of tires and probably a bearing or shaft to replace during the season. As you can see, the cost is not cheap. Even the availability of parts becomes a factor.

Special Roller Skiing Strokes

Roller skiing does have its own special strokes. For survival, the first one is a nonstroke—that is, taking off the skis. If the hill is too steep, don't be proud. I have seen enough skin left on the road in those situations. Walk down and you'll feel like skiing again tomorrow. The second special stroke—the snow plow—sounds as if it is the same as skiing and it is on 2 wheelers (see Figure 8.6a). However, in roller skiing, using the three-wheeled roller skis, the execution is different. The wheels won't slide sideways down the road, so the skis are spread in a slight plow, and an outward pressure is exerted against the wheels. To be really effective, this move requires considerable strength to stop the skis from crossing in front of you. Do not expect any miraculous slowing down in the middle of a hair-raising hill, for it won't happen. You must slow down early, because this pavement plow is not nearly as effective as a regular snow plow. In addition, the roads are much harder. The way to take steeper hills is to walk them, plow early, or half ski in the grass on the side of the road to slow you down. If you find yourself going too fast, keep your feet farther apart than shoulder width, and brace your knees with your elbows (see Figure 8.6b). This position is very stable and helps prevent the skis from crossing at high speeds. Using your poles to slow down can be effective at low speeds but is downright dangerous at higher ones. The tip can catch and you could find yourself impaled on the handle of the pole (see Figures 8.6c-e for other safety measures on roller skis).

Figure 8.6(a) The snowplow is very effective on two wheeled roller skis. The technique is almost identical to snow. The three-wheelers, however, require an outward rather than inward pressure.

Figure 8.6(b) Traversing—for the steepest roads. Better yet, WALK down.

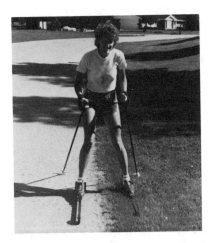

Figure 8.6(c) Using the side of the road to control speed.

Figure 8.6(d) Never use your poles to slow down in this manner. The next time you try it could be your last.

Figure 8.6(e) Elbows act as a brace to keep roller skis from crossing on high speed downhill.

Figure 8.6 Three proper and one dangerous method of controlling speed on roller skis.

The downhill turns are even more insidious. On snow the knees are angled in to set the edge to create a turn. On three-wheeled roller skis, however, the ankles are tipped outward to turn. One would therefore expect time spent on roller skis to ruin downhill snow technique, but the reverse is 'true. Even though the angle of the ankle is different, the time spent on roller skis has helped our skiers get better on snow. The snow is softer, and the confidence and ability to balance at speeds helps the skiers in the winter. Some of those tough downhills look a lot easier covered with soft snow when contrasted to the hard pavement of roller skiing. And it's even a bigger plus with two wheelers. They handle and turn much like snow.

On the other side of the coin, roller ski racing and its demand for more speed has introduced its own strokes. The main difference is the double pole. On fast roller skis it is more efficient to keep up your rolling speed by using short strokes. Because the resistance is not there, it is not too tiring to do this on roller skis. However, a longer stroke is needed when double poling on snow. The resistance is greater, so more active involvement of the stronger muscles of the torso is required.

Three-wheeled racing roller skis also force racers to skate turns differently, both on the flats and the down-hills, whereas the two-wheelers are much more like snow. When skating around the flat turns on racing three-wheelers, a slip or even tip will occur if too vigor-ous a motion is used. However, the turns on race courses will, at times, be very tight. It is not uncom-mon to come to the end of a road and make a 180° turnaround. Some quick stepping rather than big powerful thrusting on the fast skis is required.

If you are serious about your skiing, especially if you live in a marginal snow area, roller skiing is not just another way to train, it is a necessity. If you truly love to ski, roller skiing is a way to extend your enjoy-ment through the other 9 months of the year.

Technique Differences Between Roller Skiing and Snow Skiing

Three things make roller skiing different than snow: (a) There is no need to set the wax, (b) there are no tracks for the skis, and (c) the pavement is much harder than snow. Each is a factor and can cause differences in technique, so some awareness of the pit-falls is necessary.

1. In diagonaling, there is no need to set the wax. As a result, the careless skier can get into bad habits unless he or she is careful. The following are ways to avoid this pitfall:

- Try to keep your weight on the heel and initiate your kick from the heel.
- On occasion, concentrate on kicking down as if you were setting the wax.
- Feel the slight lofting of the body and try to feel light on the glide ski as you pole.
- Have someone check you out to see if your leg is flexing too late. This can be detected without video by the abnormally low foot carry of the trail leg resulting from the late kick.
- As a last resort, do the hop-and-glide drill concentrating on an early kick. But intersperse this with the poling drill where you ski slowly with rhythm, extending your glide by the pole push while delaying the return of the trail leg. These drills are good in combination because they are two extremes and, when used together, guard against deviation too far in either direction.

2. There are no tracks for diagonaling on roller skis; as a result, bicycling the foot, short glide time, tenseness and too smooth skiing can result. To combat this, the following may be done:
   - Wear knee and elbow pads if you are a beginner or feel extremely awkward. This security will allow you to better relax on the skis and the pavement will not look so forbidding.
   - Try to relax on your skis, letting the roller skiing come to you rather than "horsing" the outcome. A good attitude is just observing what your body is doing rather than forcing it to do something. This is one of the best ways to beat tension. Use this attitude in all of the following points.
   - Intersperse short-step skiing with uninhibited skiing, always planting the pole early. Be as relaxed as you can. After you conquer this stage, you may go for a more powerful technique.
   - Relax on the glide ski, allowing the trail foot to swing next to the glide ski, not lifting it in a bicycle motion. Relaxed balance is the key. On roller skis it is permissible to ski with a wider stance than on snow. This may be the only

way a skier can relax and not worry about crossing his skis. The only pitfall is that the skier's stance is so wide that he cannot stay on top of the glide ski.

- Too smooth skiing is the result of both insecurity and the removal of the requirement to set the wax. An attempt to preload the leg and loft the body onto the glide ski is a good way to cure this problem. This flaw is one very few skiers have, but those who do are usually very good.

3. The hardness of the pavement can compound many of the above problems and introduce one of its own—road shock.
   - The double pole can easily become a collapsing movement if the poles are planted too forcefully. Try to accelerate through the motion, building speed as the stroke continues. Slow roller skis can compound this problem because it is very difficult to accelerate through.
   - Tennis elbow is something I've heard of but have never seen in any of our skiers. However, if that is a problem, soft and padded gloves rather than bouncy pole tips are the answer.

4. Skating should be at least 50% of your roller ski workouts. Include marathon, free, and uphill types of skating.

In conclusion, I would like to restate that most people do not develop grotesque skiing styles on roller skis but ski pretty much the same as on snow. This is especially true for skating. One last thought for the advanced skier: If you own more than one pair of roller skis, don't save your fast skis only for races. Some of the slower models have a slower rolling speed than snow. Taking a few workouts on the fast models will allow you to use your muscles as fast or faster than you do on snow. This type of training will make sure that power as well as strength is the result of your summer training. Pulse rate can determine what kind of workout you are doing. So pay attention to that important indicator because even the hills are easier on light, fast skis. The heavier but faster two-wheelers can be used, but then skating or double poling should be the prime strokes because it is almost impossible to turn over the heavier skis fast enough in the diagonal stride.

Training

9

Basic Fitness for the Skier

Training—to some a nasty word, to others a thing of joy. It connotes seriousness, a commitment, a dedication to a goal. Training is something that requires active participation; it is not a spectator sport. While training, it is important to realize that a person is composed of two parts: One mental and one physical. To neglect one at the expense of the other is folly. The two are not as separate as they may seem.

A poor mental state can easily affect the physical well-being of an individual. This is often reflected by the quick passing away of a person after the death of a spouse or death right after retirement. The physical state can just as easily affect the mental. A person who is overweight, out of shape, and has trouble moving cannot help being affected mentally. On the other hand, being supple, light, and in shape cannot help but cause a positive frame of mind and greater productivity.

A friend of mine who is a surgeon claims that if all those people in a hospital who are overweight or who smoked were removed, the beds would be almost empty. To make matters worse, the overweight person in surgery is much harder to operate on, and his or her chances of survival are less than that of a lean individual's. An anatomy course I took as a youth proved this concept to me. The cadaver on which my group worked was extremely fat. We had trouble finding even the most elementary parts of the anatomy, hardly getting anywhere, when we noticed that some of the other groups were not in the same situation. Those groups with lean cadavers had laid open the entire body while we were still on the first part. At that time, I really became aware of the difficulty an obese person caused a doctor in operating—just in finding what he or she was looking for under all those layers of fat.

The relationship of body to mind is apparent in the difference in individuals as they age. My father always prided himself on physical condition. Earlier in life he was an acrobat, champion weightlifter, and participated in many sports. Today, at 73 he is as spry as ever, whereas many other men of his age are barely able to move. He can still do more push-ups than I can and has a morning resting pulse of under 40. One of our cross-country skiers in his 20s made the mistake of playfully wrestling around with my dad. (The two are about the same size.) Much to the young man's chagrin, he soon found himself helplessly pinned to the ground, unable to move, and this skier is one of the strongest people, pound for pound, I know.

I cannot help but compare that situation to what I have seen in the nursing homes as various relatives enter their senior years. As an example, an uncle who was mentally alert broke his hip. Becoming sedentary, he never recovered physically and had to remain in the nursing home. It was sad to see a person with his abilities trapped with all those people who were senile or of failing mental capacities.

In contrast, a near tragic accident happened to my father several years ago. He was clearing some brush in the woods behind his home when the rotating cutting blade of the power-driven brush clearing tool rebounded off a rock into his lower leg, cutting his leg through the calf to the bone. He went into shock but, fortunately, my mother heard him shouting for help. She pushed the exposed muscle, which was hanging out, into his leg, wrapped it, and applied a tourniquet to his leg above the knee. With the help of a neighbor, they made it to the hospital. Fortunately, no nerves were severed and the bone was not damaged, but the leg required quite a bit of internal stitching and had to be cast for 6 weeks.

Realizing that people of his age have difficulty recovering from operations in which lower limbs are cast, causing stiff joints and a loss of mobility, I assumed this was the end of my father's active life. I failed to reckon, however, with the mental toughness of an old man and the therapeutic effects of cross-country skiing.

About 3 years prior to his accident, I had gotten my dad hooked on cross-country skiing, which is a natural activity in the snow belt of northern Wisconsin. Cross-country skiing is easy on the joints and relatively safe. It develops the heart, lungs, and circulation as well as building muscular strength and flexibility. My father's first bout with the slippery skis were rather comical, as he repeatedly fell into the soft snow, even on the smallest downhills. I figured he'd never learn, but to my surprise a year later, he was not only skiing the more difficult trails of the area, but even entered a local citizens' race. His progress as a skier was amazing, showing that learning a physical skill need not be limited to the young. Then came the tragic accident with the brush cutter. It looked as if northern Wisconsin's oldest citizen racer's skiing career was over.

When the cast came off in November, the results were predictable: He was unable to walk and the ankle was extremely stiff and swollen. After several weeks the improvement was minimal. He was getting around slowly with a walker but was almost completely unable to use a cane because of pain and stiffness in the ankle. Being a teacher, I have seen many high school students with their legs in casts and it took many of them over a year to regain their mobility. But my dad was 71 years old, so I figured his active days had ended.

When the snow came in late November, I called up North to see about the early snow and was amazed to discover that my father was out skiing. Still unable to walk across the room without a cane or walker, he was out skiing. The recovery was remarkable. By Christmas, his leg seemed to be normal, and he was walking without a limp and skiing every day. To me it was a miracle. I had never seen a teenager heal as fast.

That season he was a much faster skier, cutting 10 to 15 minutes off his previous times and capping his season by skiing the Birkebeiner. This in itself was another minor miracle, for he was still a relative newcomer to skiing, and I remembered well his first bouts on the skis just 2 years before, where even the slightest inclines brought him down. When I heard the weather conditions, icy and purple klister, I knew the course was fast and dangerous. Rather than worrying about his goal of finishing, survival was my concern. He made the cutoff, and, considerably bruised and battered, he finished some 8 hours later. (Incidentally, a few friends of mine who were excellent skiers had some horrible experiences and were hurt badly in the fast conditions and the expressway-like pileups.) This man who I had written off as an active individual not only regained complete mobility, but went on to surpass his previous achievements and finished the Birke in very dangerous conditions. This to me is one of the great stories of the sport (see Figure 9.1).

Figure 9.1 Oldest racer in Northern Wisconsin. Walter Borowski, at 73, shows that skiing for fun has a training effect that keeps you young, physically and mentally.

The moral? Training should be a lifetime activity and cross-country skiing is one of the kindest and best ways for your body to maintain cardiovascular and muscular condition. It should not be considered something that is only done to ski faster, to make the Junior Olympics, or to win the club championship, but it should also be something that is enjoyable enough to continue for a lifetime. Goals are important and give a person incentive to train, but something should be left when the races are over. Thus, I define training as a lifetime activity that should be followed by everyone who is physically able.

I recently read an article by an "expert" on physical fitness. She claimed that a study of Norwegians showed that those who cross-country skied lived "only" 2 years longer than their sedentary countrymen. Her point was that you have to like what you are doing because the benefits are not worth the effort. That may be partly true. If you don't like it, you probably won't do it. But I have to disagree about the benefits. Quality of life is something this study said nothing about. From personal experience, I have seen that those individuals who remain active are able to do much more at an older age. For the inactive and overweight septagenarian, just getting up from a chair or even a fall can be a very difficult situation, whereas this feat is nothing for the fit 70-year-old. Quality of life is not just the years on earth, but also how they are spent. Once you reach age 65, 2 more "good years" are not that little a deal. Cross-country skiing is not the only way to do this, but it is one of the most enjoyable and easiest on your body. If you want to be fit for a lifetime, today is the day to start training. I am hopeful that it will become a way of life.

There are as many ways to train as there are people. Some of our skiers train because they race, others race because they train, and even others just plain ski or race for the fun of it. Some do 21 hours a week (I think they're a little overmotivated), and some ski themselves into shape in the winter. Some ski to keep themselves in shape for backpacking, biking, running, or canoe racing; others backpack, bike, run, or canoe to train for skiing. Some lift weights; others run hills or row. Some compete in triathlons, some in roller ski races, whereas others foot race, canoe, row, or do nothing competitively in the summer. The choices are endless. What you end up doing will be highly individual and you may be the only person in the world who trains just like you. In fact, some of the things you do may be as innovative as those of any champion athlete in the world.

The first question you should ask yourself is, "What are my goals?" The levels of cross-country ski training can be broken into the three following parts, although there are as many levels of intensity as there are individuals. (a) Level 1 is fitness, (b) level 2 is citizen racing, and (c) level 3 is serious competitor. The next question is, "How much do I presently train?" Big jumps in training hours usually lead to injuries.

You do not want to become injured or sick from doing too much too soon. This is especially true if most of your training is running where it is easy to become injured through overuse injuries. Biking, swimming, and roller skiing can help prevent some of the running injuries.

General Fitness

Exercising aerobically for three 30 minute sessions per week is what the specialists claim is necessary for good cardiorespiratory fitness. That is where the pulse is elevated to approximately 70% to 85% of the maximum. (An estimate is maximum 220 minus age, although in practice, I've seen quite a variance to this rule of thumb.) In general, the pulse is in the range of 110 to 165 bpm. This will keep you beneath the anaerobic threshold where you are going too hard for your muscles to produce energy aerobically. There are complicated formulas for this, but a simple talk test is sufficient. You should be exercising at a low enough intensity that you can comfortably talk to a friend, but the pulse should be elevated to a rate of 110 or better. Later on in training there are other types of workouts that will involve efforts outside this range, but for now, easy is the word. You want to go fast enough to achieve the benefits but slow enough to enjoy them. You are trying to build a lifetime habit. If it hurts too much, you won't continue.

A note for the experts: The three workouts a week for basic fitness is also an excellent maintenance program for even top competitors. Even for the elite, very little is lost on such a shortened program. Many skiers follow this or a similar program each spring. I recommend a period like this for everyone—a time where the enthusiasm is allowed to build up.

I have observed some real progress made on this abbreviated program. One 40-year-old woman went from running 10-minute miles for 2 miles to 7.5 minute miles for 4 miles, and doing only two and sometimes three workouts a week. This improvement occurred in the period of about a year with weekend skiing being the only winter activity and with many layoffs in between.

What kind of workouts apply to this formula? Running, roller skiing, cross-country skiing, swimming, or running with poles—some activity that easily elevates and sustains the pulse.

Which method of training should you choose? Much depends on your environment, what you like to do, what you can do, and a host of other factors. Some variables might be hills or lack of them, roads for roller skiing, or even the climate. Lakes and rivers are another consideration or even indoor pools. Injuries, your ability to run or swim, and many other personal factors go into your decision. If you live in the mountains, walking can be enough. Three, half-hour sessions spent walking continuously up a mountain pass or trail, preferably with poles, is as difficult as running, and for most people, much harder.

Running for Fitness

For many, running is the most convenient training method. All you need to start is a pair of shoes. Furthermore, you are not limited by daylight, so you can work out at anytime; it doesn't take any travel time if run from your doorstep; weather is not a factor, for rain gear or layers of clothing are easily put on; and no time is wasted. The warm-up period can be the gentle jog as your muscles start to feel the flow of blood. Elaborate stretching exercises are not really needed, although you may want to spend a few minutes stretching the Achilles, hamstrings, quadriceps, and lower back. If you are a TV addict, the workout can be slotted in between two shows you want to watch or even between loads of wash. It's simple to get started.

Many beginning runners suffer when they first start and thus give it up. This is usually due to an overzealous approach to their training. It is important to start slowly, not just in pace but also in amount. Too much, too soon again can be the killer. Shin splints, Achilles problems, hamstring pulls, and joint problems (knees, ankles, and hips) can develop. Most runners develop soreness when they first start training. How this is handled will determine whether or not they continue to train.

Most skiers go through an adjustment period every spring, for no matter how good their intentions to keep up the running, January and February are hard months to run. When spring rolls around and running again becomes a part of the training regimen, initial soreness results. The way to beat this is twofold, assuming you have good shoes. First, start by running a short distance, for example, 1 mile. This distance will vary with individuals. Follow that with a day of rest. If you had no soreness or felt pretty good, you can increase the running up to 2 miles the next time out. Rest again the next day. If you felt good, you may increase the mileage on the third day to 3 miles. (*Note:* This is for experienced "trainees." Beginning runners might take a more gradual approach.) If you feel that you were a little too sore or problems started to develop, back off by taking extra rest days from the running; in addition, do not increase the mileage but back off a bit. You can bike, swim, and such, but give your body a break from the pounding of running.

Run-Walk Training

The run-walk method is the second way of breaking into running in the spring. Break up the running with walking in either a planned or impromptu method. The varieties are endless. You can run aerobically, pulse 110 to 165, for a mile, then walk for 200 yards; or it could be just 200 steps of each, alternated throughout a workout. The walking is very therapeutic for the body and less stress is offered by the joints, tendons, ligaments, and muscles. You can travel more miles and suffer less using this system. Then as your condition improves, gradually decrease the walking distance and increase the running or just continue to run-walk as the training form.

Hard core runners and elite athletes usually feel guilty about walking; however, I strongly recommend walking, especially when soreness or other signs of overuse are felt. Walk for about 100 yards, then continue running. In the same respect, any skier should stop and walk when any symptom of overuse develops during a run. A little prevention can save a whole season. In many cases the brief pain will go away after a short walk and the athlete can continue running. There is no need to feel guilty about the walking because, as some coaches have shown, the results from running with occasional walking are as good as continuous running.

This run-walk method was established by Ernst Van Aaken of Germany as an excellent way to train, even for world class runners. He had much success coaching women runners using this method. He would have his athletes run-walk at a very slow pace and then spend the last 10% of the workout at race pace to develop leg speed. The run-walk has also been used successfully by ultramarathoners to cover such distances as 50 and 100 miles. These runners intersperse many feedings with their running and walking and go farther and faster than they might otherwise do. I find it rather humorous to think my old scoutmaster was not too far off when he advocated the "Indian Method" of travelling great distances. Walk 200 steps, run 200 steps, walk 200 steps, and so on.

Getting Started

One note to the beginning runner: It will not feel good immediately. All this talk of runners' highs will escape you for a while. You will plod. Your body will feel like it weighs a ton. But the feeling will pass if you pursue the task intelligently and if you do not overdo it at the start. Make your distance increase smaller than 1 mile. Go from 1 to 1-1/2 miles and do not run initially more than three times a week. A woman runner in my neighborhood typically exemplifies the stages of a beginning runner. When she started, her feet seemed glued to the blacktop. Almost imperceptively she improved. I didn't notice it until a friend of mine commented on her excellent running form. When I saw her running early in the morning and again later in the day, I asked her if she was on two-a-days, and she said no, which surprised me. She was still on the same workout, her distance one of the week, in that case a 17-miler, and was training to run her first marathon—a remarkable feat from a woman who could hardly move when she started.

I used to laugh at runners, calling them "brain pounders." I told them their brain cells were being destroyed by all the jarring on the pavement. However, after taking up cross-country skiing and running, it was not too long before I found myself lined up in a 16-mile race next to these very same brain pounders. I still much prefer skiing and roller skiing to running itself, but it does provide some diversity in the off-season.

Many top skiers do much of their training by running, much of it using poles on hiking trails (see Figure 9.2). One of the side benefits of trail running is

Figure 9.2 Running with poles over ski type terrain is fun and rewarding for any skier.

relieving the stresses on the legs because the forest paths are softer; some even have bark laid on the trails. In addition, the use of poles relieves some of the pressure on the legs. The result: less leg injuries, more distance, and an exercise that greatly simulates skiing. One season I could run for 2 hours in the woods and hills with poles before pain in my hip began to bother me. However, 30 minutes on the roads had the same effect.

One note of warning: Be prepared for occasional jibes from hikers on the trails—some in fun, some rather vicious. "Where's the snow?" "It's the wrong season," and "Aren't you a little confused?" are a few of the recurring comments. This used to be irritating, but now we simply ignore the obnoxious and are friendly to the rest. We follow the same policy while roller skiing.

If you are getting your basic half hour in three times a week, you will be physically fit and will be able to enter the shorter citizen ski races as fun-type events without worrying about finishing. If you want to be better than that, read on.

Making Your Run-Training Time More Effective for Skiing

The basic difference between cross-country skiing and running is that skiing is a power-endurance sport, running an endurance one. The word *power* is the key. This not only means the powerful upper body bursts of the skate or double pole and the use of the arms in the single stick, but also means a powerful use of the legs. In running, the legs cycle continuously, merely maintaining the momentum of the body. In skiing, the legs work in an explosive manner, not only on the hills but on the flats. The body is thrown forward by this explosive action of the legs, even when diagonaling in the fastest conditions. Then the arms take over giving the legs a rest. Each stride is a mini-fartlek in itself.

I've always been amazed at the number of publications that recommend running as the main form of training in the off-season. For most skiers the season is only 3 or 4 months long. To train for cross-country skiing in such a nonspecific manner for most of the year seems foolhardy if you have high aspirations. While the experts were touting running as the main form of training, mere beginners seemed to have problems with that concept. I remember hearing questions such as "How can running help you that much when the same muscles are not even used?" or "If running is so good, why aren't the best runners the best skiers, even when they are serious about their skiing?"

The answer is obvious. The best runners are not the best skiers because running and skiing are really quite different. First of all, technique and coordination considerations are tremendous. Not only are different muscles being used, but in skiing they are also being used more powerfully. The real kicker, though, is that the arms have to be trained to use oxygen.

Several years ago Dr. Robert Arnot did some oxygen uptake studies, both with and without arm involvement, of some cross-country skiers. Oxygen uptake is a measure of fitness: The higher the number, the more oxygen is used and supposedly, the more fit the person. The results were amazing. You would expect a skier to be able to use more oxygen when both arms and legs were involved as compared to legs alone. However, the elite skiers, USST members, actually used less oxygen. These were highly trained cross-country skiers, national team members. The results for the average citizen racer were even worse.

Dr. Arnot's conclusion was that the arms and legs must be worked together so the arms learn to utilize oxygen in an aerobic manner and that even the highly trained elite skiers did not do this enough. Subsequently, the USST members began to train more specifically, and they actually improved their oxygen utilization when they used both arms and legs compared to the legs alone—the opposite of what had happened earlier. The moral of the story? Use your arms and legs together as much as possible, in a manner as close to skiing as possible. Do activities that also build up power endurance as well as endurance. This means that double poling alone is not enough. Double poling will build up the arms but will not help when the arms and legs must work together.

Other Activities for Training in the Off-Season

If faster skiing is your goal, which are the best ways to train? The following training alternatives may be used:

Roller skiing, when properly executed, is the closest thing to skiing except skiing itself. A study showed that roller skiing on the flat was not as good oxygen-wise as running. Wow! Any roller skier could have told you that. He or she also could have told you that it depends on the speed and weight of the skis. With some slow roller skis, you could even diagonal stride on the flats and get a good workout. It also depends on road surface, and on how hard the skier was going. A later study confirmed what any experienced roller skier knows: On a hilly course, roller skiing actually pushes your pulse much higher than running. Most importantly, you are not only training your heart and lungs but also your muscles.

Hill walking is one of the best ways to train in the off-season. It is not just used to create a break in training or for an easy workout. If you can find a hill that is over 2 minutes long, you can easily bring your pulse to the maximum. Those lucky enough to live in the mountains can get much of their training on long up-hill hikes with poles. Most hill walking should involve poles, because of the better workout. The goal of these skiers is not to walk fast, but to go slow enough to keep their pulse in the aerobic training range if that is the desired workout.

Running the ski trails with poles is vastly superior to road running or running without poles. Not only do the poles relieve the stress on the legs, helping to avoid running injuries, but the arms and legs are worked together. The skier uses his or her poles on the uphills and runs normally on the flats and downhills. This workout is definitely harder to do with poles than without. Several of our athletes run without poles because the workout with poles is too hard on them. Some pretty good runners have been brought to their knees on their first run through the wooded trails, demonstrating the validity of Dr. Arnot's study on the use of the arms and legs together. After a while the arms adapt, and the runs become enjoyable.

Rowing with a movable seat exercises the legs and upper body together. If you have the equipment, it's great. Only one serious skier I've known had access to this method of training; therefore, it would rank low on the scale of training. The indoor machines, however, are effective for training during inclement weather or when injured.

Swimming is one of the better options if you can swim well enough to reach and maintain an effective pulse rate. Its natural limitations are the need to be near a facility and to have access. The obvious advantage of swimming is that it exercises the total body, especially the upper torso. The not so obvious aspect of swimming is that it allows you to train when injured. Several years ago, an article appeared in *Runner's World* about the many personal and national records set in the tryouts for the ill-fated Olympic Games of 1980. What was most interesting was that many of the athletes had been injured for much of the time during training. How did they go on to achieve such success, despite the injuries? Biking and working out in a pool were the two predominant alternate methods of training.

For their workout, the athletes, without touching the bottom, ran in the deep end of the pool. Some needed flotation devices to keep going in their attempt to imitate the biomechanics of running as closely as possible. They would do their actual scheduled track workout in the pool. If it called for a long, easy day, they would run long and easy. Because they weren't touching the bottom, they didn't get very far, but the workouts were measured in time rather than distance. On the interval days, they would do the actual intervals in the pool, matching the time and intensity of the track workout.

Cross-country skiers could do the same thing easily. If the injury was not as severe, the running could take place in waist- or chest-deep water, the legs producing the striding motion of skiing. One advantage of running in water is that beginners can improve their technique by paying attention to the first key of the diagonal: That is, the opposite hand and knee come forward together. Most beginners are a bit out of synch, and a little time spent on this activity in the water in the summer can pay dividends on the snow in the winter.

However, because the crawl is an excellent upper body developer, the skier is probably better off just swimming if conditioning is the goal. The motion of the arms in this stroke is very similar to skiing. Also, because most skiers would probably be swimming because of leg injuries, the crawl is ideal in preventing reinjury of the legs while still working many of the same muscles as skiing.

Running is perhaps the most convenient and popular way to train. Most of the top cross-country skiers run in the off-season. Its weaknesses are the lack of arm involvement and the enormous amount of stress-related injuries. But because of the convenience and cost, it will probably continue to be the best way to train for many skiers.

Biking remains an enjoyable and popular way to train for cross-country skiers. Like swimming, it is especially effective for skiers who are injured or who cannot run. Standing on the pedals in high gears makes this activity much like skiing hills. Bill Koch trains often on the bike using this method. Biking does usually take twice the time to get the same training effect as running, and the arms are not at all involved.

Biking combined with swimming and running is a balanced way to train. This is the magic of the newly popular endurance event—the triathlon. The three events do work the entire body and are much better in combination than any one of them alone. Although they are not really specific to skiing, they are an excellent alternative to spring and summer training. I would suggest, however, that the serious skier get in at least two ski-specific workouts (roller skiing or running with poles) a week, even when training for triathlons.

Weightlifting is an extremely important part of the training regimen for most serious competitors. The special section on weights later in the next chapter will cover this subject in depth.

Training for the Serious Competitor 10

To Be The Best You Can Be

Assuming you're serious, how do you go about increasing your training from the basic three 1/2 hour workouts a week? First of all, you should do as much of the really specific activities as possible, that is, skiing, roller skiing, running and/or walking with poles. These activities produce immediate results. They force you to use your arms as well as your legs and specifically train you for what you are trying to improve—skiing. In addition, they force you out to the hills. Cross-country courses are hilly. Too many running loops are on flat terrain. I have seen some pretty fair runners become mere puppies when confronted with the type of course skiers use. To be good on the hills, train on the hills. There are ways to get around this if you live in an area without hills, and we'll get to them later. But if you have hills, you're lucky; so use them.

Increasing the hours you spend training is the next way to upgrade your training schedule. The two ways to do this are to add more training days per week or to increase the amount of time you spend working out each day. Extending the time spent on each workout is the best way to begin increasing your training time, but situations can vary. Later in the chapter the different intensities of workouts (i.e., fast or slow) you will want to incorporate into your program will be discussed. Extending your training time is best pursued by gradually adding time to one workout until the 1/2 hour becomes 45 minutes. Then a second workout can be upgraded to 45 minutes. Then you can go back and increase one of these workouts to 1 hour. You will now have three workouts which look like this: 1/2, 3/4, and 1 hour. You may now increase this schedule to 4 and then 5 days a week, by adding 1/2 hour workouts. This will give you 2 rest days a week, which is ideal for most people. This schedule gives you a margin of safety against overtraining and the resultant sickness. The total hours for this program are 3-1/4.

You can add to your hours in many different ways and include many types of workouts. If you add biking or canoeing, for instance, the hours will be different than if you roller ski or run, as these activities require about twice the time to get an equivalent workout. The choices are innumerable. One general guideline is that you can vary your methods of training more in the spring and summer, but you should gradually increase the hours and specificity in the fall. In other words, biking, running, and swimming are fine activities for the early season training, but come September most of your training should include using poles in some way.

One commonly asked question is, "How many hours do I have to train to be good?" That is easier to answer than, "How much do I have to train to be the best?" Let's try to answer the former question first. One of the saddest things I see as a high school teacher and especially a former basketball coach is the tremendous number of youngsters who aspire to become basketball stars. They spend hours practicing with the dream of playing in high school, college, and in the pros. Unfortunately, Mother Nature plays some strange tricks on these youngsters. You have to be fairly tall to play basketball; however, many tall players do not reach their growth spurt until after their freshman year in high school. In addition, only five kids make the starting team. So what has happened? Many players who never grew spent years practicing, wasting countless hours trying to develop these skills. Mother Nature's cruelest joke is on the early maturers, once the hopeful stars, who will spend the rest of their high school days wondering what happened as the late bloomers pass them by. I have seen some kids develop serious problems in trying to cope with this situation.

Fortunately, it is easier in cross-country skiing. A skier can determine if he or she has any potential by training 5 hours a week. I know. I've seen it often. I've seen some skiers make their biggest improvement when they cut their hours from 10 to 5. These skiers trained faster and were more rested. A surprising number of skiers actually train too much and, as a result, are sick at critical times of the year. This includes citizen as well as classified racers. The citizen racers have the added stress of a job, family, and home. Skiing 5 hours a week is a safe and relatively easy way to see if you have potential. If you discover you do, then you must find the answer to the more difficult question of how much to train to become the very best— but more about that later.

Finding Your Potential—the 5-Hour Program

The following is a sample program that will enable a person to discover if he or she has any real potential for this sport without spending the rest of his or her whole life trying to find out. Of course, the race results are the test of this program's effectiveness. Five workouts a week with rest days as insurance against sickness make up this schedule. The workouts are one at 1-1/2 hours, two at 1 hour, and two at 3/4 hour. The longest one will be a slow workout for endurance, the two 3/4 hour ones are tempo (race pace) or hills, and the hour workouts will be medium. These numbers are flexible and may be changed at will, but they do offer a good starting point. The hours may be 3 per week in the spring, and 6 in the fall, or 5 all year long. In fact, anything between 4-1/2 and 6 hours per week would fall into this type of program.

The important thing is that the hours spent are specific to skiing and that the intensity is adequate. Any serious competitor should read Bill Koch's article on training in the November 1981 issue of *Cross-Country Skiing*. Koch's main point was that the total number of hours trained was not as important as the way these hours were performed and their intensity. Long, slow distance may be good if you are training to avoid a heart attack, but if you want to go fast, you must at some time train fast. There should be at least 1 long, slow day of training in your week, but 5 slow days would be folly. It would be equally poor to go hard every day of the week. Many skiers train this way and find themselves run-down and worn-down by December, the time when a skier should be building both physically and mentally. (*Note:* World class athletes and many serious competitors will be in top shape by December and will only try to increase their race speed and hold a peak for the important races; however, this will not apply to the large majority of skiers. Thus a balanced training schedule is required; one that will allow you to have days for speed and fast coordination, days for long endurance, days for hills, and so on. To be physically and mentally ready for the season starting in December, your training schedule must include rest days.

When setting up a training program, the skier must realize what he or she is trying to accomplish. Skiing and running are different. If you are training to be a skier, you must spend hours specifically training to be a skier. Although they are serious about their skiing, many good runners and bikers do not perform well during the ski season. Cross-country skiing is a sport of power/endurance, emphasizing the power. This is especially true since the skate came into prominence. Most skiers realize that the endurance is important but many seem to be unaware of the power aspect. You must learn to ski with explosive movements if you want to be one of the best. It must not, however, feel that explosive to you, or you are probably using too much of your own potential strength on each stride and will tire well before the race is over.

Components of a Weekly Workout

With the use of some common sense, let's analyze the components needed in the weekly workouts. First of all, remember that you are designing it for *you, yourself,* not for anyone else. Ultimately, what you do depends on your environment and your own strengths and limitations. However, the following workout components will help you get started. (*Note:* Roller skiing itself is not included as one of the basic workout types. It could be fast, slow, medium; short, long, hilly, double pole, diagonal, skate; or easy, or hard. The roller skis themselves are only a specific tool to accomplish your training goals.)

LSD—Long Slow Distance

First, you must learn to go long, especially if you are involved in the longer races. One long, slow workout a week will suffice. Exercise physiologists claim that you can increase the distance you can go by training your body to use fat for energy in addition to carbohydrates. The following are the guidelines: The workout must be over 1-1/2 hours. It must be slow enough to allow you to burn fat. If you go too fast, you will be utilizing mainly carbohydrates. The USST training manual suggests that a pulse rate of 120 to 140 is the proper intensity, varying from skier to skier. We have some juniors whose pulses are over 190 at a slow pace, yet they are very good endurance athletes. One of these athletes' pulse rates has dropped considerably in the last year, but the performance has not increased commensurately. Use common sense, for pulse is not the final answer. An athlete who learns to internally monitor his or her physical reactions is definitely in the best position to tell how hard he or she is going.

Hills

Cross-country skiing takes place on the hills, so hill work must be included if you wish to be successful. (How to cope if there are no hills in your area will be discussed later.) If you want to be good on the hills, train on the hills. You don't want to beat yourself to death by "maxing out" on the hills every day; however, you can train on the hills every day if you internally monitor the stress and take the hills slowly on the easy days. It is best to avoid the tough hills several days a week to avoid overtraining and becoming run down. A good approach is to vary hilly with less hilly courses. I would never suggest that you avoid the hills altogether on any day, just find easier ones and/or go slower. The following two types of straight hill workouts may be included, even though most of your workouts should occur on hilly terrain.

Long Hills. Walking or striding with poles, skiing or roller skiing long hills (at least 2 to 3 minutes) should be included once a week. The intensity of these workouts should be at or a little above race pace. This means a 5, 10, or 15 k race pace, not a sprint up the hill. These are meant to be mainly aerobic, not anaerobic workouts. That is, you should not be going all out. These are workouts that will build during the season. Make an attempt through the year to increase the speed at which you walk or stride the hill. If you desire to do straight anaerobic workouts, that's fine, but this hill workout is not meant to be that.

Do not go too hard on these workouts too early in the season, for this will be impossible to keep up. These workouts become too brutal for the mind and result in skiers backing off and quitting them altogether. In fact, if this workout at race pace gets to be too brutal and you hate to face the hill, do it only once every 2 weeks. This is especially true if you have hills in your other workouts (see Figure 10.1).

Figure 10.1 Making the wax work on a fun type training session in late spring.

Many of our athletes claim that this workout is the most beneficial because it has made them better on the hills. When they are on a tough, never-ending hill during a race, the memory of the hill workout keeps them going. They know how to judge the pace and know that when they reach the top, something will be left. For this reason, this workout should not be an all-out effort, for if it were, its training effect on the mind would be lost.

Short Hills. The second type of hill workout is the short, explosive one. This one usually follows the regular hill workout. The duration of these shorter hills is 40 seconds or less. This is not a tough workout for your system because the time spent is too short to build up much lactic acid. If you only have short hills, they would be an ideal second workout for the day. Their main purpose is to build up explosive power—more of a weight workout for the legs and arms. Again, poles are used for this workout. Each stride is done explosively and even bounding is acceptable. On snow, bounding is usually a waste of effort because of unnecessary jumping in the air. But here we are looking for an explosive use of the muscles. Double poling and skating some of the intervals is recommended.

A Fast Workout

A skier's goal is to go fast; therefore, he or she must train to go fast. The skier must include a fast workout once or twice a week. Experts used to say that you should avoid fast workouts in the summer because you might peak too early. The experience of many athletes has shown this idea to be false. You must not only train the muscles to go fast, but you must train the mind to endure the discomfort of going fast. You must overcome the fear of going fast and soon you will be going faster than ever. Fast skiing is a necessary ingredient to a successful program. But fast skiing is like weight lifting. Your real improvement takes place on the easier or rest days when the muscles rest and recover. To ski fast on the fast days, you must be fairly rested.

One and maybe two fast workouts should be included every week. These workouts should last for 15 to 90 minutes depending on the race for which you are training and the time of the season. Early in the year, this workout may be done only once every 2 weeks; later in the year, twice per week if desired. One workout can be short and the other can be longer. These workouts teach you to race faster, so there should be an attempt to increase the speed during the year. Steve Gaskill has written much about pace training where he has put real numbers on the training times that his athletes are trying to accomplish. This has the added benefit of giving the athlete short-term goals, and they can easily monitor their improvement. Gaskill's method, briefly described, is as follows. You can refer to his articles and booklets for further information.

The athlete measures a loop or out-and-back course, preferably about 1 kilometer. He or she then skis the lap several times as fast as if in a training or unimportant race, keeping track of the lap times. From there the skier tries to improve 1 second per kilometer per week for the season. Steve's athletes have had much success with this training method. We had trouble in our only attempt because of the way roller skis vary in speed due to the weather and the wear on the tires and bearings, but will attempt it again, trying to measure the speed of the ski and making adjustments. Pace training was successful for us until the fall when our skis became much slower due to the cold weather. We will try a lighter lubricant this year to see if the skis can retain their summer speed.

One other type of fast workout must be mentioned. Once called technique workouts, the USST now calls them 200-meter pace workouts. At a distance of 200 meters or less, a racer can go quite fast but will not have gone long enough to build up much lactic acid. (Our skiers have found 80 to 100 meters to be right for them—not too taxing.) These short technique intervals are good for learning to ski faster in a coordinated manner. Many skiers start to thrash when they try to ski fast. One of the goals of these workouts is to learn to increase speed but maintain coordination. The other goal is to improve your technique by skiing in a short stretch, making it easy for you to concentrate on what you are working. The correct terrain can be selected depending on the stroke used.

These intervals can be interspersed in the medium workout or added on at the end of a medium day, winding down with 15 minutes or so of speed technique work. At this time, skiers can observe each other without ruining the continuity of the workout. In the spring or summer, we may spend an entire hour workout doing technique intervals, which amounts to an easy workout and is good at this time of the year. It's nice to get the technique out of the way early so that the fall and winter may be used mainly for conditioning; however, you should always pay attention to technique during the entire season. I have seen world champion skiers who have varied their technique tremendously during different time periods and not always in a positive manner. If the best can slip, so can anyone. So get checked out occasionally. Poor technique hampers speed because it's inefficient.

Medium-Paced Workouts

The in-between, medium workouts are aerobic workouts, somewhere between the long, slow ones and the fast ones. They are definitely slower than racing speeds but may vary considerably in pace from day to day. If you feel stronger, they will be faster. If you feel a little tired, they will be slower. Avoid going too fast on these buildup days. They can be active rest days or they can be just a little below the fast days. But they must be slow enough that you feel refreshed when you are through and are rested by the next day. The USST manual suggests a pulse rate between 140 and 180 for this type of workout.

Perhaps the best way to judge the intensity of your workout while you are doing it is the old talk test. If you can talk easily and do not notice your breathing, it is a slow workout. If you have considerable trouble talking, it is a fast workout. If you can hear your breathing but you can still talk, it is medium. There are times, on long hills, when you will breath a little harder on a medium workout, but you should definitely be below race pace. Again, there are all sorts of varieties of medium workouts. These will be straight aerobic workouts staying below the anaerobic threshold, the bread and butter workouts for the heart and lungs, as well as specificity training for the muscles. They can vary in intensity from low to high aerobic. On the days you feel a little down, they can be near the long, slow workouts in intensity. On other days, they may be closer to the speed or hill days. They will be the workouts that compromise most of the week between the long, slow workout and the more intense ones.

Designing Your Weekly Training Program

Exercise physiologists, coaches, and athletes do not agree among themselves as to which workouts achieve which results. I have seen high oxygen uptake improvements credited mainly to medium distance, race pace work, 2- to 3-minute aerobic intervals, and anaerobic intervals. The conclusions are confusing. But if a skier remembers to work all the systems needed in a ski race, he or she cannot go far astray. (I myself believe the most productive workouts are those in the medium plus range, just below race pace but above middle aerobic. They are around the anaerobic threshold. Our athletes get one of these in each week. We feel they are more taxing physically than the hill intervals or tempo workouts.)

How do you set up your weekly program to avoid most pitfalls? First, decide on how many hours you can or are willing to handle. Then slot in your long workout, your pace workout, and your hill workout, spacing these so they are not back to back. Then slot in your medium workouts until you have the needed hours. The critical question is, how much? I have already answered how much you need to find out if you have any ability (about 5 to 6 hours), and how much you need to be pretty good, such as a top junior (about 8 hours). But if you are striving to be as good as you can be, that may be a different story. Bill Koch claims that he only trains 8-1/2 to 10-1/2 hours per week.

Some international competitors train 15 to 20+ hours per week. How much for you? Marty Hall says you find your limits by overtraining.

How can you tell if you are overtraining? Many symptoms can measure your physical state. These signs relate to stress on the body and range from scientific studies such as urine tests to noticing whether or not you have a cold. Some foreign teams prick the ears of their athletes and test their blood on interval days to see when they've had enough work.

Fortunately, the best symptoms of overtraining are also the easiest to recognize. The first and most important symptom is how you feel. If you are always tired and run down, then you are training too much, not getting the proper nutrition, or sleeping too little. Do a self-analysis and take the proper measures. Sleep is extremely important to an athlete. If you are getting enough sleep and you are still tired and run down, cut back on the training or take a rest day.

Resting pulse is another way to measure whether or not you are training too much. If the resting pulse is up over 5 or 6 above normal, and the sleep has not been good, take a rest day. If you continue to be run down with an elevated pulse, cut back on the training. If the situation is extreme, think about seeing a doctor. It may be mononucleosis, which is devastating. It took me over a year to recover from its effects when I was in college. If all seems OK, yet you are still rundown, take a closer look at your diet.

This brings up the question of when to take a rest day. (*Note:* To some athletes a rest day can be an easy or even medium workout.) Some schedule a certain day for rest and do not deviate from it. Others never take rest days until they are forced to by travel, scheduling, or illness. I believe you should take at least one rest day a week. If you are like most cross-country skiers I know, the trouble is usually too much rather than too little, so play it by ear. Take the rest day when you feel you need it. But if you have gone 6 days without a rest day, take one whether or not you feel you need it. If you monitor your internal feelings, you will soon have a good handle on when to rest and when to go hard.

This brings us to the ultimate type of trainer. Bill Koch relayed his training philosophy to me after winning the World Cup. He trained no more than 10-1/2 hours per week; he always kept in mind why he was training—to go fast in the winter; he made his hours count by training hard; and he really "tore one on" whenever he felt like it during a workout. Bill said he was always aware of his own body and what he was trying to do and where he was at.

Most people need a little more structure than that, so two suggested weekly schedules are included. One is for an 8 to 9 hour week, and the next is for a week of over 10 hours. The rest days are taken when needed. This schedule is for fall. The intensity of each workout would depend on the time of fall and the condition of the racer.

Table 10.1 8 to 9 Hour Training Program

Day 1	Day 2	Day 3	Day 4	Day 5	Day 6	Day 7
2-3 hr LSD	1 hr medium	1 hr fast	1.5 hr medium	1 hr hills	1 hr medium	rest

Table 10.2 Over 10-Hour Training Program

	Day 1	Day 2	Day 3	Day 4	Day 5	Day 6	Day 7
A.M.		3/4 hr medium		3/4 hr medium		3/4 hr medium	rest
P.M.	2-3 hr LSD	1 hr medium	1 hr fast	1.5 hr medium	1.5 hr hills	1 hr medium	

To increase the hours, second workouts may be added. For example, three times a week the skier can take medium workouts of about 3/4 hour, thereby getting his or her total up to over 11 hours a week and still keep some quality in the workouts.

The above program should again consist of mainly roller skiing, running or walking with poles, and possi-

bly rowing with a movable seat. In the spring and
early summer, the amount of this specific work will be
less but will gradually increase into the fall. The hours
should have reached their dryland peak. At this time
you should be thinking about the racing season. Every
workout should achieve some specific purpose.

In October, there are several options from which to
choose. Some say to increase both the hours and intensity, but I disagree. If you do a good job of increasing the intensity, increasing the hours at the same
time is hard to do. Instead, I recommend a slight de-
creasing of the hours while adding a hard workout,
whether it be a hill, tempo, or long interval (3 to 5
min) workout. You are really bearing down at this
time, trying to increase the speed at which you will
race. You are not going all out but are always trying to
go a little faster, knowing there is still a little left.
Sometimes you may even go all out, but this is not the
rule.

When the snow arrives, things start to change.
This is the critical time of the year for skiers in our
area. It is hard to train when it is cold, rainy, icy or
when there is too little snow on the ground to ski, too
much salt, snow, or ice on the roads to roller ski, and
too slippery a surface on the shoulders of the roads
and on the trails to run. One note, however, is that it
is possible to train on those days. Each skier must
make individual adjustments according to the environment.

Some alternative ways in which skiers from our
area are forced to train during this changing weather
that may also help you are as follows:

- *Pool workouts.* You can swim, imitate the diagonal
  in the deep end (wearing a vest), or ski walk in the
  shallow water. Sometimes injuries and hot weather
  indicate this type of workout.
- *Stationary bicycles, indoor rowing machines, and
  jogging trampolines.*
- *Circuit weight training.* By moving from station to
  station as quickly as possible, you can actually get
  a cardiovascular as well as a strength workout.
  Sebastian Coe trained this way during the winter
  before he started breaking all of his running
  records. An Exergenie and roller board could be

worked in here. If you live in an area with few hills, emphasize 1/2 squats for 20 to 40 repetitions.

- *Rope jumping and aerobic dance.* Music and weightlifting are a good combination, especially with the Exergenie.
- *Alternating stair running with the roller board.* First, run or ski walk up and down a flight of stairs for about 5 to 10 minutes. Next, hit the roller board for about 2 to 5 minutes; then go back to the stairs. Keep this up until you complete the workout. It would be boring to do on a daily basis, but it is a big help on occasion. This routine is a good substitute for training on hills.
- *Ski walking up the downhill slopes not covered by artificial snow.* This is one of the best, if not the best, activities at this time.
- *Ski walking up downhill slopes covered with artificial snow.* Then take your skis and ski stride or skate up the hills on the less steep parts. This can be done either anaerobically or aerobically, depending on your intensity.
- *Roller skiing.* Roller ski whenever possible if the roads are not too icy, salty, or wet. The general rule is, roller ski on the days you can, for there will be plenty of the other days. You can fit in the other alternatives when forced to do so.
- *Ice skating.* This is an especially excellent training method true with the advent of skating. Poles may be used in this activity.
- *Utilizing the snow on weekends.* The last several years have been so bad in our area that most of my life seems to have been spent in the van, shuttling between home and the North woods. However, our skiers have improved tremendously during this period of no snow.

Dave Schimp, for example, was a beginner in the spring of 1982. He had skied some with his family, but was not proficient at the time. He had just started to think about racing when the season ended. His accomplishments in the off-season were inspiring.

Dave bought some roller skis and started working out. On one of the first times out on the roller skis, he made a mistake by trying to keep up with the best skiers in the area. The experience was so discouraging that Dave considered quitting immediately. However, he endured and the technique changes he made during the summer were astounding. By fall he was skiing virtually without a flaw. His progress is recorded on videotape, which is enjoyable to watch every so often.

When winter came—no snow. Nevertheless, Dave did well at the Gitchi Gami Games and moved up on some of the better juniors—this with no snow experience and virtually all of his experience on roller skis. After the Gitchis, when other skiers were able to get up North, Dave had to remain in town. He improvised by skiing on the downhill slopes where there was artificial snow, by roller skiing, by hill running with poles, and by ice skating on a backyard pond. On many days he did all of these workouts. By January Dave had improved so much that he won two large citizens' races in northern Wisconsin. Finally, he made Junior Olympics in a year when the central division was deepest in junior-one boys. He did well at the Junior Olympics, placing in the top third: Imagine, all of this from a boy who couldn't ski the year before, who had no snow to train on until the second week of February, who had to learn on roller skis, and whose background was mainly weightlifting, not an endurance activity. Moral? If you want to be good and the conditions are not perfect, improvise! You can achieve more than you thought possible.

The main problem of training in the transitional season was compounded in Wisconsin several years ago when the state legislature dropped daylight savings time for the winter. What is even worse is that we are in the eastern part of the time zone. The resulting problem is lack of daylight. This does not affect running and ski walking up hills, but running in the woods and roller skiing are out. There are enough legal problems trying to roller ski during daylight without compounding the problem by roller skiing at night.

Fortunately, we usually have snow in the upper areas of our state, so the weekends are our salvation. Six hours of training are not uncommon or unreasonable on these weekends. Then, of course, the rest of the week's training must be adjusted. Friday usually becomes a rest/travel day and Monday a light or rest day. This varies from athlete to athlete, but it is the healthiest approach. If you are in good shape at this time, it is silly to jeopardize your gains by trying to squeeze in an extra day of hard training. Tuesday and Thursday now become the hard/fast/hills days, and Wednesday becomes the long day of the week.

Some fast skiing must be done on the weekends because the early races are important to our juniors. This is not necessarily bad. Our skiers do not have any noticeable difficulty adjusting to snow after roller skiing and vice versa. It works to our advantage in the long run. Going back and forth between snow and roller skis allows a skier to adjust his roller ski technique so it is more like his snow technique. In a year, much more time is spent on dry land than snow. These dry land months spent on the roller skis then become more productive when the roller ski technique is correct. Thus, there can be advantages in a supposedly poor situation.

Training During the Racing Season

If you have been increasing your intensity through November, you probably will be ready for the racing season. But, perhaps not. There are basically two types of serious racers. The first has trained systematically and is in the best shape possible at the beginning of the season. This skier only has to ski, keep doing what he or she is doing, and gradually ski faster during the season, using his or her basic program as well as races to become as good as he or she can be. It is a matter of shaping and adding a little to what he or she already has. The physical gains will not be that great, but the speed will increase because of racing and speed workouts. This skier will benefit more from rest as he or she hones down his or her skiing. Unfortunately, very few racers fit into this category.

Most skiers enter the season in less than ideal shape. They must increase their hours and try to ski into shape. They need work rather than rest and must use the races as the vehicle to get into the best shape possible. This skier is looking for long races that will provide a good workout, whereas the other skier might prefer the shorter races to learn to go fast. I have seen skiers have much success using both methods at the citizen level. Beth Schluter, one of our coaches who was a two-event world master's champion in 1983, sort of skis herself into shape each year. However, although she does not roller ski or run with poles, Beth has a good base from canoeing (she and her husband, Errol, are past national marathon canoe champions), biking, and a little running in the off-season.

Most serious skiers are usually a mixture of the two types. They are probably in very good shape but need a little more work to get the physical base that they would like to have. The following is a program that can be adjusted to individual needs but that can be used once the racing season is here.

Table 10.3 Race Season Training Program

SUN	MON	TUE	WED	THUR	FRI	SAT
race 1-2	rest	long 2-3	tempo 1	medium 1-1 1/2	rest	race 1-2

Let's assume that the skier will be racing twice on the weekend and once during the week, on Wednesday in this case. If you are not racing, a hard workout over hilly terrain or a time trial (pace workout) can be substantiated. If you only race on Sunday, Saturday can be easy or whatever if the Sunday race is unimportant. If the only race on the weekend is on Saturday, then Sunday can be a long day. Also, you can do an easy distance workout immediately after the race.

So a winter schedule has Saturday, Sunday, and Wednesday filled. Friday will be a travel or light day with the same for Monday. Tuesday then becomes the long workout of the week, which is needed to maintain an endurance base. This can be a medium or slow workout depending on how you feel and what the rest of the week will be like. This workout should be 2 to 3 hours long. Thursday then becomes a medium or slow workout of about 1-1/2 hours. (These hours will vary according to the individual.)

The basic winter schedule is depicted in Table 10.3. Each week will be different, depending on the races, your snow condition, and how you feel.

It is important to realize that these are the crucial weeks of the season. Do not be afraid to take a rest day if you feel down or a cold coming on because failure to do so can ruin the entire year. I know a number of skiers who became slaves to their schedule and lost their winter skiing due to illness. When you feel illness coming on, take large dosages of vitamin C and get plenty of rest. An afternoon nap can often salvage lack of sleep and can cure the onset of illness. Don't be afraid to take a nap and train later, using an alternate workout.

One thing that a skier must be able to do is analyze his or her own weaknesses. If you are short on endurance and your races are long, then some added long workouts are in order. If you are weak on the hills, emphasize the hills. If you are weak on technique, add a workout where you do technique intervals. Concentrate entirely on form for short stretches that do not tire you enough to inhibit your movements.

Weight Lifting

If you feel you are not physically strong, try weight lifting. I firmly believe that weight lifting is important for most skiers, especially for juniors. It seems to me that skiing is behind the times in its attitude toward this type of strength training. Almost every other sport extensively utilizes some form of weight training. It is no accident that the modern athlete is bigger and stronger, and the increase is so great that it cannot be attributed solely to diet.

Exercise physiologists have claimed that in order for a muscle to benefit from weight training, the exercise must be executed, at least, the speed of the movement needed in sport. Physiologists have based this on controlled studies of groups that have worked out for short periods of time. But simple observations of participating athletes have shown that weight lifting, even when done at a much slower rate than the motion of the sport, is still very beneficial.

An example is baseball, a sport requiring perhaps the quickest reaction time and speed of movement of any sport. For years, weights were thought to slow one down, therefore, baseball players avoided them. Today's baseball player makes the ballplayer of the past look like the guy who got sand kicked in his face. There are many examples of "singles" hitters who miraculously became homerun hitters after a winter of working out at Nautilus, for example, Robin Yount, the league MVP of the Milwaukee Brewers. Lifting weights at a slower speed than swinging a bat has not seemed to stop him from developing power as a hitter.

Similarly, one only has to look at the average top sprinter. These guys are bench pressing over 300 pounds, and it has not seemed to hurt their ability to develop explosive power. Sebastian Coe made his biggest gains during the winter when he weight lifted aerobically (circuit training) for a large part of his training. Football and swimming are more obvious examples of sports that profit from weight training programs.

It has always seemed to be a matter of common sense that if a skier is stronger, he or she will have to use a lesser percentage of his or her strength in each stride or double pole. He or she will be able to go faster because he or she is more muscularly efficient, tiring more slowly than his or her weaker counterpart of the same genetic background. So if you want to be faster, strength is one of the keys and weight lifting is the quickest way to get it.

For many skiers weight lifting may be just what they need to make their program a success; however, this may not be the case for everyone. Some natural mesomorphs, or mature athletes, may not need this type of training. Only a few, however, would not benefit from supplementary weight training.

The first thing to realize when entering a weight program is that you will be doing other types of training many hours during the week, and the weights should not cut into this time. Second, your goals are different than a power lifter's or body builder's. Third, you will be fairly exhausted from your other workouts. The result is that two times a week is all you will need to build up your strength, and these sessions do not need to be marathons; 20 to 30 minutes is enough. Some weeks need only have one workout if you are particularly run down. I have seen many athletes gain on such a program when three or four times a week brought no gains. The muscles need rest to grow stronger.

You will be getting plenty of endurance strength in your other workouts if you train specifically. This is like light weight workouts for the whole week. The result is twofold. If you try to weight lift three or four times a week, you will not gain but only get discouraged and quit. The other thing that follows from this is that you are already getting the endurance, high-repetition workouts. The gym should be used for pure strength. This means the repetitions should be kept under 20 with the emphasis placed on increasing the weight or number of repetitions each time. A basic program of 8 to 12 exercises should be followed with special emphasis placed on the muscles used during skiing: The lats (upper back), triceps, thighs, stomach and gluteals. If you want to prove to yourself which muscles are needed for cross-country, just notice which ones get sore when you first start skiing. The ones which are used the most will do the most complaining the next morning. One of the surprises I had was the realization that the gluteus maximus plays such an important part in good skiing, especially if you go up the hills properly.

In addition to weight lifting, weight control is also an important concept. Each skier will have to analyze him- or herself. Some should lose weight, some should gain. If you are weak and thin, then weight lifting and more food is the answer. If you are too heavy, weight lifting and less food is the answer. Why is weight lifting part of both answers? Obviously, in gaining weight you want to put on muscle, not fat. But in losing weight, one of the biggest problems is getting weaker and losing muscle as well as fat. Cross-country skiers need to be strong. By weight lifting and proper dieting, you can lose weight and become stronger. Last year one of our skiers went from 215 to 185 pounds and got stronger each time in the gym. I might have been skeptical if I had not witnessed it myself.

How you eat to lose weight is very important. *Do not go on one of the fad diets. Do not only eat protein and drink water. You need carbohydrates to supply energy for training.* In addition, muscle mass is lost when you go on a high-protein diet for any period without eating carbohydrates. Eat balanced meals, just smaller portions. Changing eating habits is the key. Training during a snack time is a good way to lose weight. By weight lifting while you lose, you can tell if the lost weight starts to take away your strength. This is the best way I know to find your ideal weight. It is the lightest weight at which you can maintain your strength as measured by your poundages in the gym.

Studies have shown that excess weight is definitely a hindrance, especially on the hills. If you are weak on the hills, perhaps this extra weight is one of your problems. Whatever the case, self-analysis is the key to good training. Note where you are weak and work to correct it. The preceding material gives you a framework from which to start. Each person is different, lives in a different environment, and has a different set of potentials. Blindly following a program is not the answer for you. If you want to be the best you can be, you must develop an internal awareness and adapt your training to meet your needs.

If you are interested in an in-depth analysis of how to train and the physiological reasons behind such training, read Brian Sharkey's (1984) *Training for Cross-Country Ski Racing.* It's the best and most practical physiological presentation of training that all serious competitors should read. I also strongly recommend Marty Hall's (1981) *One Stride Ahead* and Steve Gaskill's USST publications for exposure to training ideas. But remember, you are the final judge.

Weight Lifting Programs

The ideal progressive resistance program in my opinion is the Nautilus system. If you are interested in the complete rationale behind these machines, see the literature published by Nautilus. From my weight lifting experience of well over 20 years, I feel most of what Nautilus says is true. I have lifted free weights and Nautilus equipment. There are some weaknesses in the Nautilus system that might be significant if you were a body builder or a competitive weight lifter. However, the convenience, the lack of soreness after a workout, the ability to develop strength in a short time with short workouts, and the way the various muscle groups are isolated make this an ideal training technique. The cross-country skier's main upper body muscle groups are the lats, and the Nautilus system, especially the torso pullover, really works these muscles. In addition, the legs can be effectively worked with less of a chance of back injury in comparison to free weights.

To do a Nautilus routine, simply work through their entire system, following their instructions. Anyone with access to these machines will also have the workout schedules, so I will not include them here. However, keep your workouts to twice a week, or once if you're particularly tired that week. Your normal cross-country training is like an endurance weight workout, so don't feel guilty.

If you do not have access to Nautilus, weights can accomplish the same thing but with less convenience and slightly more time. The following is a program that develops overall strength by working all of the major muscle groups. Start with a weight that can be lifted comfortably 8 times. Try to increase your repetitions (reps) each workout. When you can make 12 reps without cheating, increase the weight by 5 pounds. For the legs and roller board, the reps may be greater. If you desire, you may make these reps almost anything you desire within reason, that is, 30 to 40 reps. I really don't believe that reps over 12 build the kind of endurance we are talking about for skiing. In comparison to the number of reps a skier uses in a 50 k race, 30 reps are much closer to the strength factor than to the endurance factor. Maybe not to a weight lifter or football player, but to a skier the frame of reference is much different. So if your weight set does not include huge poundages, go for more reps. It'll still be a strength workout and your endurance will be from your aerobic workouts. In Figures 10.2a-e you can see some weight lifting exercises.

Figure 10.2(a)   Squat to parallel.

Figure 10.2(b)   Bench press.

Figure 10.2(c) Curl.

Figure 10.2(d) Military press.

1. Warm-up. Clean and press a medium weight about 10 times.
2. Squats to toe rise—1/4 to 1/2, not deeper. Start with 20 reps and work up to 40. You do not have to really grunt out the weight on this one. It's tough enough on its own. Guard against back and knee injuries by keeping your back straight and head up, not going lower than thighs parallel to the floor. This workout is especially important if you do not have many hills in your regular workouts.
3. Chins, pulldowns, or roller board. These all work the muscles needed for skiing. In fact, both chins and roller board should be included in the same

Figure 10.2(e) High pull.

Figure 10.2 Some weight lifting exercises.

workout. On the roller board, I suggest raising the
incline or adding weight to your body once 20
reps are attained. If you want to, at the end of
your workout, you could add a couple of sets of 40
or more on the roller board or pull the Exergenie
for 2 to 3 minutes, et cetera. (See the Special
Roller Board Workout.)

4. Bench press. This develops the chest, deltoids,
   and triceps. This is important to balance the back
   development predominant in cross-country skiing.
5. Strict curl for the biceps.
6. Military press for the shoulders and arms.
7. High pulls (upright rowing) for the deltoids. (*Note:*
   Avoid horizontal rows as there are better ways to
   develop the lats without endangering the back.
   I've seen many back injuries from this one.)
8. Incline situps or hanging leg ups or both.
9. Any favorites you may have.

The Miniworkout With Little Equipment

The following is an excellent way to maintain and
to develop muscular development in a short period of
time with little equipment. They are "compound"
exercises that work several muscle groups at once.

1. Chin-ups. A couple of sets. (Roller board may be
   substituted if you have it.)

2. Dips. May be done between two bars or tables or whatever. If you are strong enough, handstand push-ups may be added. If you are weaker, dips between chairs alternated with push-ups may be added.

3. Half squats. Bicycling while standing up or intensive hill bounding up a steep hill for 30 seconds may be substituted.

The Special Roller Board Workout

A roller board workout can be as effective as a workout on Nautilus. The roller board workout is demonstrated in Figures 10.3a-c.

Figure 10.3(a)   Normal halfway point in roller board pull.

Figure 10.3(b)   Normal finishing point of roller board pull. Do till exhaustion.

Figure 10.3(c) Finishing point of second half of exhaustive roller board workout. Do till exhaustion.

Figure 10.3 Effective roller board workout.

1. Set the height of the board so that 10 to 15 reps are possible. Add weight if the board will not go high enough. Go to exhaustion in normal roller board workout while lying on your stomach.
2. Immediately, with no rest, continue working the lats to exhaustion by pulling yourself up the incline by using your lats only. The elbow should end at your side but the arm remains bent. Do one to three sets.

In normal roller board exercise, the workout is finished when the arms (triceps) give out. The lats still have not been worked to exhaustion. However, the above will allow you to isolate these important skiing muscles and will make sure they get their maximum development.

Equipment Selection   *11*

You Don't Run Marathons in Hunting Boots

Before running out and buying equipment, the beginning skier should define his or her goals. The choice of skis and overall gear depends on the type of skiing you will be doing. In other words, you don't go running in hip boots and you don't go snowshoe rabbit hunting in racing flats. The equipment must match the goals. Unfortunately, every ski shop goes through a similar routine with each new customer, but the result is often the wrong or inferior equipment.

What I am going to present is a highly opinionated way to purchase your first equipment. First of all, I am assuming you are into skiing for the fitness, and most or all of your skiing will be done on groomed or at least skied-in trails. If you're into mountaineering or backpacking, your goals will be very different and you should see a specialty shop. The percentage of readers who will fit into this category is probably small. There are some skiers in our area who do ski with heavy equipment with the idea that they may be going off trail in the mountains, but they never seem to do so. The result is that they're doing the equivalent of running in hunting boots. So I'm assuming that most of your skiing will be done on trails and that you will want equipment to make your experience an enjoyable one. That means that your skis will be lightweight and easily maneuverable. The first two criteria for buying equipment are lightness and comfort.

Waxable and Waxless Skis

Unfortunately, the beginning skier doesn't know what he or she wants to do and then doesn't know what equipment will do it. Waxable versus waxless is the first decision. Waxless skis usually are nothing more than skis with permanent brakes. This may change with new developments. But for now, the waxless ski does not perform nearly as well in all conditions as the waxable ones. If it did, the best racers in the world would be using them. So, some guy won a world championship medal with his waxless skis, but how many other races did he use them in? There are tons of races each year, yet only once or twice in the last decade did a racer do well on commercial waxless skis at a world class level. It is interesting to note that the best results have come from the USST contingency of Koch, Galanes, and Simoneau, who have created their own version of a waxless base by roughing the base of a waxable ski. Waxless skis still remain the last resort when no wax seems to work at those difficult times around the freezing point. Waxless skis may be the way to go if you are buying for a large family with young skiers and if you have to do most of the waxing. Still, you'd be much better off in the long run by teaching the kids how to wax their own skis.

Choosing the Proper Type of Ski

Now that you've decided on waxable, how do you pick the proper ski? The usual question asked is, Are you a beginner or an intermediate? If you are either one, the ski shop will usually set you up with the all-around compromise package: The good old touring one. Forget that. The average touring ski is way too heavy. In fact, the very skier who gets this package is the one who can least handle it. The beginning jogger does not buy heavy jogging shoes, so why should the beginning skier do the same? The regular touring ski is a wider ski (lighter, wider skis are available) and is more durable, but unless you intend to jump streams

and ford creeks in the wilderness, the light touring ski
is fine. Modern fiberglass skis are fairly durable, even
the racing skis, so a skier does not have to keep that
as a priority anymore but can rather concentrate on
performance.

Light touring or racing skis are the two choices.
Light touring skis are skis which have the same width
as touring skis but are made out of lighter materials.
These skis will do anything a touring ski will do except they are lighter and easier to handle. Their wide-
ness is supposedly an advantage to balance; however,
it is only slightly easier to balance on these skis than it
is on racing skis, which are a little narrower. Most intermediates and beginners do not notice much difference between keeping their balance on light touring or
racing skis.

The other advantage, supposedly, of touring skis is
that they are better in untracked snow and off-trails.
This may be true in the mountains, but it sure isn't
true in the Midwest where there are basically two
types of untracked snow: skiable and unskiable. If it is
skiable, the snow is not too deep, as in spring when the
snow has been compressed or when there is a layer of ice
several inches under the snow. This happens when
rain is followed by snow. The rain covers the old snow
with a layer of ice and makes an excellent base. This
type of snow can take the skier's weight, stopping him
or her from sinking too deep. These are the only times
that off-trail skiing is enjoyable.

Deep, soft snow is unskiable because you can sink
down so deep that you might as well be hiking or be
on snowshoes. Most of the time, off-trail skiing is just
not that enjoyable unless you're into the backpacking
type experience; and when off-trail skiing is enjoyable,
the snow is such that racing skis do as good a job as
touring skis. In order for the touring skis to be effective in deep snow, they'd have to be about twice as
wide as they are.

So to my way of thinking, racing skis are the best
way to go for an athletic beginner. Ask yourself, Am I
in it for fitness? Am I athletic at all? If the answer is
yes to either, your first pair of skis should be a low-
level racing ski but, at the worst, a light touring ski.
This type of ski selection will just make skiing more
fun.

One of the women in our area whose husband did some racing forced her into getting in an entry level racing ski during their second year of skiing. In addition, she was coerced into purchasing some racing type boots to replace her three-pin 75 mm norm. She was embarrassed because the skis said racing and she wasn't a racer but only a beginner, and the light touring skis she had were good enough. After one day on the new equipment, she has never used the old light touring skis again. These were *light* touring skis. Think of the difference she would have noticed if they were a heavier model. With her new racing skis, she claims skiing is much more fun and it is easier to turn because of the ski's lightness and the better boot and binding system. For turning on trails, lightness far outweighs any sidecut considerations. This woman weighs about 110 pounds so she really notices any heavy equipment.

I get a kick out of racing husbands who have the lightest and most responsive gear while their wives have the heavy touring models and a boot and binding system that offers little control. The chances of their wives enjoying themselves as much or even getting interested in citizen racing is rather slim because of the equipment differences. Husbands, give your wives a break. Get them light equipment with good boot and binding systems. Give them a chance to feel what it is like to move across the landscape with ease.

Before I alienate every ski shop owner, there are many that do an excellent job of fitting and selecting skis for their customers. This is especially true today as the boot and binding systems have improved, and the beginner does not automatically get the three-pin system, 75 mm norm. However, I do not believe that a shop would ordinarily fit an athletic beginner immediately into racing equipment. The idea of a return customer who will need an upgraded set of equipment the following season probably plays a small part, but I'm sure the main reason is their genuine belief that what they are saying is correct. In other words, their philosophy is different than mine.

If you are still undecided or confused, the only answer is to try different skis. Many shops have demo days when you can try out the equipment. See for yourself whether or not a skinnier ski is too hard for you to handle. Don't rely on an expert. Even the experts don't agree among themselves.

I was lucky enough to rent skis the first time out and be part of a group on several different types of skis. We switched skis several times, and it made my first selection much easier. I realized the importance of a light and fast pair of skis. Although I didn't go all the way to racing skis, the light touring skis I bought still perform almost as well as my racing skis. They are very functional, just a little heavy. Of course, if I had to do it all over again, the choice would be racing skis.

Once you have decided on the type of ski you need there are still many other variables to consider. How do you find the ski that is right for you?—one that is fast yet easily climbs the hills; one whose wax won't wear off after a short time. Many of the salesmen are getting very good at this aspect, but they are still in the business of selling skis. If a shop doesn't have just the right ski for you, most will sell you the next best option. Only an exceptional few will send you to another store. Never fear, what I am about to describe is a way to select skis that will take you out of the clutches of the salesman.

Criteria for Selecting Skis to Fit You

Much of the material here has been derived from observation and from fitting various skis for skiers of differing abilities. A large portion of our starting assumptions were borrowed from Marty Hall. In fact, I think Marty opened the door for the average individual in ski selection. Until he wrote about it, only a select few knew this process, so many of our criteria are actually his ideas. It only makes sense that in choosing skis, who would have the most knowledge?—a national team coach who earns his living by producing fast skiers. Who gets the first selection of skis?—the average citizen racer? No way. It's the elite skier. So if you want to talk about fast and good skis, no one is better qualified than someone like Marty. In fact, both Marty and Steve Gaskill have been very helpful—maybe patient is a better word—with all of our questions.

However, one area where Marty and Steve have not had much experience is in fitting the average skier or citizen racer. These skiers are obviously not as fast, may not kick as strong, and may run out of gas in the middle of a race. These are some of the types of skiers with whom we deal on a regular basis. Getting to know these skiers, as well as some very good ones, has given us a base of information. These skiers just don't buy a pair of skis and disappear as they do from a ski shop. By skiing with these skiers, we learn their strengths and weaknesses well. If a ski doesn't fit, it becomes obvious. The skis can be slow or fast. The skiers may have trouble getting up the hills. By trial and error, we have established some solid criteria, enabling a skier to select an appropriate pair of skis.

Weight of the Skier

What are the criteria for choosing skis? Contrary to popular belief, ski selection is not directly related to the height of the skier. It is more related to weight. You can see for yourself that skis don't vary that much in height if you line up a pair of 200, 205, and 210 centimeter skis. In some cases, one manufacturer's 205 may be the same length as another's 200.

For instance, I am 6′4″ and used to ski on 220s. Downhills are not my strength, and I am very glad that I have made the switch to shorter skis. They give me more maneuverability on the turns and are easier to skate with, not to mention the lightness, which translates into quicker feet. It makes a long day in hilly terrain less tiring, so skiing becomes more enjoyable. What's more, my shorter skis are actually faster than the old 220s. If you are in doubt between two sizes, choose the shorter one. The old test of holding your hand above your head to see where the ski comes to your wrist is not a good way to select a ski. As you will see later, the *camber* (stiffness) of the ski is much more important. A general guideline has been that the average-sized skier takes a 210, but with the advent of skating, that has dropped to 200 or 205. I know some racers who have several different length skis in their bag. Contrary to popular belief, a long ski is not necessarily faster than a short ski, especially when used on a hard track. It is more stable fore and aft at high speeds, however, and, all things being equal, is faster in soft snow where the smaller ski would tend to sink. But on normal hard tracks of well-groomed trails, the amount of friction with the snow is the same.

Camber

Camber is the property of a ski that keeps the midsection, or kick area, off the snow while gliding. This property of a ski allows the skier to wax the middle of his or her skis so they do not slip when a downward force is applied, yet allows the wax to ride free when the skier is gliding. A properly fitted ski will have a good kick, allow the kick wax to contact the ground effectively, yet have fast glide, part of which is keeping the wax off the snow as much as possible.

There are two ways in which a skier can "weight" the skis while gliding. The body weight will be either equally distributed between the two skis (as on downhills or while double poling) or entirely on one ski (as in skating or diagonaling). Thus, there will be two waxing pockets on a ski: The longer one, which will be off the snow when the skis are equally weighted, and a shorter one when all the weight is on one ski. These are the two critical determinants of performance when choosing the proper stiffness of camber. Therefore there are two wax pockets to measure when choosing a ski.

The Poundage Meter and Paper Test

A skier can select his or her skis rather accurately by two methods: The first is the poundage meter, found in most ski shops; the second is the paper test. Either of these two tests can fit a ski very well.

When you are choosing a pair of skis, you must avoid two traps. The first is not to get a pair of skis that are too stiff. These skis will not be much fun to ski on, for the skier will have trouble getting up the hills because he or she will not be heavy or strong enough to compress the wax pocket to the snow.

There are ways to get around a poorly fit ski that is too stiff. Blue klister may be layered on as a base. This will bring the base closer to the snow and will form a good cushion to make your waxes more effective. Wax may be applied on top of the klister. As you can see, this will require more work, but it will make the skis effective.

The second pitfall is more subtle: The too soft ski will be a good climber, but the wax will always be dragging. The result: The wax will wear off quickly, and the skis will be slow; so in both cases enjoyment diminishes. There is no way to help skis which are too soft. You can make an attempt by using thinner coats of wax, but the bottoms will still drag and the ski will be slow most of the time. The bright spot is that there is considerable leeway in selection if the skier follows the guidelines presented here.

The poundage meter, which is really a *C clamp*, gives the skier a fast way to find the skis that are the proper stiffness. If you are in a ski shop that has a number of skis from which to choose, it can take quite a while to run paper tests for all of the possibilities. The C clamp is much faster. We have found that there is some leeway in the proper poundage that a skier can use effectively. However, here are some guidelines.

See what your longer, double pole, pocket is by setting the clamp for half of your body weight. This pocket should be from around the heel to about a foot or more in front of the toe of the boot. I've seen fast skis that have had short pockets and some that have had long pockets, but generally the skis with the longer pockets tend to be faster and easier to wax.

Then start applying pressure to the clamp until the skis just pin the feeler gauge. This will tell you how much force is needed to compress the ski to the snow. If you are a beginning skier or one who does not have a strong kick, or even one who is not in good shape and would have trouble setting the wax later in the day, a weaker poundage is indicated. In this case, the clamp should close at about 30 to 55% body weight. The average citizen racer can handle a ski in the 55 to 70% body weight range; the top racers in the 80 to 105% range. These numbers will help you select a ski that will perform well in all conditions. Some advanced skiers have skis for many different occasions: A softer one for when the track is not as hard, such as in new snow or sloppy tracks, a stiffer one for when the tracks are hard or icy, and even a shorter one with a hard sharp edge for skating. However, coaches have told me that many of the best skiers in the world have a favorite pair of skis that they use in all conditions. These skis are the fastest, and they have characteristics that make them versatile.

One word on poundage testers, or C clamps. As they are used now, the force is applied to only one point of the ski, usually at the placement of the ball of the foot. The skier, however, has his or her whole foot in contact with the ski when determining the double pole pocket and has the ball of his or her foot in contact during the kick phase. Therefore, the pressure distribution will be different than when actually skied on. Because the ski is not a completely rigid system, a slightly different pocket will be found on snow than when using the poundage tester. Skis that touch together when 50% of your body weight is applied to the poundage tester should have no pocket on snow. But, they usually have a very nice double pole pocket. This is because the feet distribute the weight over a larger and different surface area. If the ski has a pocket that starts in front of the heel, a skier standing on two feet with the weight mainly on the heel will actually have much of his or her weight behind the wax pocket.

The best way to determine the waxing pockets and correct stiffness is still the old-fashioned paper test. It tells you more about how the ski will react against the snow, because the flat surface approximates the surface you will be actually using the skis against. This method requires a level surface (a kitchen counter is adequate) and a friend to help. Some skiers actually take a flat board to the ski shops with them.

First, you need to find the balance point of the skis. Place your toes about 1 inch behind it. Stand on both skis with your weight mainly on the heels (see Figure 11.1a-c). Then, have a friend slide a piece of paper back and forth under one ski. This determines the maximum wax pocket for most situations. (*Note:* See waxing chapter for explanation of shorter application of stickier waxes and longer application of harder

Figure 11.1(a) The double pole pocket—two feel equally weighted with weight mainly on heels.

Figure 11.1(b) Single stick pocket—there should be paper movement for the better skier. The softer waxes should not be applied outside this pocket.

Figure 11.1(c) Setting the wax. For most skiers the paper should be completely pinned. This guarantees the ski is not too stiff. Some elite racers and/or klister skis would still have movement at this time.

Figure 11.1 Locating the wax pocket.

waxes.) This paper shows the area of the ski that will not be in contact with the snow during any gliding when both feet are equally weighted. Again, this distance on a good pair of skis should be from the heel to about a foot or more in front of the foot.

The second part of the paper test determines the wax pocket while gliding on one foot. The skier now stands with his or her weight entirely on one foot, again mainly on the heel. An attempt is then made to move the paper under the foot. If it is pinned or moved with considerable friction, the ski is soft and suitable for a beginning skier or soft snow conditions.

The paper test has one area of weakness in the soft ski or beginner range. Any number of ski stiffnesses will show a pocket on two feet and none on one. These skis can range from very soft to just soft. But with a very soft ski, the wax will dig into the snow and really slow down the skier. Squeezing various skis with your hands can supplement the paper test if no poundage tester is available. To be safe, when choosing a soft ski, pick the stiffest ski which will still pin the paper while standing on one foot.

A stiffer ski should allow movement of the paper for about a foot or so under the toe. Now the paper test can be made even more discerning. There are two parts to this test. First, the skier stands on one ski with the paper under that ski. He or she then rolls up on the ball of his or her foot and makes an attempt to move the paper. If the paper is pinned, the ski is an ideal all-around model suitable for any skier who is able to transfer his or her entire weight to one ski. In other words, an average citizen racer would find this ski enjoyable to use. The C clamp reading would be about 60 to 80% body weight. If the paper tears when an attempt is made to pull it out, the ski will still be fairly easy to use. However, if it pulls out with resistance on a smooth surface without tearing, it may be bordering on the stiff side. It would require strong weight transfer to set the wax. Some of our better skiers find that stiff skis are too much for them to use without the use of a klister or some kind of cushion or binder.

If the paper is still not pinned when on the ball of the foot, make one final test. Bounce up and down on your toe while someone moves the paper. If the paper just grabs, it is a hard powder or klister ski for an elite skier. This ski will be way too stiff for most skiers. Most of the top international team members of the U.S. and Canada have skis about this stiffness. That is, when rising to the toe of the foot, there is still a pocket centered around the toe and is usually about a foot in length. Because these skiers are almost always racing on hard tracks, this ski is used by some of the racers for all diagonal races. I guess they get a favorite and stick with it. This ski would also be an excellent klister ski for a serious citizen racer, especially one who races marathons. A layer or layers of klister can be covered with hard wax. The waxes can be kept off the snow, and wax wear will not be a problem because of the ski's stiff camber.

For an elite racer a klister ski may be a little stiffer, but for the average and even the very good skier, I would never recommend skis that stiff. I know from personal observation that some elite racers ski with skis that are softer than that. These skis would test out at 100 to 120% body weight on a clamp. I've

seen some top skiers use skis that are in the 60 to
90% range and use them for all conditions.

I have some definite ideas as to what type of stiffness or pocket will make for a fast ski. First, we have
to examine what we are trying to accomplish with the
wax pocket, and why a ski has to have stiffness or
camber at all. The major goal is twofold: It should be
stiff enough to keep the kick wax off the snow when
gliding, yet easy enough to compress when kicking.
But here is the catch: There are two different gliding
situations—when the skier is on two skis and when the
skier is on one.

A skier must usually compromise when choosing a
ski. If he or she gets one that still keeps the wax off
the snow easily when all of the weight is on one foot, it
will be very stiff and hard to set the wax. Only the
best skiers can handle these types of skis. The compromise, then, is for the skier to get the stiffest (most
camber) he or she can handle without having to make
a special effort to set the wax, which would be tiring.
This is why someone like Bill Koch has a real advantage over the average citizen skier. Because he is a
stronger skier with an explosive kick, he will be able to
use skis that keep the wax well off the snow. His kick
wax will drag less, and he will have no trouble setting
the wax, even at the end of a long race. Then, because
he will be carrying more speed into a hill, he will not
need the grip in many situations that a slower moving
skier will need. So he can use a harder wax. The moral
of the story is, the better your technique and conditioning, the more things you have going for you.

But the average racer can find a ski that will close
the gap and be easier to ski. Why are skis cambered?
Think about it for a while. Skis are cambered to keep
the midsection of the ski off the snow to reduce the
drag of the slower kick wax. Then, the key is not stiffness but wax clearance; therefore, the ideal ski would
give good wax clearance yet be easy to set. In other
words, the softest ski with the highest pocket would be
ideal.

Sound like a pipe dream? I have already seen this
type of ski and some of our skiers are lucky enough to
get them, accidentally, by the way. When we started
closely examining the fast skis in our area, we discovered

two main characteristics. One was the way in which these fast skis flexed (which we will cover next), and the other was the characteristic of the wax pockets. We measured the height of the pockets with little squares of paper. The height of a pocket was measured by how many sheets of paper could be slid under it while the skier was standing on two feet and then on one foot. Skis that were fast in colder conditions but bogged down in warmer snows with stickier wax had the same overall flex patterns but did not have a high pocket when one ski was weighted.

Surprisingly, we found that this was not always related to ski stiffness. Some stiffer skis actually had less clearance than some that were softer. Until this discovery, I had assumed that a skier would have to ski as well as an Olympic skier to get adequate wax clearance and, therefore, be able to ski on very fast skis. Now I feel that type of ski is within the reach of every citizen racer. The only technique requirement is that the skier be able to balance on one ski until the next kick. The kick itself need not be very powerful.

Let me explain. Some of those fast skis with high pockets completely pinned the paper when the skier rolled his or her weight onto the ball of the foot. In other words, they flattened out completely at less than total body weight because they were soft. Anyone with good balance could handle a ski that easy to compress, easily getting up the hills, yet having plenty of glide in both single stick and double pole situations.

The challenge is to the manufacturers to make more skis like these. As the average racer becomes more enlightened, he or she will demand more from his or her skis and place the burden on the ski manufacturer to come up with better skis. The manufacturers that do will sell the most skis. It's as simple as that. It's possible to make these skis because I've seen them—a soft ski that will have a high pocket when all the skier's weight is on one foot. In addition to all the other benefits, the ski will perform well in all conditions; it will keep klister off the snow, yet be flexible enough to ski in soft conditions; it will be an ideal klister ski for sloppy tracks above 32°; and, finally, it will make a good skating ski.

Proper camber alone does not make a good ski or even determine which one to choose. However, the wrong camber will guarantee that your skiing will not be as pleasurable as it could be.

The Tips and Tails

Another critical area for selecting a fast ski is the flex in the tips and tails. Place the bottoms of the skis together and squeeze them until most of the camber has been removed. Then pull the tips apart, one at a time. Notice what happens to the other tip. If it dives toward the middle, it will be a ski that plows and digs in the snow so it will be slow, especially in soft snow conditions.

Next, set the ski on a flat surface and compress the middle with one hand and pull up the tip with the other. It should curve gradually throughout the entire tip region right into the pocket area of the ski, rather than at just the end of the tip. From my experience, those with a sharp bend at the end tend to break easily, especially if they seem really bendable. Those that have flat sections in the tip will plow snow and not ride over the little irregularities in the trail. Some tips will be stiffer than others, so if you are only buying one ski, a slightly softer tip will ride on top of the snow better in a very slushy or soft track.

The tails of the skis should be considerably stiffer than the tips but should still have a smooth bend throughout the entire section. They need to be stiffer and torsionally stable to allow the skier to skate and turn with ease. Most of cross-country ski turning and maneuvering is done with the tails, which must be fairly resistant to twisting so they will hold an edge, especially for skating and turning. Twist the tails of the skis; there should be a fair amount of resistance. I have never run into a top-of-the-line racing ski that failed this test, however.

Length and Weight of the Ski

Two other factors are length and weight. We have already covered length and its relationship to ease of handling, but it also has an effect on weight. The shorter ski will be lighter. In addition, some of the racing skis are considerably lighter than others. The lighter ski makes skiing more enjoyable, especially on a hilly course. This is magnified as the size of the skier diminishes. If you have your choice between two equal skis, go for the lighter model.

Other Criteria

Another criterion is the type of base material. All of the top skis now have bases which are fast and hold wax well. A few years ago some of the skis had bases that did not have the proper porosity to hold wax. Nowadays this is not a problem. Almost any racing ski will have a P-Tex 2000 or equivalent base. However, the bases should be scrutinized for defects such as bubbles or holes in the P-Tex.

What are some of the other properties besides proper stiffness that make for a good ski? First of all, the bottoms should be square. Check by placing the skis back to back to see if they are flat or square in the areas that they contact. They should not come together in a concave or convex manner.

Second, they should be about the same height when sitting side by side on a flat surface. This is one indication that the skis are matched fairly well. Another test for this is to check their pockets using the paper test. The pockets should be very close to each other. Not too many skis will have identical pockets, but they should be close. Then squeeze the skis together and see if they close nicely. If there are some easily seen spaces where light comes through when the skis are compressed against each other, these skis should be discarded. If the ski tips come apart slightly as they are squeezed, you may have a fast pair of skis. This is not mandatory, but is a good sign.

Tip style is something that everyone should consider when getting a ski. The modern javelin tips are more enjoyable to ski with while diagonaling because they rub less against the side of the tracks and are lighter and easier to handle. However, beware the extreme javelin if you are not very good on your skis. They tend to wash out when the tracks deteriorate and do not hold a turn quite as well. The reason is that there is less of a straight line along the edge to keep the skier going straight. In fact, it is like having negative sidecut. Edging the ski in softer snow can tend to make it turn out. This is especially detrimental to skating.

One final question: Do I need a special ski for skating? For the serious racer, it wouldn't hurt to have one glider waxed and ready to go. Then one of the specialty skating skis may be fine. But they offer no real advantage over a nonjavelin tipped ski, selected by the preceding criteria, except in one instance. On icy or very hard trails, the hardened or metal-edged ski will be able to be edged when the normal ski will not. However, in normal circumstances, the specialty skis are sometimes slower than a well-selected pair of all-around skis. If you want a pair of skating skis and can afford them, go ahead. But the low-budget racer with one pair of well-selected skis is presently at no disadvantage. However, who knows what the ski manufacturers will come up with next?

Boots and Binding

The boot and binding system, is, in my opinion, almost as critical as the skis to the enjoyment of skiing. One of the biggest crimes committed against the beginning skier is giving him or her inferior equipment such as heavy and wide skis, very slow skis if the skier is unlucky enough to buy waxless, baskets that catch in the snow, and boots that offer almost no control of the ski. So the beginner with his or her uncontrollable skis is given boots offering less control. The system I'm talking about is the old Nordic 75 mm norm. These boots are connected by three pins through the sole and offer no real way to keep the skier's foot from slipping off the ski. (*Note:* Some very stiff telemarking boots have three-pin bindings, but these are specialty items and are heavy. The regular three-pin boots aren't so stable.) So when the downhill gets a little fast and hairy and the skier tries to torque his or her foot for a little control, the result is the foot twisting off the ski and the ski continuing to move straight ahead.

There is no excuse for this to happen nowadays, but all too often it does. Many different manufacturers offer boot and binding systems which have a positive system of control. These systems have wedges attached

to the ski that fit into the underside of the shoe. As a
result, the skier's foot is guided onto the ski and kept
there when a sideways pressure is applied. In addition,
these boots usually offer a freer foot lift off the ski.

One point should be made, however, about a widespread heresy. A boot that allows the toe to lift off the
ski will not give you a longer kick, which in itself may
not even be desirable. It does, however, allow a free lift
of the foot off the ski and maybe allows a better glide.
If you stop to think, the kick is over before the shoe
has lifted off the ski. Any stiffness will drive the tip of
the ski into the snow on the follow-through. In fact,
the stiffer boot promotes a higher follow-through to
clear the top off the snow. But we're not looking for
artificially high foot movements, just efficient ones,
and the new boot and binding systems do just that.

One of the best things to happen recently for the
tourer has been the improvement of touring boots and
bindings, which now have the same modern system of
control as the racer and the warm style of the touring
boot. One of our local shop owners says beginners
renting packages from him often come back and say
they haven't decided on a ski, but they know the boot
and binding they'll purchase for sure. Most of the
major manufacturers have touring systems that now
offer foot control and warmth, so there is no longer
any excuse for a beginner to get a poor system. Unfortunately, many of the carload and bargain packages
still are dumping the old boots and bindings on the
market, and skiers who think only of price are getting
just what they pay for.

What are we looking for in a boot? It must have a
positive locking system to the ski, that is a wedge or
something that keeps the boot from slipping off to the
side. The binding should pull the boot when it is engaged.
This ensures a good fit with no play. If the boot wiggles
in the binding, controlling the skis will be hard and
turning will be difficult. The sole should be stiff and
resist twisting. This can be tested by just taking several
shoes and twisting them. In addition, the shoe should
allow the foot to bend at the metatarsal joint (see
Figure 11.2). Failure to bend here can cause plantar
fasciatis or Achilles' problems. In other words, the
shoe should allow the foot to bend in a normal
manner.

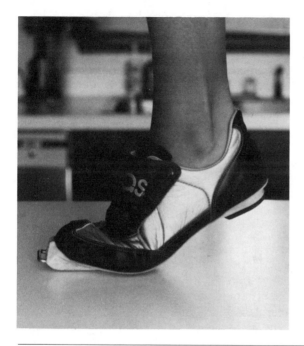

Figure 11.2 A comfortable boot must be flexible at the metatarsal joint.

Above all, the shoe should fit. There should be room for two socks unless you are an experienced racer who will use only one sock because of the lightness gained by the smaller shoe size and one less sock. Don't laugh! Some racers do just that. However, I believe in a big and comfortable shoe that will allow the use of two socks because comfort and warmth mean more to me. Racers usually do not have to worry about warmth unless their boots are too tight, cutting off circulation. They usually go hard enough, even in workouts, so that the feet are kept warm by the circulating blood. Overboots can be used if a racer is standing around.

The last consideration is, Are the boots waterproof? If you are skiing above 32°, it becomes extremely critical. Surprisingly enough, cold feet are more common on the days when the snow is wet than on the colder and drier days. Once the feet are wet, the heat is absorbed directly away from the foot and the cushion of dead air insulation is gone. So waterproof boots or waterproof overboots are the solution. Some

skiers spray their boots with silicone but I have not
had too much success with this. I have not had too
much luck with anything but overboots on those wet,
sloppy days. Sometimes the only solution is to carry
spare socks and change occasionally. If you are skiing
twice during the day, a second pair of boots may be
the only answer. (This season a Goretex boot has hit
the market which may even be the better solution.)
Above all, change into dry shoes and socks immediately after skiing. It's a good idea to make an entire
change of clothes, especially if you have some driving
to do before you get home for the evening.

Poles

Pole selection is another area where the beginner
often gets shortchanged. Several factors must be considered in determining which type of pole to use. The
cheapest fiberglass and bamboo poles have baskets
that are round and have tips made of soft metal. The
tips are usually no problem until ice is encountered;
then, anything can happen. Because icy trails are the
hardest on which to keep your balance, having a pole
that slips does not help. This problem could be simplified
by getting a pole one grade up. These poles have carbide tips and are excellent for ice or even roller skiing
on pavement.

In addition, better poles usually have baskets that
protrude only in the rear, allowing them to release
from the snow. A basket protruding to the front will
catch the snow as it is pulled out on the forward
stroke. In addition, if the skier is going to ski often off-
trail or in soft snow, a solid basket is recommended.
These are very light and come standard on many
poles. The solid structure is needed to stop the pole
from sinking too deeply into the snow. Most racers
now use this type of basket because it works well in
hard and packed snow as well as in powder.

Pole size is an important consideration. A pole that
fits comfortably under your armpits while you are
standing is about right (see Figures 11.3a and 11.3b).
Some experienced skiers vary from this a little. The
rise of skating has caused some racers to use poles 5
to 20 cm longer than normal. This is something that
each skier will have to determine for him- or herself.

Figure 11.3(a) Choosing the correct length ski pole. *Note:* An elite racer might have poles up to 4 inches above the shoulder.

Figure 11.3(b) Skating poles may be shoulder height, and even higher.

Different manufacturers have poles with various handle designs. I feel a skier can get used to any of the handle designs on the better poles, and which is chosen becomes a matter of individual taste. I happen to prefer the handle that curves away at the top, but I know others who prefer the ones that lock the thumb into the straps.

This brings us to the critical determinant in choosing a top racing pole: stiffness and weight. Here, stiffness, not weight, is the main factor. Once you plant the pole, it is important that all of the energy is used to push you forward. If the pole bends, some of the push is lost or absorbed by the pole. It used to be that lightness and stiffness meant a loss in durability. This season the newest poles are wrapped in Kevlar so they are stiff, light, *and* durable. They may even be confidently used in mass start races, where breakage was previously a factor.

Clothing

All skiers could learn from the racers. A racer will dress to the level of his or her activity and to the weather. Too often, tourers do not. The biggest mistake is to overdress, the second biggest is to wear cotton. Overdressing can result in excessive perspiration. Cotton, undergarments in particular, holds the moisture against the body, so the skier can find him- or herself in real trouble when he or she stops moving. The water will conduct the heat rapidly away from the body. The result: Hypothermia, a dangerous lowering of the body temperature. At that point even dry clothes won't help. An outside source of heat is needed if it is nothing more than another skier huddled close for warmth. This book, however, is not meant to be a primer in first aid, for better sources are available.

Dressing sensibly can keep you from having to be in that situation. This is where the average skier can learn from the racer whose secret to dressing is layering. The tourer will have more layers because he or she is generating less body heat. The first item to get is an undergarment made of material that does not absorb water, but instead wicks it away to evaporate without keeping the skin wet. Then for temperatures down to 15° without high winds, a racing suit over underwear is all the average racer needs. These suits also wick moisture away from the skin and are made to resist penetrating wind. A warm cap and thin gloves complete the outfit. With this combination, a skier will not overheat during the race. It took me years to learn that I only needed a light sweater in addition to the above gear for temperatures in the 0° F range.

The secret to good clothing is layering—the way the racer dresses before, after, and on workout days. Warm-up jackets and pants before and after the race are the rule. If it gets too hot, take off the warm-up; if it gets too cold add a light sweater. In addition, most racers have a thicker pair of gloves for real cold days, especially during workouts.

On workout days, many racers carry a fanny pack if they are on a course that may take them any distance away from civilization. This pack usually contains a dry pair of mittens, which are warmer than gloves; racing versions can also be purchased. You can easily carry a space age blanket (a thin plastic blanket that folds up into a small square), a dry pair of socks, a small container with water, and maybe a breakfast bar or two. In addition, toss in a few waxes with an old cork. This may seem like a lot, but it all easily fits into a fanny pack. The blanket is a must because racers cover more ground and can find themselves far from the touring center. If they are injured and stranded while skiing alone, it could be critical.

The average skier can learn well from this. Racing suits are much better than knickers, especially wool or cotton ones, for several reasons. First, the racing suit is an excellent wind shield; second, it is not as heavy as wool and does not hold moisture like cotton. One of the side effects is that the skier does not have the heavy wool socks in contact with the snow as in the traditional knicker suit. This is the area where the skier is first likely to get wet. A few falls into the snow on the side of the trail can leave the socks covered. Then the body heat melts the snow, and hypothermia sets in. However, snow does not stick to a full-length racing suit.

It is easy to layer over a racing suit, even with a cotton tee shirt because it is not against the skin. A warm-up jacket as well as a sweatshirt or sweater can be worn and then removed and tied around the waist. If you feel yourself overheating, take off a layer. The only disadvantage is that many skiers feel self-conscious in a racing suit. It is possible to get these in styles that now look like knickers even though they are full length.

For the racer, the racing suits are better aerodynamically and are stretchy enough to ensure freedom of movement. There are generally two styles of suits. Some suits are double-fronted and some single. I prefer the single-front because it is usually warm enough and certainly better on the warmer days. On the colder days layering can again take over. Wearing a light sweater, made of a synthetic material so it will wick away the perspiration, can easily turn the single-layered suit into a warmer one. However, if you own two suits, the second could be double-fronted for the cold days. (*Note:* Some of the new suits are single-fronted but very wind resistant.) One slight note of warning: Every once in a while you will find a super bargain, but be cautious. Some of these bargain suits can be real bargains, but many are made of an inferior material that is not very wind resistant, and this could result in frostbite. The same thing can happen if you use a cheap pair of warm-ups. Another note of caution: If you are skiing in a two-piece warm-up, be careful that there is a good overlap between the top and bottom, for the stomach is another prime area for frostbite. It can happen without you even knowing.

Frostbite, however, usually attacks the extremities such as the nose, ears, face, hands, and feet. Beginning tourers and good racers seem to be vulnerable to this malady—the tourers because of the lack of experience, and the racers because of the light dressing and the excitement of the competition. If a cap comes off a little and leaves the ears exposed, the racer seldom will stop to adjust it back again. That is why earmuffs are a good idea on those cold days. There are specially designed muffs that are light and comfortable. Another alternative is a thin nylon overpiece, or balaclava, which covers the head, chin, and ears. You can wear a hat over it. This tends to get too warm in a racing situation, but is ideal for touring. The part of the ear that is especially vulnerable to frostbite is the lobe, for it can easily be uncovered. Do not take this lightly. I remember watching one young racer's ears swell after only a 5-k race. A little protection can go a long way. Special face creams, designed to help prevent frostbite as well as chapped skin, are effective and are available on the market.

The feet get in trouble when the shoes are too tight. You are better off with one pair of socks and a loose fit than two and a tight fit. The tighter fit cuts off circulation and removes the dead air space that acts as insulation. It's no fun when the water in your system starts to freeze.

This is also true in one special area for men only. Man's extra extremity is best protected by a pair of polypropylene undershorts with a plastic wind shield. If you cannot get a commercial pair, you can improvise with plastic bags. This is one of the most painful areas for frostbite and should be protected even when the weather is not down to 0° F.

The mitten is the last protection against frostbite. I know that many racers wouldn't be caught dead wearing them, but as mentioned before, there are racing styles that are comfortable and not too bulky. Mittens allow good pole control yet are much warmer than gloves. Every tourer and racer should own a pair of mittens, carry them in his or her fanny sack, and have the good judgment to use them when necessary.

A little common sense, combined with the idea of layering and the proper type of clothing can go a long way. Any clothing that holds in moisture is bad. Likewise, overdressing can also be disastrous. Get those wet clothes off as soon as possible and carry some dry socks and gloves or mittens along. Protect against frostbite on the windy and/or cold days and you should be all right.

Choosing Your Roller Ski Equipment

It is very important to select the right equipment for roller skiing. As in skiing, different individuals may require different equipment. Selecting the right ski may mean the difference between successful off-season training and frustration. All of the following opinions are based on the experience of many skiers. They are not only one man's opinion.

The Ski

Evaluating and choosing a roller ski is not easy. Many factors determine the final choice, and it is easy to make a wrong selection. Speed, weight, durability, cost of repairs, stability, and the number of wheels are some of the main considerations.

However, the big question is, am I training for diagonaling or skating or both? I know a number of serious competitors who use their three-wheeled roller skis for both diagonaling and skating. I know one or two who use their two-wheelers for diagonaling as well as skating and double poling. But for the serious trainees, an increasing number have one of each; a light three-wheeler for traditional training and a two-wheeler for skating. Some of these even have the wheeled ice skating boots as a third option.

For the serious skier, weight and speed far outweigh the other factors. We have found that for traditional training, using the diagonal, the ski should be a little slower than snow and should be as light as possible. This is one of the supposed inconsistencies in evaluating roller skiing. For gliding purposes alone, it would seem that the ski whose speed most approximates snow would be the best, but that is not the case. A roller ski that is that fast will not give a skier an equivalent workout to snow, even if the skier goes faster. The reason is that the roller ski kick is so effective that a skier can really tear up hills where he or she might even herringbone on snow.

In addition, because of the more automatic kick, less energy is expended because no downward force is required. The result is a longer glide for the effort. To get the same effect as on snow, the skis should be a little slower. The slower ski actually causes the arms to work a little harder than on snow for the same type of glide, but on snow, the skis slip more and cause a greater pressure on the arms during herringbone and other marginal wax situations. The result is that the arms get approximately an equivalent workout.

Pulse rates were used as a partial indicator in analyzing the effect of faster and slower skis. On workouts where skiers perceived themselves to be working hard, but not quite racing, pulse rates over one flat to rolling course dropped from an average of 160 to 110 when the light but slower skis were changed for the heavier but faster skis.

One other interesting observation was that although the lighter and slightly slower skis gave a fairly equivalent workout to snow in an average workout, they are much harder to use on a long, slow workout. We have found that slower and longer workouts are much more taxing on these roller skis than on snow. This is because of the slow rolling speed. So when going slower, you still have to put forth more effort to keep rolling. In other words, at slow speeds, snow skiing is easier. I suppose to get an equivalent long, slow workout, a skier could have a faster pair of roller skis for that purpose. No one roller ski on the market now offers everything.

The weight of the skis is very important to the lighter or weaker skier. While a big skier may not be bothered by heavy roller skis, the smaller skier might feel as if he or she has logs or bricks attached to his or her feet. Just looking at a light roller skier using a heavy roller ski, you can see that his or her legs look like they're in slow motion. Small skiers will find they exert too much energy actually moving the skis and will not have very much fun if the skis are too heavy. So the lighter skier should get a light pair of skis, even if he or she is a beginner. In fact, all skiers learn better on light roller skis. A heavier ski definitely comes forward at a slower pace and makes it hard to get any kind of turnover for any but the strongest skiers. In diagonal training the majority of elite skiers opt for lighter 3-wheeled roller skis.

Roller skis have come a long way in the last 5 years, and this is just one of the indications. A skier can hardly go wrong if he or she buys a new pair of three-wheeled roller skis. Some will be a little heavier, more or less durable, slightly more stable, but all will be skiable. This was not the case a few years ago.

Some excellent two-wheeled roller skis are now on the market. Almost all of them skate well. There is even a much better selection than for 3-wheelers, which tells you something about the skating revolution. Try several out and choose the one you like best.

Skate Boots

The ice skating training boots, with a single set of wheels down the middle of the foot, are the last training ski to consider. Their wheels roll free in both directions, so they cannot be used at all to diagonal stride, making them truly a specialty device. They do make skating up hills easier to master and a skier feels a sense of freedom while using them. You can even leave your poles behind and go ice skating down the road. They also can be made to perform quite similar to skis on slalom-type runs. But despite all these fine points, I feel the two-wheeled roller ski is still the choice for most skiers. The two-wheelers more closely approximate the feeling of skating on snow. They have better fore and aft stability. The skate boots are fitted to the athlete's foot size and are therefore not very interchangeable. But most of all, the skate boot is the most dangerous on steep downhills.

So what do you buy? The choice is yours and you may have some idea already, but here are a few suggestions. If you primarily train by running, especially if you run with poles, your first choice should be a two-wheeler. This fills in your weakness. If you are unable to run, and many fall into this category, start with a light pair of three-wheelers. Ideally, each skier should have a 3-wheeler for diagonaling and a 2-wheeler for skating. However, many are skating well on 3-wheelers, by economic necessity. Finally, if you have money to burn, get a pair of skating boots.

Poles

The poles are the second item to consider. The main concern for poles is that they must have carbide tips; otherwise, they will not stick in the pavement. If you have a pole with a carbide tip, it will suffice for roller skiing. The length of the pole should be the same as on snow. On snow the pole sinks into the snow, and on roller skis the road is lower than the skis. The result? Use the same pole. As far as tips are concerned, I have never seen a skier with a real tennis elbow from shock against the pavement. So the tips that have a built-in shock absorber are not needed. In fact, they are very hard to ski with, as the tips keep bouncing out of the asphalt. Instead, a skier should consider a softer pole for road skiing as it will lessen the shock. In other words, don't use your expensive, stiff racing poles. But if you do find your elbow getting sore, the hands are the best place to start. Thick gloves will help absorb the shock. If this fails, add sponges. However, this problem will probably never arise if you use softer poles. For roller skiing, the cheapest aluminum or fiberglass pole with a carbide tip is the ticket.

Shoes, Bindings, and Pads

The shoes and bindings can be the same as in winter. Most skiers use their older and outdated boots and bindings because roller skiing will scrape up your good boots. Contrary to popular belief, roller skiing does not require a boot with more control, so old boots are OK. You are not herringboning or making sharp downhill turns with the pavement skis. The roller skis are a little heavier but do not require much torquing action. So any old shoe and binding system is adequate. I am presently on the fifth year of roller skiing with my old Adidas boots. I also used these boots for several winters, and they still work fine. However, if you use very heavy roller skis or have to do a lot of snowplowing to slow down, your boot and binding system may not last as long, and neither will your roller skis, as quite a strain is placed on the tires, axles, and bearings.

Sore feet can become a problem because some of the roller skis have rather narrow shafts and create pressure on the middle of your feet. A solution is to tape carpeting on the shaft. If your feet still get sore, add a wider platform. Do this by purchasing another plate, placing it under the ball of the foot, and adding a carpet cover. The wider roller skis do not usually present this problem.

The last items on the agenda are knee and elbow pads. If you are just starting out, I would highly recommend them, for many beginning roller skiers have suffered bad falls. Also, wear long pants for a while until you become confident on the skis. A helmet is appropriate for a beginner with little confidence. For some, roller skiing comes naturally; for others, unfortunately, falling is a common occurrence. One bad experience has stopped several skiers I know from continuing roller skiing—don't let it be you.

Waxing   **12**

A Path out of the Labyrinth

I have to thank Marty Hall for his help in finding our way out of the morass of waxing. We developed many of the things we do, but hints and advice from Marty were very helpful. Many of our waxing "discoveries" were really the reinvention of the wheel, for we discovered many other racers waxing the same way. At first, I thought we had hit on something quite unique and I was going to call this chapter the "Milwaukee System of Waxing." However, what we have discovered, even if others have done the same, is a quick and easy way to wax which has not, as of yet, filtered down to the general public.

Waxable Versus Waxless

To wax or not to wax? That is the question. Shakespeare's famous quotation has its modern counterpart for the cross-country skier. Actually, it is only a question for the beginning skier. If you are motivated enough to be reading this book, the question is already answered. Waxable skis outperform waxless skis by such a large margin in most conditions that unless you are unbelievably lazy or have a large family of young children, there is only one choice, waxing. In most situations, waxing is really very simple. There are some conditions, usually at or around the freezing point, where waxless skis will outperform waxable skis, but for the average skier, these days will be few and far between. The serious racer or skier will already know about these days and will have decided about them for him- or herself.

On my first outing, I was fortunate enough to go skiing with some experienced skiers. They had waxable skis and I rented waxless. The immense difference in speed of skis was readily apparent. Even as a beginner, I quickly noticed that I was trudging along while they were easily gliding. We switched skis for a short time, and there was the proof. That first tour in the Kettle Moraine of Wisconsin did two things for me: It hooked me on skiing, and it convinced me that a waxable performance ski was the only one to use. I noticed that the thrill of the kick and glide rapidly diminished as the glide disappeared. Skiing was still fun, but the thrill of flying like a bird across the landscape became the trudge of the turtle.

Unless you own more than one pair of skis, make your decision to go waxable. At the end of our first winter of skiing, we were fortunate enough to participate in June in a Peter Davis camp in Oregon. One of the ski reps had a pair of "hot" waxless racing skis that we could try out. We did a speed test down a slight incline, comparing our touring skis, which were waxable, to the "hot" no-wax racing skis. I, with my waxable skis, had trouble keeping up with my son who was on his crude, waxable touring skis. Then he switched to the no-wax skis. I followed him down the incline. He double poled as hard as he could. I had to step out of the track and snowplow to keep from running him off the hill.

So in most conditions, but not all, waxable skis will outperform no-wax skis. If you only ski once or twice a winter, if you have many skis to wax or if the terrain which you ski on is very steep, you may also want the slower waxless skis. However, we are talking about skiing faster, not slower.

The Glide and Kick Wax

Before waxing, the first decision you must make is where to put on the glide wax and where to put on the kick wax. The glide wax is very slippery and helps the skis go faster, just like the glide wax on Alpine skis. The kick wax grips the snow and is what allows you to climb hills. The kick wax goes in the middle of the skis and the glide wax on the tips and tails.

As explained in the equipment chapter, camber is the bend of the ski which keeps the middle of the ski off the ground when you set it down. When you are gliding, camber will keep the kick wax from contacting the snow, at least too heavily. It is in this section, which is kept off the snow, that you want to apply kick wax. Why? The kick wax is sticky, and if it drags forcefully on the snow while you glide, it will slow you down. It would also wear off quickly and require much rewaxing. However, the force of your kick will flatten the ski and cause the kick wax to grip the snow. Conversely, you will put the glide wax, which is faster, on the tips and tails that are in contact with the snow during the glide.

Locating the Wax Pocket or Kick Zone

How do you locate the wax pocket where the kicker wax is applied? The easiest way is to find a flat surface. We use the kitchen counter at home. To keep peace in the family, make sure all of the wax is removed from the bottoms of the skis. Then stand on the skis with both feet being equally weighted. If there are no bindings on your skis, place the toe slightly behind the balance point. Place a piece of writing or typing paper under the ski and slide it back and forth. The wax pocket is the area where the paper slides freely. Mark the spots where the paper stops with an indelible pen. This may be slightly different on each ski, so don't let it surprise you. You may wish to test the skis on different parts of your flat surface to make sure it is really flat (see Figure 12.1).

You can also determine the wax pocket in the store where you purchased your skis if the store has a poundage tester. Tighten the tester until it registers half your body weight. Then slide the metal testing device between the skis and mark where the metal stops sliding. This is an approximation of the wax pocket. These results will be close to those obtained by

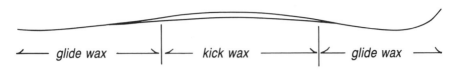

Figure 12.1(a) A soft ski only has a glide wax and kick wax area.

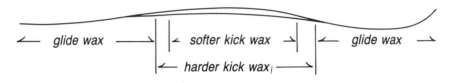

Figure 12.1(b) A stiff ski has three or more waxing areas: A glide wax area; double pole pocket for harder kick waxes; and a single stick pocket for softer kick waxes and klisters.

Figure 12.1 Various waxing zones on a ski.

standing on a flat surface because each ski was supporting half of your body weight.

After locating the wax pocket, you should still keep an eye on how the kick wax wears while skiing. If you wax out of the pocket, it will wear off rapidly while slowing you down at the same time. If you see that your practical wax pocket, derived from snow testing and observation, is shorter than predicted, adjust it in the future and re-mark your skis.

As you can see, it is very important for your skis to fit properly. If they are too soft, the kick wax will always be dragging on the snow, resulting in slow skis and much rewaxing. If they are too stiff, you may need to put on more layers of kick wax to get up the hills.

Prepping the Base

Now that the wax pocket has been determined, it is important to prepare the base for skiing. If you are not a serious racer, omit this step. Even if you are serious, you only need to prep your skis when you first buy them. The section on advanced waxing will cover when to reprep your skis.

The purpose of base prepping is to ensure that the ski bases are square and to prepare the bottom of the skis for wax retention, the result being faster skis. Some skis now come with instructions not to prep them, but you should always look the bases over for yourself, for they may still need to be prepped.

Sanding is the safest and most common way, today, of prepping the base. Some of the oldtimers still use metal scrapers to do this, but a slip at the wrong time can gouge the base of the ski. I've seen some real butcher jobs. It's just hard to get a level bottom using a scraper. It is too easy to get a convex bottom if you are not careful. You should use silicon carbide sandpaper in grits of 100, 150, and 180. Swix has a regular kit for preparing the skis. It includes other items for advanced waxing as well as instructions for sanding the bases.

Before you start, you may be like a friend of mine who asked why he should prep his skis because it was the wax and not the actual ski bottom that was on the snow anyway. His reasoning was, why bother to sand the base? He soon found out the hard way—in a race. After the race, he wondered why his fast new skis were so slow. As he glided along, his skis were so rough that they made a grating sound. You could plainly hear it while skiing next to him. This lack of prepping had ensured that he had slow skis, even though he had just spent over $200 on them. If he had skied on these for a month or two, the scraping of glide wax and wear on the snow would have smoothed the base for him. However, sanding is a much faster way. In addition, natural wear does not square a base very well.

So if you want fast skis, they must be prepped. (Most shops will only hot glide wax and scrape your skis, not really prep them.) First, you need a square sanding block, a place to hold the skis, and different grades of sandpaper, starting with 100 to square up the base (i.e., make sure that it is not concave or convex). Then use 150 on the whole ski, and finish by doing the glide zone only with 180. This is the general outline for an all-purpose ski.

Start with the roughest sandpaper, 100 grit, and sand until the base is level. Check by using a metal straight edge. There are two ways a base must be flat.

The first is across the width of the ski, which is easy to check with a straight edge or true bar. The second is the lengthwise section of the ski bottom. Here the sandpaper can be your judge. Use a sanding block, which is as long as possible, parallel to the sides of the skis. Look at your base as you sand. Note any areas that are not being sanded. If you have a level sanding block, these will indicate low spots on the ski. Sand with the 100 grit until the base is level in both directions. It is important to keep the strokes as long and straight as possible. The longer sanding block will encourage a flatter base from front to back because a shorter block might follow any wave-like irregularities in the base. Also, always sand from front to back. As the quality control has improved for the various manufacturers, most bases are now square to begin with. In that case, start with the next step.

When the bases are square, repeat the entire process with 150-grit silicon carbide paper, again sanding the entire bottom of the ski. You are now done with the wax pocket area of the ski, which does not have to be as smooth because its main purpose is to hold kicker rather than to serve as a gliding surface. A stopping point of 150 is a good compromise of gliding ability and wax holding ability. The glide zones on your all-around skis can be finished off with 180 grit. As you will see in the advanced waxing section, the base prep process will be different for warmer snow. As the temperature approaches and exceeds the melting point, suction between the ski and the wet snow becomes a big problem, so ways to break it up must be devised.

Applying the Glider

First of all, you must select which glider to use. Contrary to popular belief, the actual choice is not that critical, as any differences in speed due to glider wax are slight compared to the choice of kicker. I would select a glider which has a temperature range for most of your conditions. The general rule of thumb is that the glide wax and the way it's applied becomes more critical as the temperature rises. For that reason, many skiers including some top racers, glide wax with a wax that is right for about 32° F and use it for all conditions below, the only modification being that of scraping it thinner as it gets colder. Skiers in our area use purple glider, a wax that is used more or less as a universal glider. Of course, if the race is important, then the proper glider is applied.

The traditional method of applying glider is to melt the wax with an iron and drip parallel lines down the glide zones of the skis. It should not be applied to the kick zone of the ski. The wax is then ironed in for several minutes to ensure penetration into the pores of the skis.

The temperature of the iron is of extreme importance. If it is too hot, the wax may be changed in structure and/or worse yet, the base of the ski may be damaged. If the wax smokes, the iron is too hot. Once you have waxed with your electric iron, it is easy to note the setting where the wax melted but did not smoke. Some hand irons made for skiing have a temperature indicator that can be used the same way.

After the wax is in the ski, allow it to cool. If this is the first time your skis are being waxed, you should scrape the warm wax off immediately, getting as much wax out as possible. This is done to clean the pores and remove any dirt or residue. A soft wax such as a red is usually recommended the first time after base prepping. However, some of the experts are now recommending that the type of wax most often used with that ski is the one with which you should prep the base. Hot wax in the preferred glider wax, then let the ski cool overnight.

In the morning, the ski is scraped appropriately for the type of wax. The colder waxes are scraped closer, the warmer ones left thicker. Choose a metal or plastic scraper. The metal is faster than the plastic but also requires more care. One slip with the metal scraper can gouge the bases of your skis. The strokes should be from front to back, and the top of the scraper should be angled toward the tails of the skis to prevent gouging.

There are two concepts for glide waxing: Thickness of glider and roughness of surface. So how much wax is left on the ski becomes all important. As the temperature drops, the wax is scraped thinner and the surface left smoother. This, again, is because of the hardness of the crystals and the lack of moisture in the snow. As the temperature rises, the glider is left thicker by scraping less, with a rougher surface presented to the snow. To achieve this surface, use a wire brush or file to introduce striations into the wax surface. This will allow the water to run out without developing a suction. Pull the file or wire brush in one motion through each area of glider wax. The path should be parallel to the sides of the skis. At first, it is hard to run a wire brush over that new pair of skis, but after a while when you see that no damage is done, it won't seem so bad. (It gets a little more frightening in the section of advanced waxing.) If you are touring, leave more wax on the ski and allow the snow to wear it off. Then you won't have to rewax as much.

In the warmer snows that create suction with the skis, the warm gliders with the grooves wire brushed into a thick application of wax showed noticeable advances in speed over the colder and well-scraped gliders. So as the glider gets warmer, less scraping is needed. But for general run-of-the-mill waxing, put on your Swix purple or its equivalent and scrape it smooth, leaving a layer of wax on the ski to wear off as you work out or tour.

One last hint in shortcutting on the glider waxing: Look at the base of your skis periodically. When you see spots where the glider has worn off, crayon on the glider cold and then heat it in with an iron. A light corking will finish the job. There is no need to scrape. Unless you are in a situation where you want to make sure you have the fastest skis possible, this is a quicker and more economical way to apply the wax. It has always seemed to be a big waste to me to have to clean off all my glider wax just because of a few wear spots. This may disturb the purists, but skiing is not a full-time job for me or for almost anyone I know or coach. Less time waxing means more time skiing. That makes sense to me.

Kick Waxing . . . What Most People Mean by Waxing

When we first started skiing several years ago, the salesman told us that kick waxing was simple. He proceeded to show us how to read the label on the can, check the temperature, and proceed to wax. Step 1 was to crayon the wax on the middle of the ski bottom. Step 2 was to either cork it in or, even better yet, allow the snow to smooth the wax for us. If the ski slipped, the first step was to make the wax longer. If it still slipped, then the wax should be applied thicker. If after three coats of kicker it still slipped, the same procedure was to be followed with the next softer wax.

With this good advice, waxing turned out to be a nightmare. What he didn't tell us was that the temperatures on the labels were not applicable to our local snows but were derived in a foreign country where the wax was made. Snows are different in different geographical areas because of moisture and temperature, and such. The wax that was supposedly correct for the temperature of the day almost always slipped because the snow is usually moister in the Midwest. So after waxing through several colors—each color thicker and longer—each ski ended up with about 2 pounds of wax. Even if the right wax was finally achieved, there was so much wax on the bottom that the skis were slow. On rare occasions, we were lucky and hit the wax right away.

The second thing we noticed was that our wax wore off quickly and we were rewaxing every 5 miles. I could not envision how anyone could wax for a race like the Birkebeiner. Our mistake was that we were not corking in the waxes. We were crayoning the wax onto the ski bottom and allowing the snow to cork it in for us. What the salesman did not tell us was that wax needed to flow, slightly melted, into the bottom to have any bonding ability to the ski. The heat of the friction caused by corking, melted the wax slightly or at least made it more fluid and allowed it to penetrate the pores of the base. Having the snow apply the friction lost this advantage. Instead of being corked in, the wax was sanded off.

Nowadays, in normal snow conditions, we generally hit the wax in a very short time, put on only two layers, and ski for the whole day. Our breakthrough came at an early season race about 3 years ago. Marty Hall was waxing some skis in seemingly easy waxing conditions. It was about -10° F and polar seemed to be the best choice. The polar was just a bit slippery, but other waxes seemed to be slow. Marty told us to put on a layer of extra green covered by polar or special green. It worked, getting both good kick and glide. This was our first experience with *cushioning*, which means putting a colder wax over a warmer one. Now it is the way we wax most of the time. Rarely do we apply only one wax; it is almost always a mixture of two or more waxes.

I can hear you now. "How can it be simpler to wax when you're mixing all sorts of waxes? How do you know what to put on and what you have?" First of all, the temperature ranges on the cans are always different than the actual use in our area. It took quite awhile for me to get over this. I thought if it said green, it must mean green. So the first year or so we tried to get the wax to work at the temperature on the label. We figured we were wrong because the label had to be right. Now we know! The labels are usually off by one or more wax colors for our area. If it says green on the label, we know the correct wax is blue or even extra blue.

How did we find this out? The ultimate experts—the skis themselves—told us. If they slipped, a warmer wax was needed. Waxing is really quite simple when you use your skis as the judge and do not get bogged down by preconceptions. The wax can is a good starting point, but only a starting point. It gives some ideal temperature ranges for the waxes, which supposedly work in the country of their origin; however, there are so many other variables that the reaction to the snow is the final judge.

Before we go into too many details of kick waxing, some concept of how snow and wax relate is helpful but not mandatory for precise waxing. The wax works when the snow crystals are able to penetrate into the wax enough to get a good kick, yet the crystals do not imbed so deeply that they won't release when gliding.

When this happens, the skis ice up. That is, the crystals never are freed from the bottom, and ice and snow build up on the ski's bottom. There are two basic factors at work in determining the effectiveness of the snow crystals biting into the wax: The age of snow and its moisture content. The older snow has lost its sharp ends through aging and is not as effective at penetrating the wax as younger snow. The same holds true for moist snow. So the rule of thumb is that the older and/or wetter the snow, the warmer the wax.

Some veterans can look at the track, take the air and snow temperature, estimate the air and snow mixture, and come up with the correct wax. I saw Mike Marciniak, Central Division Junior Coach, do this at the Junior Olympics in Ishpeming during some of the toughest waxing situations I've seen (see Figure 12.2):

Figure 12.2   Mike Marciniak, Central Division's waxing wizard.

Temperature ranges of 32° to around 50° during a race; icy tracks in the morning becoming soft from sun as the race progressed; rain on and off; and, to make matters worse, fresh snow in the tracks. However, if you can't duplicate Mike's expertise, never fear. The action of the ski on the snow will tell you soon enough if you are waxed correctly.

The basic principles have now been established. The wax tables published by the manufacturers will probably be different from what you will experience, especially when old or moist snow is encountered. But we're not worrying. The snow will tell us if we made a mistake. After a while you will be able to be pretty close on your first educated guess.

The following is a system of waxing that we have developed which runs counter to most standard instructions on waxing. At first, we thought it was unique to us, developed from that first hint from Marty Hall. Now we realize that many racers actually wax this way. You can use this method with any brand of wax. Initially, you may want to stick to one brand of wax, but you can easily mix brands as the color coding is pretty close. Some brands may be one-half wax softer for a given color, but most are in the same ballpark.

Temperature is the first factor to consider in choosing the wax. Age and then moisture come after. Choose a wax that you think will be a little sticky. If you think it's a blue day, start with purple or special purple. Cork in a light layer. We never wax out of the double pole pocket at this stage. In fact, advanced skiers seldom wax out of the single pole pocket with waxes softer than X-tra blue. (*Note:* The single stick pocket was the pocket while standing on one ski.) If the glider is supposed to be faster than the kicker, why flirt with slow skis by having your kicker drag against the snow needlessly? If you need more kick, go with a thicker layer or a stickier wax. While kicking, not much pressure is imparted to snow on the areas outside of the kick zone, so wax applied there does not give a much better kick but can sure slow you down during the glide. Now try that stickier wax, purple in this case. You might be surprised to find that it is a little too slick, or it may be just right. We will assume, however, that it was a little sticky and come back to the other two instances later on.

If it seems just slightly slow, you will cover it with the next harder wax (extra blue in this case). If it is very slow, you will cover it with the wax two or three

levels harder (green in this case). Remember to cork
the wax so it bonds well to the bottom. The corking
should make the bottom smooth and the wax difficult
to see. Go out to test the wax again. If it's still not
right, go through the process again—softer if the ski
slips or harder if the wax seems slow.

This method has several advantages over the traditional longer and thicker method. First, you will find
the correct wax in a very short time. By moving in
wide sweeps and narrowing down your field, you get
in the ballpark sooner. When you find the right combination, you will not have a lot of layers of wax to slow
your skis. If you are only touring or working out, you
are ready to go. If you are racing, you may want to try
some other combinations or single wax around the
area you have determined as effective waxing.

The second advantage of this system is that the
temperature usually rises during the day. As the top
layer wears off, the softer wax underneath will come to
the surface. Then the softer wax will work in the
warmer temperatures. This waxing method has proved
very effective for skiing all day and not having to rewax. Many times two layers have been more than adequate for 3 hours of continuous skiing, and this is for
some pretty fast skiers who cover a lot of ground in
those hours.

I prefer the harder over softer combination for several reasons. First of all, the harder wax touches the
snow directly and therefore glides better. When the
wax is set during the kick, the softer cushion underneath allows the snow to penetrate the wax for better
grip. But this only happens during the kick. However,
there are no absolutes in this game. How much you
have mixed the waxes when corking is a variable. Assuming you have not mixed the waxes too much, the
combination of hard over soft gives you insurance
against warming conditions. At times this may be only
mental, but if it gives you confidence, so what?

If you are in a serious race and hit on a combination
that works such as blue over purple, you could use
that as your starting point for waxing some other skis.
You might put extra blue by Swix on one ski, super
blue by Rode on another, and special purple, applied
shorter on a third. You might even try extra green

over binder. The point is that once you've located the ballpark, you can do any number of things.

After the first year of skiing when we allowed the snow to do much of our corking and had very little wax durability, we went to the other extreme. We always ironed in the kicker. The wax was definitely more durable when applied in this way, but waxing became very tedious. It was a big production to apply the wax. No longer could we simply add on a quick layer. In addition to being harder to do, ironing can change the way a wax works on the snow. I will say this though: When we hit the wax, it worked forever.

Then one day at a race we happened to be waxing next to a car load of USST skiers. To our surprise, they had no torches and were corking their wax in like any group of novices. Well, almost. They did do an exceptionally good job of corking the wax. When they were done, you could hardly see the wax. The corking was thorough and the layers were thin. So now, unless the conditions are drastic (very abrasive) and/or the race very long, we never use an iron. This has made waxing not only much faster but, more importantly, more consistent. I'm convinced that the ironing process does things to the wax. After ironing, the wax does not have as much grip. This fact can be used to make a ski a little faster if desired. The racer could find the "right" wax and try the same combination, but this time iron it in.

Most of the time you will have no trouble applying a harder wax over a softer one. But once in a while, it is hard to accomplish. In these cases, the hard wax just pushes the soft wax around but does not bind to the ski. In these circumstances, usually when you are dealing with waxes that are softer than purple, you can get around this very nicely. Simply heat the hard wax in the tin with your torch. Then apply it while it is momentarily softer. The torch does not have to be used very long on the wax—a quick pass will do. Once the wax is on, it may be corked or heated in. Experience will dictate your exact technique as you become more adept.

Klisters . . . Where, When, and How

Choosing and mixing klisters is generally done in the same manner as for hard waxes although the application varies. If the klister is too sticky, a harder one may be mixed in, and if it is too slippery, one with more bite may be added. The trouble with klisters is that many skiers do not have much experience using them, they can create a sticky mess, and there is much confusion as to which klister is softest. Unfortunately, some of the manufacturer's instructions are not very good. The hardness follows the same color codes as hard waxes. (Rex OV and OI are a couple of exceptions.)

When do you use klisters? and When do you use klisters and hard waxes in combination? To make it more confusing, some klisters are also used as binders for other klisters. In general, snow that has not been melted and refrozen requires a hard wax. If it is icy or the snow has lost much pointedness by refreezing, klister is indicated. For fresh snow on top of hard snow or ice, a kick wax over klister is the answer. The hard wax will stop the skis from icing up when the snow crystals are encountered, and the klister underneath will be a cushion into which the ice or granular snow can penetrate. In fact, the cushion of klister will allow a colder, hard wax to be more effective than might be expected.

The pure klister conditions of ice, corn snow, or very wet spring snow are rather obvious and easy to detect. If it is icy, a base of blue klister or skare (to bind tightly to the base) mixed with a warmer klister such as purple and maybe a hard wax (usually extra blue) ironed or melted in usually works. If it slips, try adding a warmer klister or hard wax to the mixture. Many times the last layer will be corked on if it is a hard wax.

If the snow is very abrasive, the wax will wear off the ski quickly, such as on artificial snow or some conditioned snow (regroomed many times or very thoroughly). A similar condition may be when there is snow over ice or hardpack. Here a binder or klister may be used as a base to help hold the wax to the ski. The way it works is that the klister or binder grip much tighter into the ski base than a hard wax. The main idea behind a binder is in its name: To "bind" the wax to the bottom of the ski. The hard wax is then melted into the klister and a final layer or two of hard wax is corked in.

There are several effective methods of applying klisters or binders, all of which require heat of some kind. Klisters and binders may be ironed or torched in and the application is similar. If you are only worried about wax wear and not about kick, apply a thin layer. If it is more icy and/or warmer, a thicker layer of either binder or klister is needed. The international waxing experts claim that binder covered by hard wax is faster than blue klister covered by hard wax, but I have not been able to detect much of a difference. A stiffer ski will have less contact with the snow, so any differences in speed of klister versus binder will be reduced by such a ski.

To apply the klister or binder (heated if necessary to get it on the base), dab it onto the ski and spread it preliminarily with the plastic klister scraper, which comes in the box. Then move a torch up and down the ski, melting the klister/binder into the base or iron it in with an iron set on low. If you wish to apply a hard wax on top, the skis are first placed outside to cool. When the klister hardens, apply a hard wax to the surface, which is melted in with a torch or iron. If the wax is hard to apply, use a torch or iron to soften it for ease of application. (*Note:* These mix jobs can look very ugly when several klisters and hard waxes are applied, but they can be very effective. Don't expect the same smooth look as when a kick wax is corked in alone.)

When mixing klisters, you can apply all of them together by dotting up and down the ski. The key to this application is in the mixing. An iron will do a fair job, but some skiers use their fingers to mix the klisters well. Some use a torch to melt the klisters for ease of mixing; others melt the klisters together in a pot over a stove and paint them on with a brush.

In marathon skiing where wax wear is a factor and changing conditions can be a problem, several of the above techniques may be used. For instance, a thin layer of skare, heated or ironed in, may be used as an additional binder. Then blue, purple, or even a red klister may be added. In addition, a very hot klister such as Swix or Red Rode Special Rossa may be added under the foot if a wet course is expected in places. Then a hard wax, usually extra blue, is added by heating in a layer, corking in another, and finally corking in a colder wax on top.

How it works is as follows: The colder wax has plenty of cushion underneath so it will have plenty of kick, yet its hard surface is on the snow and should be fast. As the day goes on and the temperatures go up, the blue, hard wax will be a factor and will be quite effective at a temperature much above 24° which is its normal limit in the Midwest. The reason is the cushion underneath. In addition, the bottom layers will get the skier over any ice parts of the trail and wear will not be a problem because of the holding power of the klisters. The hard wax protects the klisters from icing up when powder snow is encountered. Finally, if it rains during the day or some wet slush is encountered the hotter red klister under the foot will come into play. Sound complicated? It is, but then you're waxing for a whole day and want it to work all the time. Choosing the right combination for those long races can be a combination of listening to the weather report, knowing the trail, how the various course sections are groomed, the shape of the snow and, of course, luck. Sometimes I'm amazed at the different wax combinations that all worked on a given day. Do your thing, and as you get experience, it'll become easier. Here are two helpful hints:

1. Hard wax over blue and purple klister usually works for temperature ranges under 34° F. Extra blue has an excellent range and is usually the hard wax favorite.
2. Most marathons have waxing clinics where experts share their secrets on how to wax for a race.

A note of caution: Your skis must be reasonably stiff to take such a combination without being real dogs or even losing their wax along the way.

The following are some helpful waxing hints:

1. If your skis seem to lose their wax too quickly under normal waxing conditions, check to see if they fit you. They may be too soft and lose their wax by rubbing against the snow. Use the paper test or a poundage meter and refer to the equipment chapter for basic guidelines. Too soft a ski will also be slow under most conditions.

2. If you have trouble getting up hills and if you are always waxing one or two waxes softer than your friends, again check the stiffness of your skis. If they are too stiff, you can get around it, using a binder or a klister under the hard wax of the day. This is easier to cure than the too soft skis. One of our local skiers and fellow coaches, Beth Schluter, made dramatic improvement when she started skiing on softer skis. She won two World Masters' races at Telemark in 1983 (30 and 55 k) after switching to the softer models. Up until that time, she had a little trouble with the hills.

   Another skier we met at a clinic had a pair of skis that were stiffer than my klister skis, which were the stiffest 215 cm skis I could find. I asked him how he liked his skis, and he replied that he could never quite ski on them. It was no wonder. He was 20 pounds lighter than I and tried to ski on skis that were much too stiff even for someone my weight. They would only be usable on the hardest of tracks with klister conditions where setting the wax was no problem, and wax wear definitely would be with the softer wax.

3. Don't clean skis unless you have to. If the conditions do not change much, you may be on the same wax the next day with just a little touching up to do. In any case, you will have something to start with. If the skis do not work at all, then you can clean them and start over. The national team skiers have coaches who help them if the waxing situation is difficult. In addition, they have the organization down pat so that they have more time to wax than some citizen racers who might be rushing to get to the race.

Unless you have a lot of gook under your wax, a simple scraping will do. If it is worse you may need a wax cleaner. Apply the solvent and let it work into the surface of your wax. Then scrape it off with your klister scraper. Some people claim residue is left by this method, which is true to some degree. But I've never had any trouble getting my wax to bind to the ski after removing the previous wax with a commercial wax remover. However, if you are worried about this or if you are skiing a marathon, you may want to sand the bottoms lightly with 150-grit paper to make sure all the wax remover is gone.

This brings us to the method used by many of the better skiers—the torch and rag. The ski is heated with light and quick passes of the torch and rubbed with a rag in-between each pass. This method will not leave a residue but, unless you are confident, can be perilous. Too much heating can ruin the base of your skis, and I would never recommend it.

Waxing can be simple or complicated. Trying to make it as simple as possible will ease the situation. This means mixing the waxes and staying in the pocket, rather than going longer and thicker. Thin layers are then in order. The same applies to klister conditions. With a general plan in mind and only a few preconceptions, waxing becomes easier, especially when the final judge, the snow itself, tells you whether or not your wax is working. If the ski slips or sticks, some adjustment must be made. Just mix in another wax, either softer or harder, depending on the situation, and you'll soon be on your way with skis that both grip and glide.

Advanced Waxing

Special thanks go to Marty Hall who has provided me with much of the following update. He claims the bulk of the following information has been developed by the Swix Wax Company.

Structuring skis has surfaced recently as a method of increasing the glide speed of skis. Grooves, whose size and depth depend on the conditions, are etched in the glide zones, parallel to the sidewalls. Upon hearing this, my first reaction was "Never, not to my nice new skis." I liked those nice shiny, smooth bottoms and was more or less convinced that the smoother and shinier the surface, the faster the ski. What could entice anyone to so mutilate a base? The answer is simple—speed! If the surface is too smooth, suction develops, slowing the skis. This is analogous to the way two glass plates will get stuck together when there is moisture between them. The tiny grooves running parallel to the sides prevent this suction.

If you are not convinced enough to actually structure your base, you can structure your wax instead. At first, this technique was reserved for wet, sloppy snow. Later research showed that even in the colder temperatures, structuring helped increase glide speed. At these conditions, however, the gain was not as great and the striations were not as deep. So if you do not want to structure your bases themselves, you will not be harmed much at temperatures below 32° F.

Once the temperature reaches 32°, the glide wax may be applied thicker and striations introduced to the wax itself. Around the freezing point, a wire brush can be used to introduce parallel grooves into the wax. This will not be as durable and, therefore, not as effective for a longer period of time. However, it saves you from having to mutilate your bases.

As the temperature gets warmer, the glider can be applied thicker, and even deeper grooves can be introduced with a brush or file. Here the snow is quite sloppy, and almost anyone can feel the suction ripping at the bottoms of their skis. Texturing the wax is a big help.

However, texturing the bases themselves is much more effective even if psychologically alarming. You will choose a file, file brush, or sandpaper, depending on the conditions. The file is for wet snow above 32° F, the file brush for around 32°, 150-grit sandpaper for 30 to 20° and 180-grit sandpaper for colder conditions. The base is never polished, so it shines like a mirror. It may be pretty, but it's slow.

Swix, by the way, has a structuring tool that is faster and easier to use than sandpaper. It only requires several passes. Some teams on the World Circuit use the metal scraper to remove previous structure and for the colder snows (under 15° F). The tool has two sides, fine and coarse. The fine side is best for snows from 15° to 32° F; the rough side works best for snows above 32° F. There is also a guide to ensure parallel strokes. Of course, you need confidence, experience, touch, talent, and guts to use a metal scraper without gouging the base.

The grooves themselves are introduced into the base glide zones in long parallel strokes. These lines should be as straight as possible because any grooves skewing off will only slow the ski. Then buff these grooves with fibertex (available in many shops) to get out the microburrs left by the other methods. Then clean with fiberlene and wax cleaner. The final cleaning step is to lightly hot wax the skis and scrape immediately while the wax is still hot. This will remove any debris left behind by the other processes. Fastidious skiers will repeat this process. Then hot wax the skis with your selected glider and allow the skis to sit for at least a half hour, preferably overnight.

After the wax has cooled, scrape it down to the grooves. A too vigorous scraping can destroy the texture of the base, so use some caution. At this time, use a brass brush to get the wax out of the striations. Finally, after skiing around awhile just before the race, use a nylon brush to again clear the wax from the indentations of the base, as the cold of the snow will have drawn some more wax out of the P-Tex.

So you can see why some skiers have a special ski for warm klisters. Having a special ski for these conditions saves much time and maybe worry. Some manufacturers have a special klister ski with the base already structured. Care must be taken, however, when selecting such a ski. Because it will be used in sloppy conditions, a softer tip is required. If the klister ski has a tip that is too stiff, it will plow rather than ride above the slush. These klister skis are really warm klister skis and are not suitable in icy conditions where less structuring of the base is desirable.

The "Hairies"

When the USST team contingent, led by Jim Galanes, Bill Koch, and Dan Simoneau, first developed their version of a waxless ski in 1982, the results were amazing. The Americans swept first and second for the first time in world competition. This was followed up by other successes capped by Koch's victory in the pre-Olympics at Sarajevo. The waxless skis they developed were really waxable skis with the kick zone roughed up instead of applying kick wax. Rumors started to spread around the country about the new sandpaper method of roughing up the bases, and soon skiers who were privy to that information started to rough up their bases. I have seen 100-grit sandpaper and files used. What was amazing was that all methods worked to some degree, although none were like the USST version. Some just sanded or filed their bases, but conditions were so bad and unwaxable in Wisconsin for several weekends during the winter of 1982-83 that these combinations worked better than waxing. At least they were not icing up. I would call that season "the year of the waxless ski" in our area, and any skier with a good waxless pair had a decided advantage. But none of the skiers I saw actually roughed up their bottoms in a manner similar to the ski team.

At that time, we just didn't know. Now this information is fairly available to the general public. Would this have been the case if the Russians or Norwegians had discovered this technique? It has proved to be advantageous for those who have used it. I get a kick picturing the coaches of the various teams getting down on the tracks trying to see what the Americans had on the base of their skis. But whether or not our boys should have kept it secret is beyond the scope of this book.

Now that it is out, let's discuss it. The only reason this is an advanced waxing technique is it would be very hard for a person with only one pair of skis to mutilate his or her base to create a waxless ski. In fact, it is still very difficult for a skier with more than one pair. Because this is much more extreme than structuring, I suggest a skier only abrade his or her second or third pair of skis and even preferably an old pair of "rock skis."

Once you've made the decision to mutilate, when and how should you do it? The effective range for "the hairies" is from about 30 to 40° with the emphasis on those hard to wax for conditions, that is, newly fallen snow, especially when the conditions seem to make finding the correct wax impossible. Anyone who's been faced with that dilemma knows those conditions well.

Now, how do you do it? First, clean the skis with a wax remover and preferably lock the ski in a vise of some sort. A Sandvik abrader, marketed by Swix and hardware stores, is best for the job. Start at the highest part of your wax pocket, usually around the ball of your foot, but not necessarily so. Make small, firm parallel movements from front to back. As an area is abraded, it will start to look very porous and turn whitish in color. Tiny hairs will appear when the surface is worked with the tool, hence, the name *hairies*. Abrade an area about a foot long. Then spray maxi-glide or silicone on the conditioned surface and test it to see how close it comes to working. Experimentation will show you how far you should extend the pocket to work for you with your particular pair of skis and the given conditions. If you have gone too far, the pocket may be shortened by scraping and/or sanding. Once you've found the right combination, keep that pair of skis for the no-wax situation. Then when the given conditions arise, you're ready.

If done properly, an abraded pair of skis supposedly will retain their bite for 50 k or more in wet snow conditions. This is something that will vary depending on the conditions, the fit of the ski for the skier, and how well the base was conditioned in the first place. The ski should not be too stiff, however, especially in the tip as the conditions for waxless skis mean soft snow in the tracks. A stiff tip will plow snow and be slow. In addition, these skis should have their glide zones structured with a file or brush to reduce suction with the wet snow.

One note on waxless skis: Of all the waxless skis, the chemically treated bases have worked the best for us in waxless conditions where waxing became impossible. They were faster than other waxless skis and worked well once the snow had a considerable moisture content. This range was from 32° all the way up to the 50° range. However, once it got above 34°, waxed skis with the proper klister worked better and had more grip.

Finally, a racer who is a strong skater has one more decision to make. Are the kick waxed or no wax skis any slower than a pair that is only glider waxed? The glide test, in which the skis are equally weighted, will not work here. While skating, most of the weight is on one ski, causing more friction between wax and snow. The fastest, and not necessarily the most accurate, way we arrive at a decision is as follows: Place your kick waxed or no wax ski on one foot and your glider waxed ski on the other. Glide down a slight hill several times in the following manner. Try to keep your weight mainly on one ski, the heel of the foot upon which your balance is best. Switch skis and repeat, noting the distance of the glide on each run. This will give you a good idea of how much faster, if any, the glider waxed skis really are.

There are many other things that could be said about advanced waxing; however, the simpler the skier keeps it, the better. One of our skiers, Terry Daley, was asked to give an advanced waxing demonstration at a racing clinic. Terry, the 1984 National Collegiate Ski Association individual champion, was perplexed. He couldn't figure out what advanced waxing meant. If his skis slipped, he'd put on a light layer of softer wax. If they were slow, he'd cover with a little harder wax. The same went for klisters. If the snow was abrasive, he'd use a klister or binder, and for changing conditions he'd put a hard wax over klister. In the long run, Terry's attitude is the best. As you get to ski more and wax more, you will have a little better starting point, but when you get a simple system that works, you are well ahead of the game. I've seen more people in trouble in the limited time before a race because they got too complicated, including myself. The peace of mind that comes with a simple system is worth a great deal.

And then there's the ultimate peace of mind of the skater who doesn't worry at all about kick waxing. This system is the simplest of all. That's why many racers always have a set of glider waxed skis ready to go, for those occasions when nothing else works.

Touring

13

Still the Most Fun

It's safe to say that almost all skiers get their start touring, and the large majority, by far have touring as their major interest. I can still remember the delightful surprise I had my first time out, touring with some friends. Up until that time, winter was just an unpleasant experience between fall and late spring. After that experience in the tough and thrilling hills of the John Muir trail in our local Kettle Moraine State Forest, winter was never the same. There were things out there I had never noticed and I experienced a new awareness.

Figure 13.1 A spring tour.

I started noticing not only the beauty of a snow-covered countryside, but also the myriad of changes during the season: The way the snow was attached to trees indicating its wetness; how the color of the snow changed from day to day; how some trees continued to lose their leaves the entire season. I noticed fresh new snow, glistening snow in the sun, dirty snow, fine snow, coarse snow, cloudy and sunny days, their effect on the real length of the day, and much more. But the biggest change I noticed was in me. I realized that to truly enjoy these tours, I would have to be in better shape, so I started running in the off-season. Up until then, I had scoffed at those brain pounders, as I called them.

On that first tour, woefully overdressed, coming back soaked with sweat, I discovered warmth in sub-zero weather. Instead of hating winter, I grew to love it, now actually preferring it to the warmer months. Vibrant living became a 12 month affair, instead of 7, with 5 muted by too many hours hiding in a gymnasium or in front of a TV set. Now it's never too cold. In the words of Marty Hall, "There's no such thing as bad weather, only bad clothing." I found that it is much easier to adapt to cold weather than warm. When it's too hot, there's no relief, but when it's cold, just add a layer of clothing. Now thoughts of the first snow bring excitement to our house, and many off-season hours are spent planning the tours of the next winter. Our family now has something we all can truly do together.

It seemed that we spent the first winter trying to experience all of the different trails possible, wishing for more time to get to know each one. In those days there were very few groomed trails, and we gained a quick appreciation for those which were. The first thing we learned was that the trails in the greater Milwaukee area were extremely crowded on the weekends. After waiting on one downhill for 15 minutes, I concluded that it was more like standing in line at Disneyland than skiing. So we vowed not to ski locally again on weekends unless we were willing to get up extra early. This hardly seemed a bother because there were so many trails to discover. Our trips gradually expanded to Northern Wisconsin and Michigan and actually as far as the Cascades in Oregon.

The natural outcome was getting in better shape and wanting to test ourselves in races. Although the whole family is now involved in racing, we still enjoy touring more than anything. The races are tests of oneself whereas the tours are more of a treat, where we savor an appreciation for ourselves and for the earth we live on—the relaxation and awareness of what's happening around us, even if it's just the many changes water molecules pass through as they travel from liquid to snow to ice (and not necessarily in that order). It's the different terrain—the snow hanging on the trees and bushes, the logging roads through the woods, the pines, cedars, oaks, maples, and all of their woody relatives, the swamps, eskers, kettles, and even the rolling farm country—each trail seems to have its own personality. So for me, even though I enjoy racing immensely, touring is still the main course and dessert of skiing. Racing is the appetizer that gets me going, keeps me in shape during the off-season, and helps me set personal goals. But touring keeps me emotionally and physically healthy.

There are basically three types of touring: mountain, a more normal off-trail variety, and touring on groomed or skied-in trails. To a midwesterner, mountain touring is something else. It requires different equipment, especially if the skier is going backpacking, and certainly is more dangerous than normal skiing. The dangers of avalanches, crevasses, whiteouts, and getting lost are real. Every account I've heard about mountain touring and backpacking mentions the dangers of the sport. Even experts have close calls. I am amazed when I read the exploits of Ned Gilette, with all of his skill and knowledge, and see how close he has come to disaster. So mountain skiing is not something that can be taken lightly. I see it as more of an adventure, not normal touring, so many of the techniques in this book do not even apply. However, all mountain touring is not wild and woolly. People I know who have taught at touring centers out West have said that there are many groomed trails in the mountains. When I refer to mountain skiing, I mean skiing off the groomed trails.

Actually, skiing in the mountains is a good way to lengthen the season or even add some summer skiing to a midwesterner, or anyone else, starved for snow. There's something special about the Cascade Mountains of Bend, Oregon, I have to admit it is a different experience sleeping in a room with no screens because there are no bugs or flies. In Wisconsin an open window in the summer could spell disaster, so a place without screens awes me. Then to top it off, there is desert on one side of Bend and a mountain on the other.

Mountain Skiing

As we approached Bend through the desert for the first time, I can remember thinking that snow could only be a dream, because the outside temperature was in the 60s. But sure enough, when we arrived in Bend, it was raining in the city and snowing on the top of Mt. Bachelor.

As you drive across Oregon, the Cascades rise out of the terrain like pure and majestic monuments to winter, somehow defying the heat of summer, holding onto their magnificent crowns of pure white snow. It seems as if it is the last retreat for the cross-country skier and weaves a magic spell for those who love the snows of winter. Summer touring in these mountains offers some advantages to a foreigner or flatlander over the same activity in the winter. The weather is more stable, as is the snow. It has melted a little, and the danger of avalanche is diminished. Still, it doesn't pay to go off half-cocked, as crevasses and some potential dangers can be lurking.

One of the simplest tours is to the top of Bachelor. It is basically up the Alpine slopes on to the top of the extinct volcano. On our first trip at a Peter Davis Ski Camp, we were so intimidated by the mountain and so poor on the downhills that we never went all the way to the top. I was awed at the downhill ability of such skiers as Peter himself, and especially Dan Simoneau. It was amazing to watch Peter skiing down with the video equipment on his back, or watching Dan run some slalom gates on racing cross-country skis and bindings. Contrasted to the paralyzing fear we felt the first time down, it was incredible.

We grew to love Oregon so much that the next summer we were there again, this time for only a few days, touring back into the mountains. Our first trip to the top of Bachelor, which is a tough uphill climb, was rewarded by a breathtaking panorama of the surrounding countryside. The craters at the top and the lava rock themselves are something else to see. We seemed to be on top of the world looking out with the gods. Off in the distance beckoned Broken Top with its blown-off peak and the Three Sisters all of which were covered with snow. One can easily envision a long trek from peak to peak getting to know these precious mountains better.

The ski down Bachelor was much easier this year, although there were numerous falls, especially in the sunspots where wetter snow could bring you to your face rather abruptly. Up close these pure white peaks showed a lot more age, from the summer of alternately melting during the day and refreezing at night, than when viewed from a distance. A closer look showed the snow had acted like a sponge, picking up quite a bit of grime and dirt from the atmosphere. I could not help but wonder why there were no other ski tracks on that mountain, but then I suppose Oregonians are rather used to the snowy peaks in their backyard.

Confidence renewed, we decided to tackle the tour to Broken Top. A magazine article had suggested we set aside 6 hours to complete the trip. This would include a leisurely tour to the volcano bowl and several trips up and down the slopes to practice our telemarking and parallel turns.

The tour itself was uneventful and rather enjoyable. The snow was firm, and I could see how many skiers used racing gear for this type of touring. We could see "old Broken Top," a magnet in the distance, drawing us across the slopes and trails.

Once in the bowl we headed up to the peak for some fast downhill runs. Fun! Scary! Certainly something different than what we were used to as midwestern skiers. After several runs, we were fairly exhausted. Eating a couple of breakfast bars and drinking some water, we started for home, in this case

towards Bachelor. Because Bachelor's peak is easily
seen, we assumed the return trip would be simple. So
we decided to take a slightly different route back,
which at the time seemed more direct.

A big mistake. What we didn't realize was that the
route we took to the right had some very steep ridges
running perpendicular to our line of travel. In addition,
there was a mountain stream that we put off crossing.
We followed it for a while until it became apparent we
were going to have to cross it if we wanted to get anywhere near our starting place. What earlier had been a
relatively simple crossing of a small creek had now become a treacherous maneuver over a suspicious looking
snow bridge spanning 10 feet of rushing and ice cold
water. A fall at that time could have been fatal, not
because of the water itself, but the after-effects. Our
energy was pretty depleted from the trek in and the
trips up and down the bowl. Fortunately, we had taken
a number of breakfast bars and were not yet in real
bad shape. We also had emergency solar blankets, but
I had no desire to test them in such dire conditions.

As we continued, it became apparent that putting
off the stream crossing was not such a bright idea. It
had now branched into several streams, gathering
force as more of the melting snow from the mountain
added to its size. What was only one crossing earlier
became several, accomplished with the help of snow
bridges, slippery rocks or fallen trees. Fortunately,
there were no mishaps. But then the terrain handed us
another obstacle—a giant ridge. After attempting to go
with the flow for a while, it became apparent that the
flow was moving at right angles with our intended
path. So it was up and over the ridge. By this time,
there was no snow and we were carrying our skis, a
far cry from the other route where we skied all the
way.

Soon I began to stumble from being so tired as did
the kids (my 13-year-old daughter, and my 15-year-old
son). However, my wife, the untrained one, was the
freshest of all. She had conserved energy along the
way. While we had been hot dogging and racing
around, she had gone forward in the simplest and
most efficient manner possible. As we climbed up and
skied down Broken Top's bowl, she rested and ate

lunch. It was paying off now. She was better off than the rest of us.

We crested that ridge and were heartfallen to see another huge ridge in front of us rather than the friendly demeanor of Mt. Bachelor. Now we were stopping to rest every hundred yards or so, and things were getting pretty grim. I started to doubt the compass. Bachelor must be there, but it wasn't. Finally, after what seemed like hours but could not have been more than 30 minutes, we crested this ridge. But still no Bachelor. I felt as if a claw popped up and grabbed my stomach as I looked at my family. I began to realize that unless something changed, we might be spending the night in the mountains. Our energy seemed to be gone and space blankets or not, I did not know if we would survive the night. No words can describe the sick, cold feeling I had, not only for my family's safety, but also the knowledge that I was responsible for our position—and they were counting on me. Fortunately, my wife was still feeling good and she kept our spirits up. As I look back, that was very important. Only I know how close I came to panicking.

To this day I don't remember how many of those ridges we crossed needlessly, all because of a bad decision, to take another route back. However, I do remember sitting down on the steepest ridge of all, one which kept driving us further to the right, and making an important decision. Ditch the skis. That's how close I figured we were to not making it. We were all so fatigued that I didn't think we'd make it with the extra weight. Anyone who is a skier knows how hard that decision was and the dire physical straits we must have been facing.

Having dropped the skis, we stumbled on, half dragging ourselves up the mountain with our hands, grabbing any tree or bush we could. I prayed that this was the last ridge and that Bachelor was really there. I didn't know if we could make another. And if we could, would we then have enough energy to survive a night in the mountains? Cresting the top, I let out a shout loud enough to be heard in Bend, miles away. There it was, like a savior, Mt. Bachelor—and at the base, the road to our van. A wave of relief swelled through my body and tears flowed from my eyes as I hugged my family before we continued.

Walking down that road, I vowed never to tour into the mountains again. Later on, it became "not" without a topo map, closer advice, more food and water, and a more complete array of clothing if we had to spend a night. And that's where I stand now.

To a resident or expert in that area, our situation was never that dire unless we fell into a stream or did something stupid. But we didn't have that kind of knowledge. I learned something that day. The mountains are nothing to mess with, even in ideal conditions. I shudder to think what might have happened if it had been colder and if a snowstorm or whiteout had developed.

So if you want to go touring in the mountains, a healthy respect and certain precautions are needed. I realize that those seasoned skiers from the mountains need no such warnings, but any flatlander can use all the warnings and help they can get. To us, skiing in the mountains is a way to extend the skiing season and take a different kind of vacation.

Some other areas that might be of interest are Glacier National Park at the opening of Logan's Pass around June 15th and in the Banff area of Canada. These areas have snow when it is long gone in most of the country. Mt. Hood, another of the Cascades, also has Alpine skiing during the summer.

Groomed Trails

However, even in the mountains, most skiers reading this book will probably be trail skiers. That is, they will ski mainly on trails with set or skied-in tracks. Nowadays groomed trails are actually starting to take precedence, at least in the Midwest. When our family first started, we wanted to experience all kinds of skiing, especially off-trail. I soon found out that life in the groomed track was a lot more fun. True, we were limited to the path chosen for us, but we could move faster and, above all, get more *glide*. To me, that motion is the aphrodisiac of skiing, the intangible sensation that pulls me back again and again.

Skiing in untracked slopes sounds exciting, but in practice, all too often, it means trudging along more like a hiker or snowshoer. In addition, the underbrush is so thick in the woods of Wisconsin that off-trail skiing is not very practical unless an open field or slope is chosen. We still do it, but not very often, and then only as a diversion. I must admit I really prefer skiing along as fast as my condition and ability allow, especially on the downhills where a groomed trail gives a consistent surface and promotes greater speeds. In fact, it was the inconsistency of ungroomed snow that caused my wife to suffer a fairly serious knee injury.

I prefer groomed trails, as do most skiers I've talked to. It hasn't taken commercial areas long to catch on to the fact that well-groomed trails attract customers, and poorly maintained ones keep them away. All of the skiers I know who have gone out West for combined Alpine and Nordic vacations have skied on groomed trails. These trails are much safer, not only because of the consistent surface, but also because it's hard to get lost when all you have to do is follow the tracks that will eventually lead you to the clubhouse or parking lot. In addition, there is usually enough traffic so that any injuries are quickly reported. Most established trail systems have emergency equipment for rescuing injured skiers.

It is now up to the skier to locate a trail that is close enough to get to, not overcrowded, and fun to ski. The farther you get away from the large population centers, the less crowded it will be. The biggest Wisconsin touring centers such as Winter Park in Minocqua and Telemark in Cable can handle a phenomenal number of skiers because of their design, which offers a variety of trails (see Figure 13.2). Poorly designed trails will have bottlenecks: difficult downhill or uphill sections where everyone must ski. The better designed trails have bypasses, or even better yet, nothing very tough until the trails split off. Nothing is more frustrating than having to wait in a line to go down a small downhill strewn with beginners.

Chambers of Commerce, Departments of Natural Resources, and even published books will give you locations of various trails. But the best source of information is the local ski club. Usually, the club will have

Figure 13.2 You can't beat the tracks and trails at a touring center where people care. Luckily Wisconsin has several.

developed a booklet of information of their favorite trail systems with a map included. Better yet, they will also have skied them and can give you some insight into what to expect. And if you are looking for someone else to ski with, these clubs sponsor outings to various areas.

Dressing for touring has already been presented in the equipment chapter, but a few things are worth repeating. Layering is the key to successful dressing for any kind of outdoor activity in the winter. Getting too hot or too cold can be dangerous. By dressing in layers, the clothing can be easily adapted to the temperature and exertion. Remember, avoid getting soaked to the skin at all costs. If you are getting hot, remove a layer. If you are cold, add one. This may mean tying a sweater or warm-up around your waist. Tee shirts are good windbreakers when worn over, not under, racing or touring suits. The legs are usually more impervious to temperature changes, but on cold, windy days, warm-up pants are advised. And always carry a fanny pack with dry mittens, socks, a high-energy snack, several waxes, and a reflector blanket for emergencies. It would not be a bad idea to carry a plastic bag in case of injury. Add snow and you have a portable ice pack. The more off the trail you go, the

more you should take along. I would not go too far
from the beaten path unless I had enough along to survive the night. This, of course, will involve a knapsack
and some extra clothing.

Skiing is a highly individual sport. Each person
gets something different from it and has slightly different goals. Some want to get away from people, while
others want to meet people. Some want to walk on
their skis, others want to sail. Still others will consciously observe the beauty of the landscape, whereas
others will absorb these things at a subconscious level.
In addition, some will be more interested in what is going on in their bodies and others in what is happening
on the trail. Then there are those hardy few who want
to sleep outdoors, while others look forward to a warm
room at night and the comfort of a touring center.
Cross-country has room for all these types, and except
for a friendly argument or two, there is no real deep
conflict of interest. Cross-country skiers are so few in
number that they can't afford to be split apart politi-
cally. So whatever your interest in skiing, go out and
enjoy yourself. We can all exist side by side.

Index